GEORGE WASHINGTON'S
ONE-MAN ARMY

The Life, Legend, and Battles of Peter Francisco

REAR ADMIRAL JOHN T. PALMER,
U.S. Navy (Ret.)

STACKPOLE
BOOKS
Essex, Connecticut

STACKPOLE BOOKS
The Globe Pequot Publishing Group, Inc.
64 South Main Street
Essex, CT 06426
www.globepequot.com

Copyright © 2026 by John T. Palmer
Maps copyright © by The Globe Pequot Publishing Group, Inc.

Front cover photo: Engraving depicting Francisco's Fight in Amelia (now Nottoway) County, Virginia, by Augustus Kollner. *Courtesy of Peter Francisco Society member Ed Bowman.* Front cover inset: Peter Francisco Portrait by unknown. *Wikicommons (Magicpiano). Virginia Historical Society (Public domain).* Back cover photo: Comrades and associates of Peter Francisco. *Library of Virginia, Metropolitan Museum of Art, U.S. Senate, National Park Service, Palace of Versailles, Pennsylvania Academy of the Fine Arts, Independence National Historic Park, New York Historical Society.*

All rights reserved. No part of this book may be reproduced in any form or by any electronic or mechanical means, including information storage and retrieval systems, without written permission from the publisher, except by a reviewer who may quote passages in a review.

British Library Cataloguing in Publication Information available

Library of Congress Cataloging-in-Publication Data available

ISBN 9780811777889 (cloth) | ISBN 9780811777896 (epub)

> "**Stand forever, yielding never**
> **To the tyrant's Hell . . .**"[1]

This book is dedicated to the memory of America's first Soldiers, Sailors, and Marines who took up arms against immense odds and secured our independence. Our freedom is your legacy, and we beseech the Almighty that we may prove ourselves worthy of your sacrifice.

A grateful nation remembers . . .

CONTENTS

Acknowledgments	vii
Introduction	xi
Chapter 1: Dock Orphan	1
Chapter 2: Hunting Tower, *Buckingham County, Virginia*	5
Chapter 3: Private Francisco, *Middlebrook, New Jersey*	15
Chapter 4: Mon Ami, Le Marquis: Philadelphia Campaign, *Brandywine Creek*	23
Chapter 5: The Fog of War: Philadelphia Campaign, *Germantown*	39
Chapter 6: To the Last Extremity: Philadelphia Campaign, *Fort Mifflin*	49
Chapter 7: The Chrysalis: A Baron at Valley Forge	59
Chapter 8: Colonel Daniel Morgan: Philadelphia Campaign, *Monmouth Courthouse*	67
Chapter 9: Commando Assault, *Stony Point*	77
Chapter 10: American Hercules, *Camden*	91
Chapter 11: Cavalryman Francisco! *Scott's Lake*	105
Chapter 12: Left for Dead, *Guilford Courthouse*	119
Chapter 13: Cutting Down Tarleton's Raiders, *Amelia, Virginia*	133

Chapter 14: The Final Blow, *Yorktown* — 139

Chapter 15: Citizen Francisco: Postwar — 145

Chapter 16: Epilogue of Comrades — 165

Illustrations — 177

Notes — 185

Bibliography — 205

About the Author — 213

ACKNOWLEDGMENTS

This book is a complex hybrid that examines key battles in the American Revolution in which a great warrior—Peter Francisco—fought. The work displays a macro-micro-macro structure to balance the intricate details of Peter Francisco's biography within the grand panorama of the War of Independence. After highlighting Francisco's prewar youth, the reader is presented a macro view of the events leading up to each battle: the politics, the generals and admirals in charge, their strategies, and troop employment. Once the battle is joined, the reader is led into the soldier's world of Private Francisco and his unit (micro) to witness his individual feats of strength and courage as well as the actions of his comrades in arms. Upon the close of each battle, the lens of the book is adjusted back to a macro view to understand the outcome, aftermath, and implications of each encounter, as well as the historical pathway that leads to future combat events.

I tip my cap in gratitude to those who chronicled the life of the "Virginia Giant" over the past two centuries. Biographies by Francisco progeny offered a faithful foundation of information—specifically Benjamin M. Francisco's *Biography of Peter Francisco of Revolutionary Notoriety* (1879) and Nannie Francisco Porter and Catherine Fauntleroy Albertson's *The Romantic Record of Peter Francisco* (1929). Perhaps the most complete modern record of the life and achievements of Peter Francisco was conducted by William Arthur Moon in his 1980 work *Peter Francisco: The Portuguese Patriot*.

Academic research was not plentiful, but still some was found to be very helpful. Dr. John E. Manahan's research in 1960 especially was crucial to determine evidence of Francisco's birth, baptism, and family history on his island home of Terceira in the Portuguese Azores. Moreover, the College of William and Mary produced a foundational work "Peter Francisco: The American Soldier," *William and Mary Quarterly Historical Magazine* (1905).

Several detailed articles in periodicals added modern context, research, and insight—specifically Robert Buckner's "Peter Francisco," *Elks Magazine* (1936); Mervyn Williamson's "Peter Francisco—Washington's One-Man Regiment," *Iron Worker* (1972); Michael D. Hull's "Peter Francisco: American Revolutionary War Hero," *Military History Magazine* (2006); Donald N. Moran's "Peter Francisco, Giant of the American Revolution," Sons of Liberty California Society (2009); and Harry Kollatz Jr.'s "American Hercules, Peter Francisco, 'One Man Regiment' of the Revolution," *Richmond Magazine* (2012).

Thanks to the staff members at the National Archives, the University of Virginia Library, the Library of Virginia (Richmond), and the visitor's center at historic St. John's Episcopal Church (formerly Henrico Parish Church) for information, assistance, and access to original documents. Perhaps the most important source was Peter Francisco himself by way of his submission and supporting attestations in his postwar "Petition for Reimbursement to Virginia General Assembly" (1828).

Battlefields from New York to South Carolina were visited, and the staffs, museums, and/or displays at Brandywine, Germantown, Fort Mifflin, Monmouth Courthouse, Stony Point, Cowpens, Fort Watson, and Guilford Courthouse proved quite helpful—the battlefield hospitality was appreciated greatly. Detailed studies of each battle contained within were conducted through the review of historical books and articles that are too numerous to mention here; however, they are credited in the bibliography and notes.

Attendance at the 2023 Battle of Camden reenactment was essential to my research and marked the commencement of a chain of reenactment research by way of site visits, interviews, and video observation. To that end, many thanks to reenactor (and fellow Citadel alumnus) Ronald Crawley for his complete review of the manuscript. U.S. Naval Academy alumnus Colonel Christopher Bopp, USMC, Professor of Naval Science at The Citadel and Revolutionary War cavalry reenactor, conducted another comprehensive appraisal. The reenactor influence lent much-needed authenticity to the battlefield and bivouac passages. Author/historian Daniel Murphy provided several key insights on eighteenth-century American mounted warfare that otherwise evaded my initial research.

As always, my family assisted with review and commentary of the draft, including my wife (Brooks Palmer), daughter (Elizabeth Sanders), son (John Palmer Jr.), brother (Colonel Samuel Palmer, U.S. Army [retired]), sister (Susan Palmer McVey), sister-in-law (Claire Palmer), and cousin (James Burd, Esq.). Jim Burd also provided keen legal advice as he has done so many times in the past. Many thanks!

As with my previous book, I continue to be guided by several long-term friends/authors who offer critical expertise and advice on manuscripts and avenues for publication. These friends include Briar Hill Elementary classmate Robert C. Hall (Nathaniel Sewell), Citadel classmate Thomas L. "Roy" Jeffords, Professor Bruce Craven of Columbia University, and Rear Admiral James McNeal, U.S. Navy (retired)—adjunct professor at the United States Naval Academy.

A special note of gratitude goes to several members of the Society of the Descendants of Peter Francisco—also known in some circles as the Peter Francisco Society. Ed Bowman of Richmond was a great help as he enthusiastically reviewed the manuscript for accuracy and currency, and he contributed an image from his collection of a period engraving depicting Francisco's Fight. John Cary Francisco devoted many hours toward a complete review, and he made several value-added recommendations for revision. Anne Wilson and Peter Francisco Society historical advisor Gail Tonkens added some key details about the Virginia Giant's life that were only recently discovered and not documented in earlier biographies.

Finally, thanks to Dave Reisch and the team at Globe Pequot for making this book possible. Your guidance and coaching throughout the process are much appreciated.

Again, many thanks to all, and keep charging!

JTP

INTRODUCTION

Sunday of Pentecost—May 26, 1765: A boy and his sister play in a courtyard adjacent to their home on the Island of Terceira in the Azores. The boy, named Pedro Francisco, has not yet aged five years. His sister, Angela Maria, is three years his senior. His father, Francisco Machado Luis, had taken the hand of the striking Portuguese maiden Antonia Maria de St. Joseph do Sacramento seventeen years earlier at Santo Antonio do Porto Judeu. The couple, although a family of means, is in disfavor with the Portuguese court. But this Sunday is Pentecost, and in keeping with tradition in Terceira, it is a day of celebration. Young Angela and little brother Pedro are in their appropriate finery. The young boy is outfitted in a lace collar and cuffs, and his shoes are adorned with silver buckles with the initials *P* and *F* engraved. It is a beautiful day amid the stunning vistas of the Azores.[1]

A band of mariners, perhaps pirates from a ship at a nearby anchorage, steal quietly toward the house of Luis. They reconnoiter the surroundings and find the children unchaperoned in the courtyard. The mysterious sailors lure the children with sweets and then make their move grabbing both siblings. Angela screams, fights, and breaks away. Little Pedro is not so fortunate. The toddler is quickly bound, blindfolded, and gagged.[2] He is spirited to the waiting ship that quickly weighs anchor and sets sail immediately to the west. We cannot be certain about the reason for the abduction. Perhaps it was punishment by the Portuguese royals. Maybe Pedro was an intended hostage for barter at a later date. Was the abduction engineered by his parents to ensure he would not be taken or killed as retribution by rivals? In a theory in keeping with the brutish monarchical justice of the times, some historians postulate his execution was pending by the Crown to be conducted in front of his parents as atonement for a political offense.[3] No one is certain. What is certain is that Pedro Francisco, born nearly five years earlier on July 9, 1760, would never see his family or home again. He is a prisoner aboard a vessel on the high seas bound for parts unknown. He is terrified, but he lives. He lives to see land again in the wilds of the North American British colony of Virginia.

Nearly one month later on June 23, the mysterious ship sails up the James River toward City Point near Richmond, Virginia. At the wharf, the young boy is put ashore, and the ship sails away as silently as it had arrived. Although soiled from the voyage, the youngster bears the dress and bearing of nobility. He is big for his age and has dark hair and eyes. He has the olive skin, speech, and features of a European from the Mediterranean coast—perhaps Italy, Spain, or Portugal. The silver buckles on his shoes glisten in the Virginia sun.[4] He speaks phrases no one can understand, and he can understand no one. He conveys only his name, and Pedro is soon anglicized to "Peter." He is taken in by local housewives and guarded by the wharf watchman.

Thus begins the story of Peter Francisco, the first great warrior in United States history. He would find his way into indenture for a Revolutionary family that included Patrick Henry in their relations. The boy would grow to more than six and a half feet tall and a reported 280 pounds. His feats of strength as a soldier and citizen were Herculean and would be considered tall tales if not witnessed by third parties. As a teen, he would volunteer for the Continental Army, and he served, often with distinction, in at least ten engagements. Peter Francisco was a courageous soldier who moved to the sound of the guns. Moreover, he received wounds from the musket ball and the blade on a half dozen occasions. He was left for dead on one battlefield, but the soldier gave better than he received. As a seasoned veteran, he was heard to quip that "he never felt he had done a good day's work unless he had drawn British blood."[5] His physical prowess on the battlefield was unparalleled. In warfighting from New York to South Carolina, witnesses would attest to Private Peter Francisco single-handedly dispatching manifold British soldiers mostly by bayonet and a six-foot broadsword. This massive sword was commissioned especially for him by America's Commander in Chief—General George Washington—who referred to this man-child as a "one man army."[6]

In his capacity as a soldier and patriot, Peter Francisco participated in some of the fiercest fighting, witnessed the greatest events, and met an astounding number of luminaries from early America. As an indentured servant, Peter was present for Patrick Henry's most famous speech, hearing firsthand the words "Give me Liberty or Give me Death." Upon volunteering for military service, the orphan Francisco soon fought alongside, was

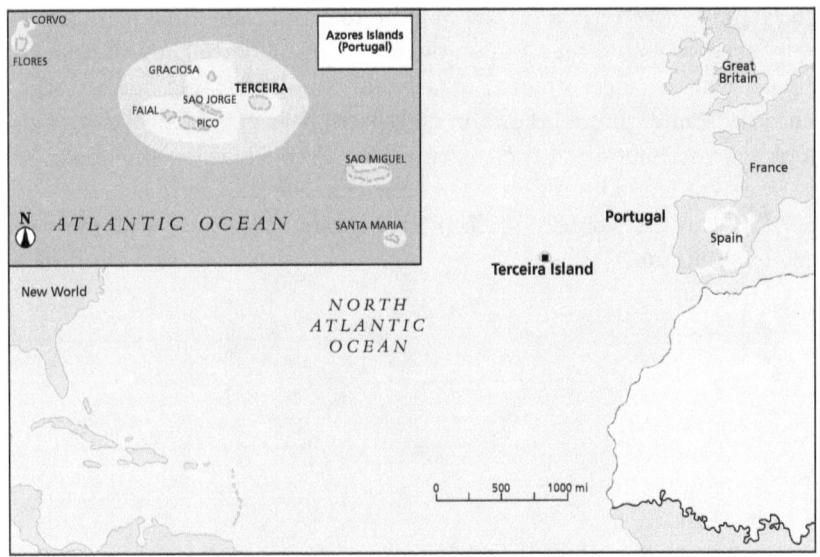

Between the Old and New Worlds, Azores and Terceira.

wounded, and convalesced with the young French General, Gilbert du Motier, Marquis de Lafayette.

Francisco and Lafayette built a friendship that extended for many years after the Revolution. Private Francisco served alongside and was well known to a host of famous patriot leaders headlined by generals Washington, Nathanael Greene, and Lafayette. After stalwart service in some of the Revolution's most pivotal battles, young Francisco was present for the surrender of the British at Yorktown. Post war, he became a planter and a businessman; endeavoring to educate himself, he developed into a voracious reader. His fame as the "Virginia Giant" was pervasive. As a veteran, Francisco was sought out for a meeting by the U.S. Secretary of State. The former soldier of repute was received in the home of the Chief Justice of the U.S. Supreme Court. He was a thrice married father of six and a fixture in central Virginia serving as Sergeant at Arms for the legislature late in life.

Sadly, Peter Francisco slipped into obscurity after his death. Twentieth-century efforts by his progeny and a few historians have resuscitated his exploits with some success. A handful of states and municipalities have established days of remembrance and monuments to his memory. To the average U.S. citizen, however, his contributions to our freedom are unknown. We are quick to say *a grateful nation remembers*, yet we have forgotten. He is arguably our first great warrior, and most assuredly Francisco is one of the greatest in the illustrious military history of these United States.

The legend of Peter Francisco should be told and retold to Americans of every age. We should reflect upon the tale of the abducted and abandoned orphan who, by sheer strength of will and constitution, became a world-renowned American soldier and an undisputed hero of the Revolution. This book is an attempt to do the citizen-soldier Peter Francisco the honor he deserves—to remind us of his fearless perseverance and sacrifice.

To echo the words of William Shakespeare, "This story shall the *good man* teach his son."[7]

Chapter 1

DOCK ORPHAN

On the morning of June 23, 1765, one can only imagine the events that preceded the arrival of Pedro Francisco into his new world. This day, the child passenger noticed a rush among the ship's crew that had captured him from his peaceful Azorean home nearly one month earlier. Years later, the kidnapped passenger would say of his trans-Atlantic trip: "Some things are best forgot."[1] During the four-week voyage, the boy received ill treatment on board the vessel. Eighteenth-century sailors were notorious for their belief in omens and harbingers of good and bad luck. Anything out of the ordinary was subject to suspicion and disdain, and this included women or children being on board a ship during an ocean voyage. Francisco would later recount that a violent storm occurred during the passage, and this event led to him being blamed by the crew. He was put to constant hard labor as punishment. Only one man, a Spaniard he surmised, tried to shield the boy from harm by the rest of the ship's company. To the crew, little Pedro was a *Jonah*, and the sooner he departed their vessel, the better.[2]

A day or two earlier off the ship's starboard beam, they passed Virginia's Point Comfort at the southern tip of the western shore of Chesapeake Bay (so named by Captain Christopher Newport more than a century and a half earlier). The boy was now permitted to peer out from the ship's weather decks, and he saw a sight he had not seen for weeks. He saw land—albeit unfamiliar land. Soon the boy and crew could see land on both sides of the ship. They proceeded west before steering northwest, upstream in a slow-moving Virginia tributary called the James River. The land closed in on both sides of the ship. To the eyes of the mariners, the river banks were mysterious, green, and lush. The boy must have pondered, *Where are we going? . . . When might I go home?*

But this morning, the crew began to scurry. Orders were barked out, men went aloft, sails were tended, and the ship's anchor broke the water near a Virginia hamlet called City Point.[3] A jolly boat was lowered from the ship's davit with oarsmen at the ready. On the deck of the ship, a sailor tied a line with a bowline knot around the child's chest—under his armpits. Another sailor—a strongback—lowered the boy into the small launch, and Pedro was placed near the stern next to the coxswain manning the tiller. From the boy's vantage, the ship that was so easily tossed about on the bounding main looked massive and still to his little eyes. The vessel's masts and furled sails seemed to reach to the clouds. The boy could see gouges in the ship's wooden hull and barnacles beneath the water line. He heard the gentle lapping of the river swells against the ship. He could smell the brine of the brack water. Pedro was transfixed by the downward gazes from the faces of the nameless crew as they assembled along the ship's rails—the men who had abducted and spirited him away to this new land. He caught the squinted stare of the Spaniard—the only crew member who had protected him during the voyage.

He was startled by the loud thud made by the seating of the two oars into the small boat's oar locks. He heard the whisper of the oars cutting through the water; the launch picked up speed, and the oarsmen synchronized their strokes. Water rushed under the boat and past the rudder with every pull of the oars. The rhythmic rattle of the wooden oars against the metal oar locks accompanied the churn in the river by the oars' blades and was followed by a gush of water under the boat's hull. The launch lurched forward with each pull of the oars, and the boat would glide until the blades reentered the water for the next stroke. From the stern, the boy could see the faces of the oarsmen as their backs were to the bow of the jolly boat and to the destination beyond—a small wharf growing larger with each pull of the oars. The morning sun was still in the east, and it warmed his back. The buildings ashore seemed to glow in the morning light, and the sun's rays twinkled in reflection from windows back toward the river. The oarsmen turned their heads occasionally toward the bow and the dock beyond to confirm the coxswain was minding the tiller and staying on course. The boy turned his head back toward the ship and saw it getting smaller by the minute. The ship's crew had returned to their duties.

After a few minutes, the City Point wharf was only about twenty yards away. The coxswain at the tiller barked an order, and the oarsmen popped the oars from the oar locks and raised them vertically with blades pointing toward the sky. Drops of river water fell from the oars' blades onto the little boy and the man at the tiller. In synchronization, the oarsmen brought down the oars and stowed them away—bow-to-stern in the boat. The boat's momentum continued to carry the launch toward the dock silently on a perpendicular course. Suddenly, the coxswain threw the tiller over to one side, twisting the rudder against the flow of water and turning the boat sharply. A "whoosh" of the water across the turned rudder disturbed the morning silence, and the boat turned parallel to the dock. The hard turn broke the speed of the boat, and it sat nearly motionless next to the wooden pier. The oarsmen jumped from the boat and tended the jolly boat's bow and stern lines holding the small craft snugly against the wharf. The coxswain rose and left the tiller to pick up the boy under his arms, and he placed the youngster on the dock. As the oarsmen hopped back into the boat, one shoved the launch from the dock with his foot. The oars were replaced into the locks, and the rhythmic pull of the oarsmen began to propel the launch back to the ship at anchor.[4] The boy watched the small boat get ever smaller as it moved toward the big ship a few hundred yards away. The child turned his back to the ship and surveyed the wharf and buildings. Nothing was familiar. Pedro Francisco had arrived in the New World.

City Point was located in Prince George County, Virginia. The James River (flowing nearly 350 miles from the Appalachian Mountains to Chesapeake Bay) constituted the northern border of the county. City Point was 25 miles southeast of Richmond and 10 miles northeast of Petersburg. The Appomattox River emptied into the James River just west of the point upon which the wharf was positioned. At least one local gentleman, Mr. James Durrell of nearby Petersburg, observed the child's arrival.[5] Little Pedro was hungry, thirsty, and dirty. He had worn the same clothes for nearly a month on the pitching ship. His lace cuffs and collar were frayed and dingy while his silver shoe buckles captured and reflected the morning sunlight. The buckles carried the engraved initials *PF*. The young boy explored the outer walls of the buildings along the dry side of the docks, and after a period of time, the wharf watchman noticed him. The watchman engaged the boy—speaking English to no effect. The child could speak, but the language was unintelligible to the watchman. He listened intently and asked the same questions in English—"Who are you? . . . Where are you from? . . . Who is your father? . . . Where is your mother?"—to no avail. Although soiled, the boy was dressed in fine clothing, and it was clear he hailed from a family of some means—foreign aristocracy, perhaps nobility. As with most four-year-old children, this youngster was only fundamentally conversant in his native tongue, and the watchman was no polyglot. He estimated the child's language to be Portuguese or Italian—possibly Spanish. This was reinforced by the boy's features. He possessed the look of a Mediterranean native with dark eyes and hair and an olive skin tone. To the watchman, "Pedro Francisco" were the only recognizable words the boy could muster.[6]

The wharf watchman alerted some local women. An unused bed was located and made ready for him in one of the buildings ashore, and the wharf guard continued to monitor the boy's activities. They resumed trying to communicate with the youngster and ascertained his name to be Pedro Francisco. Soon after, they began to refer to him by the anglicized version— Peter Francisco—a name that would be made famous over the coming decades. The neighborhood ladies fed the boy regularly, but it soon became apparent that he was fearful and lonely as his pillow was soaked each morning from his weeping through the night. The orphaned boy was missing his mother. He could not remain a ward of the wharf watchman and ladies of the local community.[7] Prince George County had a poor house, and the boy Francisco soon found residence there.[8] No doubt, the consistency and level of care was improved as compared to Peter's previous situation under the part-time but keen eye of the wharf watchman and an ad hoc collection of women nearby the City Point docks. Still, it was not long after that Peter Francisco would find a permanent home—at a place called Hunting Tower.

Chapter 2

HUNTING TOWER

Buckingham County, Virginia

Young Peter was soon "bound out" or indentured to Judge Anthony Winston.[1] Judge Winston was the owner of *Hunting Tower*, a plantation in the center of the colony. The Winstons of Virginia arrived in the seventeenth century and were descended from the noteworthy Winston Hall of Yorkshire, England.[2] Five Winston brothers settled initially in Hanover County with the county seat located approximately twenty-five miles north of Richmond. Anthony Winston was born in 1723 and made his fortune after moving to Buckingham County—squarely in the middle of the Piedmont region of Virginia and some seventy miles west of Richmond.[3] Buckingham's rolling hills made ideal farmland for tobacco, and the county was located an equidistant forty miles south of Charlottesville and east of Lynchburg. Hunting Tower represented thirty-six hundred acres—two miles southwest of New Store village. The Virginia Winstons of the 1760s were an independent lot with Judge Winston claiming as his nephew the renowned patriot, Patrick Henry of Hanover. It is noteworthy that Joseph Winston (for whom Winston-Salem, North Carolina, is named) was also a nephew of the judge.[4]

Judge Winston encountered the orphaned youth while stopping by City Point on the way back to Hunting Tower from Williamsburg. He had been attending the annual meeting of the House of Burgesses where he served as representative of Buckingham County in the legislative assembly.[5] The judge was checking on shipments that were due into the City Point wharf from England. When he met the young boy, he was impressed by his energy and bearing but took pity on his situation. Winston made arrangements to have the boy indentured and apprenticed under his care. Peter Francisco was to find a home at the judge's estate in Buckingham County—nearly one hundred miles up the winding Appomattox River.[6]

The particulars of the initial meeting between Judge Winston and little Peter are lost to history. One can imagine the eighty-mile trip over land from City Point to Buckingham County and the thoughts that must have been running through Peter's mind. To avoid two river crossings, the party would have traveled ten miles east toward Petersburg. Turning north, they would pass the Halfway House Tavern—so named because it was (and still is) positioned half way on the road between Petersburg and Richmond. There were two main routes west from Richmond into the Piedmont at the time. Three Chopt Road led northwest to Albemarle County and Charlottesville. The more likely and direct route was an old stage road that passed from Richmond through Buckingham County and finally onto a ferry crossing at the village of Lynchburg established eight years earlier. Most of these primitive thoroughfares were converted from Indian paths into tobacco roads. Horseback and horse-drawn carts were the conveyances of the day, and little Peter was likely carried to Hunting Tower in the latter.[7]

A summer trip by wagon would have been an adventure for Peter and his chaperone. Infrequent road maintenance meant the trip was a bumpy one. The slow plodding of the horse pulling the creaking cart on rutty dirt paths would require deft handling by the driver. Weather permitting, they might make twenty miles per day. At such a pace, the eighty miles between City Point and Hunting Tower would have taken four or five days requiring establishment of overnight campsites along the way unless boardinghouses could be found. On clear nights, the traveling party might sleep in a roadside clearing under the stars. In the event of foul weather, Peter and company could take refuge under the cart or fashion a tarpaulin. Upon arrival at Hunting Tower, young Peter would become acclimated to his surroundings and begin his indenture for Judge Winston.

Young Peter's thoughts were most certainly still with his family back in Portugal. We know this because, after he arrived at Hunting Tower, he began to learn rudimentary English. Enabled by his increasing ability to communicate, he related memories about his old family to the Winstons. He recalled a beautiful seaside home, a loving and vivacious mother, his father, and his older sister.[8] Moreover, he was able to describe details about his abduction—how the perpetrators lured him and his sister to the courtyard gate with some type of food. The captors unbolted the gate, snatched the two and placed a blanket over his head, and spirited him off to the waiting ship. Fortunately, his sister escaped.[9]

To view Peter as an adopted member of the Winston family would be a generous appraisal of the situation. He was indentured. He was a servant. The research and deduction of biographer William Arthur Moon is instructive on this matter. Peter Francisco received no inheritance from the Winston estate, and neither did he take on their surname. Perhaps the best indication of Peter's servant status is that the Winstons did not see fit to educate Peter in even the basics of reading and writing. He remained illiterate until he engaged in self-education after the Revolutionary War.[10] It is important to note that Peter's situation should not be confused with the lot derived by African slaves in early America. Unlike the multigenerational bondage most Africans suffered, indentured servitude presumed a term of service after which the servant was freed. The indenture was a contract, most often for labor for a stated period of time, and the parties normally entered the contract voluntarily. Before the Revolution, indenture was a common method to pay for maritime transit to America with these contracts being utilized by nearly half of the European arrivals.[11] The term of service varied from two to seven years. There was also involuntary and semi-voluntary indenture owing to the labor of criminal convicts, broken families, fleeing wives, debtors, and orphaned or illegitimate children, to name a few. Children without sponsorship, like Peter, were typically bound out until the age of twenty-one.[12] The temperance of the masters in these relationships varied from cruel to benevolent. There is no historical evidence pointing to mistreatment of Peter Francisco by Judge Winston during his indenture.

Regarding Francisco's maintenance, such were the customs of the day. With no social safety net, everyone worked to sustain themselves—even children in colonial America's agrarian society. Seldom did one derive an existence without work, and it was exceedingly rare for one to receive uncompensated support from outside the family. Even within prominent families, patriarchs often upbraided children or siblings for not pulling their weight. Signers of the Declaration of Independence John Adams of Massachusetts and Caesar Rodney of Delaware would castigate a son and a younger brother, respectively, for slothful behavior and failing to advance personal and family equities as expected.[13] In short, Peter Francisco's indenture as a child was not unusual, and it was not perceived to be abusive or cruel given the times. He had food and shelter, and he learned a trade. One unusual aspect of Francisco's indenture was length of service. His obligation to the proprietors of Hunting Tower would not extend to his twenty-first birthday. Rather, he would be released by Judge Anthony at the age of sixteen to enter the fight for American independence.

Peter would work his way through childhood learning to speak English and apprenticing as a blacksmith. For ages, blacksmiths had been an essential part of farms and communities, and this was no exception for preindustrial colonial America. Smiths like Francisco were masters of metals—artists creating both utility and sometimes beauty from iron. Although gold and silver were the elusive elements desired most by New World explorers, iron followed just behind with the mining, shipping, and smelting of Virginia ore beginning as early as 1608. The work of the colonial blacksmith was a catalyst for a multitude of craftsmen and artisans, including farmers, coopers, carpenters, soldiers, shipwrights, weavers, millers, sailors, and teamsters who all used metal parts and tools requiring fabrication and repair.

As a child apprentice, Peter was likely first trained as a *nailor*. Nails were scarce and essential in the colonies—so much so that abandoned structures were sometimes burned to the ground so that nails might be recaptured from the ashes. In keeping with the times, young Peter may have had a quota of more than three thousand nails per week that he would fashion from bar stock. First, he would heat and *draw down* (beat out) the piece of metal by making it thin on one end and then *upsetting* (beating down) the other end to create the head. As he aged and gained experience, Peter would become a master of his craft, bringing to bear the forge and bellows to achieve optimal heat . . . the anvil and a collection of hammers to shape the metal . . . and an array of tongs to safely hold iron pieces and move them from the fire to the anvil to the quenching trough. Over time, the young blacksmith would know when the eye of his fire was large enough, when forced draft of his bellows made the fire hot enough, and how to heat the iron to the appropriate *red*, *white*, or *sparkling* depending on the task. Peter could adjust his hammer strikes to fall just heavily enough to complete the job at hand.

As an expert blacksmith, Francisco could wield anvil, vise, hammer, and heat to weld large pieces of iron or braise smaller pieces by using copper. He would soften metal by *annealing* and *case harden* finished pieces with mud or clay (to cool the outside while leaving the inside metal hot for a stronger core). He could *temper* the metal at the forge, or perhaps *lay* a sharpened edge on a plow or pick with an expert weld by deft use of a hammer. Blacksmiths of the time were often farriers who would form and fit horseshoes, shoe the horses, and often develop enough equine experience to become the village veterinarian. Added expertise might include gunsmith, locksmith, and cutler.[14]

As a blacksmith, Peter would become accustomed to hot work requiring great strength and stamina. The rush of the bellow, the smell of smoky-hot coals in the forge, the clanging of the hammer against the anvil, and the sizzling of hot iron in the quenching trough filled his senses each day. Although most blacksmiths were the strongmen of their villages, Peter Francisco would grow bigger and stronger than his counterparts at six and a half feet tall and more than 260 pounds while still a teenager under indenture.[15] He could easily reposition one of his 300-pound iron anvils without assistance. He had become a teen colossus by 1775 and would eventually tip the scales at 280 pounds as an adult. In addition to his size and strength, Peter's time as a blacksmith gave him keen knowledge of metals, sharpened blades, guns, locks, horses, and equine accoutrements. Unbeknownst to him and the citizenry of Buckingham County, the orphan boy who had arrived just ten years earlier had amassed the physical gifts and knowledge that would make him a fearsome soldier—an apex warrior.

As a young man at Hunting Tower, Peter Francisco was exposed to the politics of the day. In fact, one could argue that the balance of education the youngster *did* receive was through the discussion and debate at the Winstons' fireside. The judge and his extended family were burgeoning patriots who decried the insufferable measures levied upon the colonists by the Crown to include the Sugar, Stamp, Tea, and Townsend acts. *Taxation without representation* would have been a familiar indictment ascribed to the British king and Parliament by the Winstons. Doubtless, the powder keg of revolution was fashioned in the mind of the young blacksmith at Hunting Tower. The fuse would be lit by Anthony Winston's nephew—Patrick Henry.[16]

By the spring of 1775, Judge Winston had made it a practice of taking Peter with him on trips throughout the Virginia colony.[17] One such trip in March would prove fateful for the herculean teen from Hunting Tower. The pair retraced their original path from Buckingham County eastward to Richmond on the Richmond-Lynchburg stage road. The seventy-mile trip could be made in two or three days if the party traveled on individual mounts. By wagon, it would likely take three or more days. The destination was Henrico Parish Church where the Second Virginia Convention was being held. As a judge and former member of the House of Burgesses, Anthony Winston was well known in Virginia. Even more so was his nephew, Patrick Henry.

Thirteen years younger than his uncle, Patrick Henry was born in May 1736 on the family farm in Hanover County called *Studley*. At the time, the judge's sister, Sarah Winston Syme Henry, was a twice-married wife of John Henry. Their marriage combined Henry's four hundred acres of Hanover County land with Sarah's first husband's acreage at Studley. Contrary to the Winstons' long establishment in the colony, John Henry was a first-generation, college-educated immigrant from Aberdeen, Scotland. The Henrys were Anglican (the established church in Virginia), yet Patrick's mother exposed him to Presbyterian preachers and the idea of saving society in addition to one's own soul. Young Patrick was educated at home and became a lawyer after brief self-study followed by oral examinations by prominent attorneys in Williamsburg. Patrick Henry became an adroit lawyer, winning a noteworthy victory in the damages phase of the *Parson's Cause* against Anglican clergy. Patrick Henry represented the church vestry who had lost their court battle with their clergyman. At issue was the British veto of the House of Burgesses' price-capping of tobacco as it was often used as currency in colonial Virginia. A drought had made tobacco scarce and expensive, necessitating a price control on the crop/currency by the Virginia legislature. Without the price cap, the clergy stood to make a windfall at the expense of the parish. Patrick Henry accused the parson of abject greed and argued vehemently that the veto of *good law* was tyrannical. Henry stated further that the British king had forfeited his right to his subjects' obedience. His opponents cried "treason," yet the jury deliberated for only moments before calling for damages of just one penny to be paid by the vestry to the clergyman.[18]

This was the beginning of Patrick Henry's crusade against the Crown and in favor of American independence. Henry's legal mind and oratory skills were legendary. He was first sworn into the House of Burgesses on May 20, 1765. One week later, news of the Stamp Act arrived by ship, and on May 29, Henry introduced the Virginia Stamp Act Resolves. Virginia had rapidly taken a lead role in colonial criticism of Parliament, and Patrick Henry was their firebrand. In 1774, word reached Virginia that Parliament had ordered the port of Boston closed in response to the Boston Tea Party. This punitive measure, along with the dismissal of the House of Burgesses by Royal Governor John Murray, 4th Earl of Dunmore, spawned a series of Virginia Conventions with the second commanding the attention of Judge Anthony Winston.

March 23, 1775: The Second Virginia Convention was in its fourth day. Winston and Francisco joined the assembly and onlookers at Henrico Parish Church. Built in 1741, the Anglican church was located on Church Hill in Richmond—approximately a half mile southeast of the lowlands at Shockoe Bottom and about three-quarters of a mile inland from the James River where the waterway shifts from flowing west to east and begins to turn south toward City Point. Built by Colonel Richard Randolph (Thomas Jefferson's great-uncle), the church was a white, wooden frame building along an east-west alignment. A recent addition in 1772 fashioned a northern nave to the design forming a north-south orientation with the altar at the southeastern end. Later in the 1830s, the northern entrance would receive the addition of a gleaming white tower, adorned with a cross, over the edifice.[19]

The fourth day of the convention was attended by 125 delegates. Attendees were in rapt attention. The gigantic man-child that was Peter Francisco observed the debate with other onlookers through an open window. Patrick Henry introduced three resolutions. The first parroted the Fairfax County resolutions. It stated that a well-regulated militia would not only defend the colony's interests but would obviate the need for the king to place troops in Virginia to protect colonial equities and eliminate the necessity for a tax in consideration for such protection. His second resolution stated that the establishment of such a militia was particularly necessary owing to the presence of Virginia laws. These laws (for protection and defense) faced expiration, and this situation was exacerbated by the suspension of legislative activity by the royal governor.

Henry's third resolution proved provocative. For the first time, he called for material support and supply of the militia by stating: "Resolved therefore that his Colony be immediately put into a posture of Defence," and that a committee be appointed "to prepare a Plan for embodying, arming, and disciplining such a Number of Men as may be sufficient for that purpose." This third resolution engendered fiery debate and was castigated as a "prophesy of war" that "would place Virginia in the false position of appearing not to resist armed conflict but to invite it."[20] Henry rose and took his place on the oak planking of the church floor. His steps echoed through the crowded but quiet assembly of delegates. Although cool and blustery outside, the sun shone brightly that day in Richmond.[21]

The parish was bathed in light streaming through the windows illuminating the white walls of the interior. The walls offered

Henrico Parish Church hosted the Second Virginia Convention.
Photo by J. T. Palmer

Patrick Henry. By George Bagby Matthews after Thomas Sully.
Wikimedia Commons

a stark offset from the dark brown pews, railings, and paneling. He stood below the dark, elevated pulpit positioned near the sanctuary and altar. He thunderously delivered the most famous oration of the Revolution through his "Liberty or Death" sermon. He implored the conclave for sober self-reflection through a series of inquiries followed by a call to action:

> We are apt to shut our eyes against a painful truth, and listen to the song of that siren till she transforms us into beasts. Is this the part of wise men, engaged in a great and arduous struggle for liberty? Are we disposed to be of the number of those who, having eyes, see not, and having ears, hear not . . . I am willing to know the whole truth; to know the worst, and to provide for it . . .
>
> I have but one lamp by which my feet are guided; and that is the lamp of experience. . . . Suffer not yourselves to be betrayed with a kiss. Ask yourselves how this gracious reception of our petition comports with those war-like preparations which cover our waters and darken our land. . . . I ask, gentlemen, sir, what means this martial array, if its purpose be not to force us to submission? Can gentlemen assign any other possible motive for it? Has Great Britain any enemy, in this quarter of the world, to call for all this accumulation of navies and armies? No, sir, she has none . . .
>
> They tell us, sir, that we are weak; unable to cope with so formidable an adversary. But when shall we be stronger? Will it be the next week, or the next year? Will it be when we are totally disarmed, and when a British guard shall be stationed in every house? . . . The millions of

people, armed in the holy cause of liberty, and in such a country as that which we possess, are invincible by any force which our enemy can send against us. Besides, sir, we shall not fight our battles alone. There is a just God who presides over the destinies of nations; and who will raise up friends to fight our battles for us. The battle, sir, is not to the strong alone; it is to the vigilant, the active, the brave . . .

Gentlemen may cry, Peace, Peace—but there is no peace. The war is actually begun! The next gale that sweeps from the north will bring to our ears the clash of resounding arms! Our brethren are already in the field! Why stand we here idle? What is it that gentlemen wish? What would they have? Is life so dear, or peace so sweet, as to be purchased at the price of chains and slavery? Forbid it, Almighty God! *I know not what course others may take; but as for me, give me liberty or give me death!*[22]

The reaction from the delegates of all persuasions was roaring. On the wings of Patrick Henry's passionate lecture, the resolutions passed in a close vote. Peter Francisco was exhilarated. The young blacksmith—aged only fourteen years—was determined to enlist for service in the militia, and he asked from the judge permission to volunteer. Judge Winston believed Peter to be too young to depart on such a perilous enterprise. They returned to Hunting Tower, and Peter resumed his duties as a blacksmith. Meanwhile the drums of war were beating in the distance. Subsequent to the Second Virginia Convention came Lexington and Concord, Ethan Allen's capture of Fort Ticonderoga, the establishment of the Continental Army, Bunker Hill, the occupation of Montreal, Benedict Arnold's failed siege of Quebec, seizure of the Bahamian island of New Providence by the Continental fleet, the British evacuation of Boston, an American victory over the Royal Navy at Fort Moultrie, South Carolina, a British instigated Cherokee attack throughout the southern frontier, and numerous clashes between loyalists and rebels—all culminating with the Declaration of Independence in July 1776.

The war for American independence was raging in full vigor. Peter Francisco wanted to do his part as the engagements continued through the end of 1776 to include the British occupation of New York and Washington's capture of Trenton. Much like an untamable stallion that must be set free, Judge Anthony could no longer restrain his charge and gave him leave to join the army in December 1776. There was only one problem. Peter's services had been assigned temporarily to a nearby planter, Mr. George Wright of Cumberland County. Young Francisco had two years and forty-five days of bonded service remaining. Judge Winston bought out the remainder of Peter's contract to George Wright and released the

"Virginia Giant" from indenture so that he could volunteer for service in the Continental Army.[23] The Henrico Parish Vestry Book recorded Judge Winston's purchase and subsequent release *from slavery* of the orphan boy deposited at City Point wharf eleven years earlier.[24] At the age of sixteen, his indentured bondage was over. Unshackled, Peter Francisco was free to fight for his country as a free man.

Chapter 3

PRIVATE FRANCISCO

Middlebrook, New Jersey

Peter Francisco enlisted and was mustered into service in the Continental Army on December 15, 1776.[1] His unit was the Tenth Virginia Regiment commanded by Colonel Edward Stevens of Culpepper. His company commander was Captain Hughes Woodson from Cumberland County.[2] In early 1777, the British were reconnoitering for the Continental Army from recently occupied New York City. The 10th Virginia was ordered north to New Jersey to participate in General George Washington's undertaking to contain the Crown forces. In an effort to guard land routes to Philadelphia, Washington moved a portion of the Continental Army in April to Middlebrook, which lay twenty miles south of their winter encampment at Morristown.[3] Now a soldier, Peter would spend his initial weeks in the army undergoing training in Middlebrook, New Jersey.[4]

As a formerly indentured servant, Peter Francisco was far from pampered. Still, upon his arrival at the encampment, he would likely have been surprised at the camp operations beginning with the close quarters of the sleeping accommodations. An enlisted man's tent of the day was in the shape of a wedge with two vertical poles at each end of the structure and a supporting horizontal crosspiece. Canvas would be stretched over the crosspiece with the ends staked to the ground. Upon opening the entrance flap, Peter would see the first horizontal pole where six soldiers would bunk for the night with bedrolls and haversacks contained within. The men would sleep shoulder to shoulder in cigar-box fashion, parallel to the entrance flaps and perpendicular to the crosspiece. The man bunking in the middle of the tent would be required to step or crawl over several fellow soldiers to exit the tent to assume guard duty or relieve himself.[5] Junior officers would have more space with only two men assigned to the wedge tent. With less people in the tent, the space was large enough for a typical officer to stand in the middle. In addition, there was extra room to accommodate a small writing desk to process administration, receive and write orders, and conduct small meetings. Senior officers such as lieutenant colonels, colonels, and brigadiers may have had a large marquis tent with tables suitable for conducting sizable meetings to collectively view maps, discuss strategy, and issue orders to mid-grade and junior officers.[6]

Revolutionary war camps during Francisco's service would often have large canopy-style tents for food preparation. The sides would be open to the air, and rudimentary tables would be underneath the shelter for creation of meals and rations. Alongside the mess tent would be various contraptions to facilitate cooking of food. Long-term winter encampments would give soldiers the opportunity to create multiple earthen-walled cooking stations for use by the bivouacked army companies.[7] In temporary or transient camp sites, cooking fires would be open. Over the burning embers, metal or wooden bars were suspended with baking pans, boiling pots, skillets, or meat on a spit. Chains were often affixed to the bars to hang coffee and cook pots above the flames. The cooking was either conducted by soldiers or perhaps camp followers—wives, girlfriends, children, and some curious tagalongs. Stacks of wood fuel would be staged nearby for soldiers and camp followers to continue the frying, baking, boiling, and searing of food for the army.

After dark, *jollification* would often take place. In eighteenth-century parlance, this meant music and perhaps the dancing of jigs. Fifes and flutes were commonplace in encampments. Fiddles might be played by bowing, plucking, or strumming the instruments to fill the spaces around small campfires with music. Of course, drummers could be pressed into service to set a beat to the music. Peter Francisco would have witnessed laughter, gaiety, and pipe smoke that would blend together for lighthearted evenings when the conditions permitted. If the enemy was nearby or movement of the army was anticipated the next morning, however, the camp took on a completely different tenor from the evening prior. The gear that could be struck, packed, and loaded onto the baggage train of wagons would be organized the night before. Final preparation of a couple of days' food rations for the march would be organized for issue before breaking camp the next day. Ammunition complete with powder and musket balls would be distributed to the soldiers. Surveyors, scouts, and local experts would gather at the geographer's tent to chart out maps for the intended march.

If combat was anticipated, hospital tents would be required. Typically, each regiment was allocated one or two hospital tents to be carried in the baggage train. These were open air canopies similar to the food preparation areas, complete with tables or platforms for wounded to be triaged and operations to be conducted. At times, a building might be commandeered near a battlefield for surgeons to practice their discipline. There would be no complex surgeries. Surgeons of the day rarely had anesthetics such as laudanum. Most surgical procedures would be completed in less than ten minutes. There was no understanding of cross-contamination, germs, or bacteria. There were no transfusions or methods to replace blood. Wounds had to be treated, and bleeding had to be stopped expeditiously. Time was of the essence. Splinting simple fractures and removal of musket balls and shrapnel were exercised speedily. Even for the most serious wounds, decisions to amputate were made rapidly. The removal of a limb and the application of dressings were equally precipitous.[8]

As for Peter Francisco, he would transition from provincial blacksmith to trained soldier in the spring and summer of 1777. Consistent with the early phase of the war, his enlistment would have been for one year. As a private in the army, the soldier Francisco would have been promised a monthly pay of $6.23. Soldiers of the day were assigned three basic duties: drill, guard, and fatigue or manual labor, which could include entrenching, fortification building, latrine excavation, and the clearing of land. Daily rations consisted of one and a half pounds of meat (including bone and gristle) and one pound of bread (or one and a half pounds of flour to make fire cakes—flour infused with grease from cooked meat on heated flat rocks). Two ounces of alcohol (spirits) were allotted to purify water in the soldiers' canteens. Only one daily meal was prepared—typically in the mid-afternoon with unconsumed portions stored in soldiers' haversacks.[9]

Given that Peter Francisco was a foot taller and one hundred pounds heavier than the average man of the 1770s, it is reasonable to surmise that he was not outfitted with a uniform as was the case with many enlisted men (of all sizes) who were below the rank of non-commissioned officers. More likely, he wore a hunting shirt made of light-colored buckskin or homespun linen. This was not unusual. In fact, early in the war General Washington preferred such apparel for a variety of reasons, beginning with its practical use in all seasons. A more important aspect was the fear levied upon the European soldiers that Americans dressed as backwoodsmen were presumed to be excellent marksmen with long-range rifles employing guerilla tactics. If Private Francisco had been issued a uniform, the ensemble would likely have included a blue coat over a white shirt and waistcoat with white trousers. The various states employed different colors for the *facing* (cuff and button lining) on the blue coats. Soldiers hailing from Virginia and nearby mid-Atlantic states typically had white facing offsetting the blue coats. Most soldiers, regardless of uniform availability, would wear some type of cap. The common patriot's cap of the day was a dark wool felt tricorn or cocked hat—often adorned with some type of circular cockade fashioned from a colorful collection of ribbons.[10]

The specific manual under which Peter Francisco would have been trained is unknown. Early Continental units and militia drew from a variety of sources, including the British Army's 1764 Manual Exercise. It was not uncommon for captured American officers to have in their personal papers written material for self-study in all aspects of warfare including drill, firearms manual, marching, cannonade, and the like. As such, Washington's army was hardly a force under expert tutelage and homogenous standards of drill and tactics. Often, colonels commanding the patriot regiments applied their own personal standards of drill and marching. Under the Americans' ad hoc/pre–Valley Forge model of training, Peter would have learned the rudiments of eighteeth-century marching in columns, forming of ranks in close-order (shoulder-to-shoulder), and semi-synchronized loading, firing, and reloading of weapons.[11]

As a soldier in 1777, Peter Francisco's kit would have weighed approximately forty-five pounds. Ideally, his supplies would have included a haversack with a mess kit consisting of a canteen, tin cup, bowl, and a spoon at a minimum. Other items often carried by patriots might include a knife and fork in a leather pouch, a *soldier's housewife* or sewing kit, a flint wallet with extra flints, and a repair tool for the soldier's musket or *firelock*. A personal pocket knife was a prized possession. In addition, a shaving kit with a slab of rendered soap, a horsehair brush for application of lather, a razor, and a leather strap for sharpening was necessary to meet grooming standards. A wash cloth for personal hygiene was a basic sundry, and dental care was often relegated to a *chew stick* from a small elm branch with frayed fibers to brush one's teeth. For brightwork or metal objects, sometimes a polishing kit might be found with a small bottle of oil, cloth patches, and brick dust for use as an abrasive. For smoking, a pipe with tobacco may also include a set of fire tongs for retrieving small coals from campfires to place in the pipe to light the instrument. He may have also carried a blanket and an extra shirt. When on the march, Francisco may have been issued rations of dried, salted meat or jerky; wheat, corn, or perhaps ground flour for bread; and some dried beans or rice on occasion. Frequently, the aforementioned tin cup had a top and could double as a small cook pot for the soldier to boil the salted meat. A short length of chain was an accoutrement used to suspend the cooking vessel over a fire. To start a fire, a kit of flint and steel for sparking kindling were tools of the day. A sharpening stone to keep an edge on the soldiers' various blades was in many haversacks. Musket ball tools with ladle, mold, and nippers were integral to the soldier's self-sufficiency. Some American soldiers might possess a forged tomahawk or small ax for fatigue duty around a camp, pathfinding while maneuvering, and potentially as a weapon in close-quarters combat.[12] Currency may have been kept in one of two receptacles—a leather wallet was handy for folding money, important papers, invoices, and receipts; and a silk purse was best for coin. In addition to the contents of the haversack, a bed roll would also be slung over a soldier's shoulder.[13]

Strapped to a soldier's lower back, a thick leather cartridge box would carry apportioned ammunition.[14] A cartridge was an assembly of powder and projectile wrapped in paper for use with muskets (firelocks). Although the production of cartridges was often centralized in army encampments for distribution to soldiers prior to combat, some combatants would possess cartridge equipment and training to fashion their own firelock ammunition. Regardless, cartridge kits consisted typically of a wooden forming tool (or a six-inch dowel equal to the diameter of the musket ball to be fired). The forming tool would have a concave edge for placement of the ball during assembly. Cartridge papers were trapezoidal with the longest side spanning approximately five and a half inches. A small horn for measuring out the appropriate amount of gunpowder (usually one hundred grains) was a necessity. A cartridge was constructed by laying the forming tool and ball along the long side of the cartridge paper. The paper would be rolled into a tube with the ball inside one edge of the paper cylinder. The ball would be secured by tying two separate strings of flax thread above and below the sphere at which point the forming tool would be removed to produce a tubular cavity for gunpowder. The measure of gunpowder would be poured down the open end of the cylindrical casing, and the black powder propellent would be closed off by crimping and twisting the excess paper into a pigtail.[15]

The most important part of a soldier's gear included his firelock and bayonet. The .75-caliber, short land pattern *Brown Bess* was a smoothbore, flintlock musket that was a common British military long gun employed by the Crown forces. By extension, the Brown Bess was a patriot staple at the outbreak of war and especially in the American militia units throughout the conflict. Later in the war, French support of Washington's army would bring the .69-caliber *Charleville* infantry musket into the hands of Continental regulars in good numbers. British-contracted Hessians carried their own .70-caliber muskets. As for firelocks such as the Brown Bess, she was nearly five feet in length and weighed more than ten pounds.[16] As each musket was crafted individually, the armies' armorers proved essential to effect repairs by fashioning new parts to replicate the form, fit, and function of broken parts. A soldier's expected rate of fire was three to four volleys per minute. Depending on the manual of arms employed, there were a dozen separate orders in the processes of firing and reloading. Upon command, the procedure for loading a firelock required each soldier to extract a paper cartridge from a cartridge box containing ball and powder. He would bite the pigtail end of the cartridge and dispense a small amount of powder into the bowl-shaped pan attached to the lock on the butt-end of the barrel. Near the pan, a touch hole led to the rear of the bore. The soldier would secure the powder in the pan with a hinged *frizzen*, which was shaped like the pan. The frizzen would both lock down the powder in the pan and bear the strike of the hammer and flint later in the process.

Beginning with the remaining gunpowder, the cartridge paper and ball were put down the open end of the musket barrel and rammed home with a ram rod. Quite often, the musket ball would be augmented with three pieces of smaller buckshot to deliver more hot-lead downrange. The musket was then ready to fire. When the order "make ready" was given, the soldier would pull back the hammer from its half-cocked position to full-cock. "Take aim" was the next command—as opposed to the British manual calling for the phrase "Present." After receiving the order to *take aim*, the American soldier placed the butt of the weapon firmly into his right shoulder. The soldier would point his weapon at the oncoming enemy. As with a modern shotgun, the Brown Bess had no rear sight (it was not accurate enough to demand one). The bayonet lug near the muzzle doubled as a forward sight. "Fire" was the next command. Upon squeezing the trigger, the spring-loaded hammer containing a shard of flint would strike down upon the steel frizzen and create sparks that would normally ignite the powder in the pan. The ignited powder would project flame through the touch hole to the rammed powder in the musket bore. The second ignition of the greater quantity of compressed powder in the barrel would create a small explosion of expanding gasses to launch the projectiles (ball and buckshot) down the smoothbore musket barrel accompanied by a loud report, smoke, and flame. These were smoothbore weapons—not rifled barrels (grooved in a spiral pattern). As such, a knuckleball-style motion could be expected from each ball in the volley of musketry. Some musket balls would find their target—many would not. Special care was given to keeping one's *powder dry* and having fresh flints in the hammer.[17] Private Francisco and his compatriots may have drilled as much as eight hours each day with their muskets in pursuit of calm, cool firing on command. Each firing was followed by reloading and discharging of these muzzle-loaders three to four times per minute.[18] Through these critical weeks of basic training, Peter Francisco and his comrades in Washington's Continental Army covered much ground in their pursuit of battlefield competence and efficiency. Still, the most lethal force in the world—the British Army—awaited them on various unknown battlefields. How would they fare? The untested Private Francisco would find answers at a place called Brandywine Creek in Pennsylvania.

Chapter 4

MON AMI, LE MARQUIS

Philadelphia Campaign
Brandywine Creek

During Peter Francisco's first months of service, there occurred some give and take between the British and the patriots primarily in the northern states. In April 1777, Benedict Arnold would repel the redcoats at Ridgefield, Connecticut. The Americans under Arthur St. Clair would relinquish Fort Ticonderoga back to the British in July. August would find pitched battles in the vicinity of Oriskany, New York, where the British were augmented by the Iroquois. American militiamen led by General Stark were victorious at the Battle of Bennington, Vermont. Summer also marked the arrival of a key leader in the fight for American independence—none other than the nineteen-year-old French General Marie-Joseph Paul Yves Roch Gilbert du Motier de La Fayette, Marquis de La Fayette.[1]

Francisco and his patriot brothers would face a land and sea superpower of the eighteenth century—Great Britain. On land, the foundational unit in the Crown's army was the regiment of foot (or infantry as one would say today). A British regiment contained enlisted men who frequently were assigned to their home unit for their entire term of service. Ideally, each regiment consisted of ten companies—eight battalion companies of infantry and two elite flank companies. The battalion companies operated typically in close order, shoulder-to-shoulder, to concentrate the fire of musket balls downrange as well as to serve as a physical barrier for enemy cavalry. Opposing cavalry operated at peak lethality in open spaces where the horsemen could trample foot soldiers or use the advantage of their mounted height and equine inertia to cut down infantry with slashing sabers and carbine or pistol shots. Sometimes heavy cavalry could attempt to smash through the tight lines and squares of infantry; however, a mass of men in close order with bayonets often gave horse commanders cause to attempt flanking or encircling the enemy regiments of foot.

Flank companies were aptly named owing to their positions on the flanks during parades and often in battlefield alignment. Holding the honored position on the right flank was customarily a company of grenadiers who wore their traditional bearskin hats without brims. Absent siege work or boarding action (when engaged in combined operations with the Royal Navy), grenadiers no longer carried and threw grenades on the battlefield. Still, their headgear harkened back to the days when they carried heavy, primitive, and dangerous grenades demanding uniforms that facilitated unimpeded throwing of the explosive weapons. During the Revolution, grenadiers were the awe-inspiring shock troops of the day, often manned with the tallest and most physically fit men in the regiment. Raw recruits would not be found in the grenadiers; rather, their company would be populated with experienced veterans drawn from the interior battalion companies. As such, a grenadier company would be called upon to execute some of the most harrowing action such as assault troops, vanguard, and rearguard duty.[2]

The other flank company would ordinarily be light infantry. Ideally, these units would be light-loaded, speedy, and skilled shots. As with grenadiers, light infantry were elite companies of veteran soldiers with specific skills that were analogous to a modern-day commando. Light infantrymen were able to operate semi-independently on uneven ground—climbing, swimming, running, and leaping their way into the fight. They operated in a more open order with gaps of ten feet or more within their formations. Rather than the standard infantry mode of *firing by volley*, the light infantry developed a tactic known as *firing by files*. Employing this scheme, they operated in teams of two or more with one soldier firing while other soldiers reloaded to the rear. It was common for a light infantryman forward to hold fire until he received word from a cohort to the rear that they had completed reloading. The light infantry squads wanted a loaded weapon in their presence at all times. They were sometimes commanded by whistle rather than the drum of heavy infantry. One significant difference between open-order light infantry and close-order heavy infantry was the use of the command to *commence irregular fire*. Upon this command, the two- or three-man teams would fire and reload at will and not in concert with the rest of the company.

Sometimes called *bloodhounds* for their skills of overland pursuit, these light infantrymen wore uniforms similar to normal British infantry in that they wore coats; however, they were trimmed higher from the ground to permit freedom of movement in the brush. Early British light infantry were distinguished by leather helmets. As the war progressed, these specialists had shifted to simple cocked caps of the day with the left brim bent upward to keep their headgear clear of the barrel when carrying their firelock at shoulder arms.[3] They used gaiter trousers or close-cropped breaches with buttons near their boots. These trousers often were kept taut by stirrups wrapped around the footwear of the light infantrymen. Gaiter-style trousers served to protect the soldiers' lower legs and ankles while in the thickets performing screening duty on the flanks or serving as vanguard or rear guard for the main army on the move. Ironically, their kit was often similar and not much lighter than that of typical infantry. They utilized the same firelocks and at times augmented their accoutrements to include a hatchet for pathfinding. Their cartridge boxes were commonly placed to the front for ease of reloading. They were experts in their firearms and regularly had extra powder horns and fashioned customized cartridges. The main difference between heavy infantry and light infantry was found in their tactics in firing, maneuver, and open order while fighting in the ranks.[4]

Commanded by a colonel, British regiments of foot might total between four hundred and six hundred men. Battle attrition could reduce the numbers of soldiers in a regiment to one or two hundred. Multiple regiments could be combined into divisions, wings, or corps. Artillery, cavalry, and provincial regiments often augmented the Crown's foundational infantry organization on the battlefield. The American army retained a similar table of organization as the British, but the structure was less formalized and often adapted to the exigencies of war. From the onset, the patriots' mix of Continental regulars and militia was more rapidly tailored to irregular warfare and guerilla tactics. Not until Valley Forge would the Continental Army receive the standardized training and drill sessions sufficient to match the British in linear European tactics on an open battlefield. For now, the Americans faced an ominous, highly trained, and well-equipped British *Goliath* as they brought to bear the experience and resources of a provincial *David* found in the composition of their patriot ranks.[5]

In spring and summer 1777, the British planned two major operations that were not synchronized. In May, General John Burgoyne had returned to North America after a five-month trip to England. While back in his home country, he petitioned and received approval from Lord George Germain—the Secretary of State of North America—to move on the northern colonies from Canada along the Hudson River and through the surrounding mountainous terrain of New York. The plan called for him to rendezvous with General Sir William Howe and his larger forces moving north from New York City. General William Howe had other plans. With the assistance of his brother, Royal Navy Admiral Lord Richard Howe, he intended to travel by sea from New York, down the coast to Tidewater, Virginia, and up the Chesapeake Bay landing at Head of Elk, Maryland, before a fifty-mile march to capture the rebel capital of Philadelphia. General Howe had submitted his plan to Germain, and he received approval as well.

These incongruous British operations commenced in summer 1777 with Burgoyne striking south from Montreal, and after initially securing Fort Ticonderoga, he became bogged down in the Hudson Valley. General Burgoyne was counting on rendezvous and relief from the eighteen thousand soldiers based in New York; however, General Howe left only three thousand men at arms in Manhattan under General Henry Clinton to support the Hudson campaign. Meanwhile, the brothers Howe, with subordinate generals Lord Charles Cornwallis and Hessian Wilhelm von Knyphausen, sailed with more than fifteen thousand soldiers in more than 260 ships on the circuitous course to the upper Chesapeake Bay where the Big and Little Elk Creeks merge to form the Head of Elk River in northern Maryland. The voyage took longer than expected, and excess supplies were consumed.[6]

General George Washington. By Charles Willson Peale.
U.S. Senate Collection

Upon debarkation in Maryland, the British and Hessian forces had to devote several weeks in late August to foraging for supplies to facilitate the march on Philadelphia. General Howe, now augmented by some loyalist units in the area, engaged in a period of resupply that devastated the local populace as fields, cellars, and curing houses were raided and livestock commandeered from farms. The redcoat sorties, however, gave General Washington time to move his army from New Jersey to position his forces to defend the capital. Peter Francisco was on the march south. General Washington's senior leaders included generals Nathanael Greene, John Sullivan, William Alexander (Lord Stirling), Adam Stephen, Anthony Wayne, and a Polish cavalry officer and count named Casimir Pulaski.[7] Within Major General Greene's division, the 2nd Virginia Brigade was commanded by Brigadier General George Weedon of Fredericksburg, and one of the regiments assigned was Francisco's 10th Virginia.[8] The newly arrived French General Lafayette was also on hand but not yet placed in command of troops.

Freshly supplied by early September, General Howe moved his collective forces including Cornwallis and von Knyphausen out of Maryland and into the border areas of Delaware and southeastern Pennsylvania. Washington shadowed Howe's movements. On September 8, the British contingent moved to New Castle County, Delaware, near Hockessin, and Howe set up his headquarters at the home of Daniel Nichols on Limestone Road. There, the British commander rested his men. Washington's forces camped at Newport, Delaware—a mere eight miles away. It became apparent to General Washington that the easiest path Howe would likely seek to Philadelphia would be the Great Nottingham Road. On September 9, Washington moved his forces thirteen miles due north to the road's crossing at Chadds Ford, Pennsylvania, on Brandywine Creek—eleven miles northeast of the British. On the same day, the British commander divided his forces into two columns. Von Knyphausen moved along the Great Nottingham Road with Cornwallis (accompanied by Howe) screening to the east. Marching through the night, both British columns arrived at Kennett Square on the morning of September 10 and established camps. The British and Americans were separated by only nine miles.[9]

September 11, 1777: General Howe planned a feint and flanking movement with von Knyphausen demonstrating west of Chadds Ford. Cornwallis, acting on loyalist intelligence, would sweep north to ford Brandywine Creek and then turn south to catch Washington in a pincer movement. At 4:00 a.m., on the morning of September 11, General Howe assumed command of Cornwallis's column and marched the contingent of fifteen thousand north crossing first the west and then the east branches of Brandywine Creek at Tremble's and Jeffries' Fords, respectively. Six miles to the south, Washington arrayed his troops along the east bank of the creek under generals Alexander, Stephen, Sullivan, Wayne, and John Armstrong (north to south) with Nathanael Greene's division in reserve at Chadds Ford. A heavy fog shrouded von Knyphausen's 5:30 a.m. march of his five thousand Hessians eastward to the banks of Brandywine creek—just west of Chadds Ford. Peter Francisco and the 10th Virginia were part of General Greene's reserve brigades positioned to the east and would see action in the afternoon.

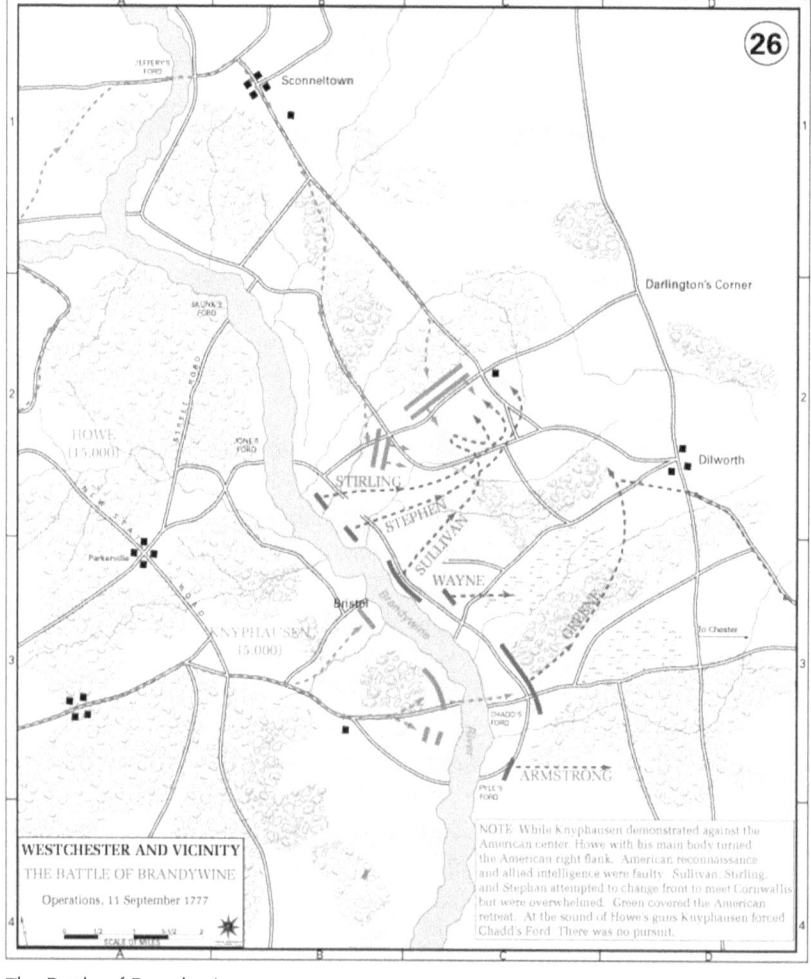

The Battle of Brandywine.
United States Military Academy History Department

Howe and Cornwallis's seventeen-mile march north, then east, and then southward to the American right flank would take until the afternoon to unfold. At 10:00 a.m., Hessian General von Knyphausen began his demonstration with cannonade from the west side of Brandywine Creek, and the Americans responded in kind.[10] Washington had established his command post at Benjamin Ring's house just east of Chadds Ford where he was evaluating conflicting intelligence regarding the enemy whereabouts and movements. From his headquarters, he was later able to determine the British had divided their force but was unsure if it was a flanking movement, a feint, or a raid of American supplies at the town of Reading to the north. Regardless, while the enemy forces were divided, Washington resolved to seize the initiative, and he prepared to order a crossing at Chadds Ford with a follow-on attack to be led by Major General Nathanael Greene on von Knyphausen's position.

While reconnoitering the banks of Brandywine Creek in the late morning, Washington on his impressive horse was joined by Count Casimir Pulaski. He fell under the gaze of British light infantry officer Captain (later Major) Patrick Ferguson. At the time, Ferguson did not know he beheld the American commander in chief a mere one hundred yards away. Ferguson not only was renowned as the best shot in the British officer corps but also was a gunsmith/inventor who pioneered some of the first breech-loading long guns. By his own estimation, the British captain stated he could have put several rounds in a target no larger than a piece of paper at such a close range. Upon later finding out that he had held Washington in his sights literally, Ferguson did not lament his missed opportunity. Washington had turned his horse away from the enemy to align his troops, and Ferguson thought it untoward to shoot such a brave and gallant figure in the back. The fact of the matter is that Captain Ferguson might have altered the outcome of the war that morning had he fired upon General George Washington.[11]

Upon Washington's order to attack, the Americans crossed the ford and made some initial gains, but they were later recalled and consolidated when Howe and Cornwallis appeared in the distance on the Continentals' right flank. Howe's troops were halted for an afternoon meal, brief rest, and reorganization. This gave Washington time to begin redeployment of Sullivan's, Alexander's, and Stephen's units to face the British to the north. Wayne, Maxwell, and Armstrong's troops guarded Chadds Ford, and General Greene was positioned in reserve to be able to support the American units defending attacks from von Knyphausen to the west.

At 4:30 p.m., Howe attacked from the north while the Americans were still maneuvering to their defensive positions. Upon hearing Howe's attack to the northeast, von Knyphausen's forces crossed Chadds Ford and pushed the Americans back along the east bank of Brandywine Creek. After two hours of fighting, Howe's column finally broke the American right flank. A rout was on, and the fate of the army would rest with the next actions ordered by General Washington and executed by Nathanael Greene. Washington ordered General Greene to move his forces four miles to the northeast to a spot near Dilworthtown to provide rearguard action and support a retreat. Washington rode ahead with Lafayette to appraise the situation. General Sullivan's men still held the high ground at Plowed Hill, but his three thousand Continentals were badly outnumbered by eight thousand British. As the redcoats advanced, Washington and Lafayette exhorted the men along Sullivan's line, but the Americans began to falter. The fortunes of the patriot forces dimmed as the British closed in, and Lafayette would take a musket ball to the left calf.[12] Incredibly, Major General Greene would arrive just in time. His troops would march the four miles at double-quick time in just forty-five minutes in the summer heat.

One can imagine the race for Dilworthtown by Nathanael Greene's division and the two Virginia brigades under brigadiers Peter Muhlenberg and Weedon (to include Francisco within the 10th Virginia regiment). At approximately 5:00 p.m., Washington's orders to Greene were issued after the patriots collapsed at Birmingham Hill to the north. Four miles separated the shattered American army from rescue by Greene's men. There was no time to spare. Doubtless, the Virginians were on the march and quickly ordered into *route step*. Rather than tight ranks and a slower quick-step at 120 steps per minute, the order for route step released the soldiers to march at a best pace and to individually carry their firelocks as they pleased. Dress and ranks were still loosely maintained, yet the Virginia regiments could move at greater speed—to jog or even to run as the topography permitted.

Chadds Ford was in a low-lying area at Brandywine Creek. Greene's destination of Dilworthtown was an elevated position four miles to the northeast. The departures from the ford were quite hilly and a mix of farmland, timberland, and swamp. This march would be a challenge. From Chadds Ford, Greene's men had a solid route through the Pennsylvania forest screened by creeks and swamps to the north and south. Moving northeast at best speed through the woods, the Virginians were unconcerned with stealth or silence. Rather, time was of the essence, and the clanking of canteens, jostling of haversacks, and cracking of brush and leaves could be heard under the feet of the onrushing patriots. Some soldiers fatigued and fell out of their formations for a quick respite only to be exhorted by sergeants and officers to get back on the march. For Peter Francisco, his firelock and kit would have been an easy load for him to carry compared to his comrades—some of whom stood only half his size. They utilized and then crossed Great Nottingham Road and covered the first two miles in twenty-five minutes before they broke out of the forest into cleared land. Swinging north, Weedon and Muhlenberg's brigades forded a small creek and passed to the east of the associated marshland. Two miles to go—no time to waste. Heavy breathing could be heard as the open ground enabled a faster pace. The regimental formations were maintained loosely, and this was important to allow officers to re-form and place their sections in appropriate alignment once the dash was concluded. General Greene rode ahead to the vicinity of Dilworthtown where Washington awaited his arrival and, more important, the arrival of Greene's Virginians. American Major General John Sullivan commanded the patriot right wing that had just collapsed at Birmingham Hill. He recommended to General Washington that Greene's division be positioned south of Dilworthtown to be able to engage the British forces pouring in from the northwest. Such a maneuver might blunt the British advance or at least provide rearguard protection to permit an orderly retreat from the battlefield for the other American divisions. Washington concurred.[13]

Greene received final direction straight from Washington where to position and make the stand. Major General Greene situated his men at Sandy Hollow Gap—astride Wilmington Road about one mile south of Dilworthtown and north of Great Nottingham Road. The formation was a semicircle with Muhlenberg's 1st Virginia Brigade holding center and facing west. Weedon's 2nd Virginia Brigade secured Muhlenberg's right flank and faced southwest. To the left of Muhlenberg's men were stragglers from the retreating American right wing that had been corralled and directed by Lafayette into taking position along the extreme left flank and facing northwest.

The Virginians went to work. The colonels who commanded the various regiments and their company commanders began to form their lines. The 1st Virginia facing the oncoming British were reconstituted shoulder-to-shoulder going several ranks deep in classic eighteenth-century fashion. They were prepared to fire by volleys or sections at the Crown forces and check them with a hail of musket balls. The flanking brigades (including Francisco's 2nd Virginia) were more loosely aligned, making use of timberland and brush cover to shield their positions until they could spring a trap on the British right and left flanks.[14]

Howe and Cornwallis were determined to complete the rout and crush the Americans once and for all. The fearsome 1st Battalion Grenadiers under Lieutenant Colonel William Meadows advanced on the British right. Elements of the British 4th Brigade under Brigadier James Agnew formed the redcoats' left. The Americans in retreat from their collapsed right wing had done a fair job in firing while retreating and then either forming up on the flanks of Greene's division or passing through the ranks to depart the battlefield. Greene called upon Muhlenberg's 1st Virginia and Weedon's 2nd Virginia brigades to halt the British advance and cover the retreating Continentals. The Virginians were formed at an angle as the 1st Virginia faced the enemy center while the 2nd Virginia was prepared to hit them on their left flank. Weedon's men (including Peter Francisco's regiment) held fire under cover until the left flank of the formation of redcoats was directly in front of them.[15]

The moment of truth fell upon the 2nd Virginia Brigade, the 10th Virginia Regiment, and Peter Francisco who would display today the first of many acts of bravery under fire. As the British advanced upon the 1st Virginia Brigade, Muhlenberg's men bravely exchanged deadly musket fire with the oncoming British—but still the redcoats came. Weedon's men would have crouched silently in the brush. Agnew's 4th Brigade fixated on their prey—Muhlenberg's Virginians fighting in the open. The redcoats gave little notice of their left flank. The patriots' weapons already

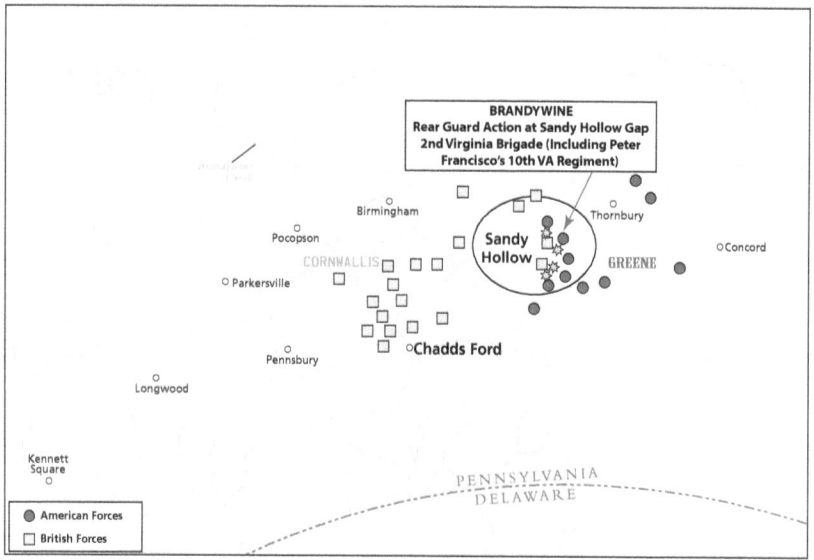

The Battle of Brandywine. Positioning of Greene's division for rear guard action: Francisco in 2nd Virginia Brigade.

loaded, Weedon's officers and sergeants would quietly give the order to "make ready!" With the thumb of his right hand, Peter Francisco pulled back the hammer on his firelock to full-cock. The clicking of the musket hammers could be heard like crickets throughout the brush among the rumble of the volleys that the men witnessed before them. The British continued to march, pausing only to volley and reload periodically—the drummers beating out the pace for the king's men. For an optimal attack on the British flank, Weedon's Virginians

Peter Francisco. Artist unknown.
Porter and Albertson (1929)

would have to hold fire until the British column was nearly perpendicular to his men in the brush. The leaders throughout the 2nd Brigade would then pass orders to "take aim." Francisco and his comrades slowly placed the butts of their muskets into their right shoulders and leveled their long guns at the Crown forces—supporting their firelock stocks with their left hands. Gripping the small of the muskets behind the locks with their right hands, the Virginians placed their index fingers alongside the trigger guards and awaited their next orders. As the drums beat on, the British would re-form their ranks as some men were cut down by Muhlenberg's musketeers, and they advanced within one hundred paces of the 1st Virginia. For the men of the 2nd Virginia, hearts pounded and breathing was heavy, but discipline was maintained. Peter looked down the musket barrel, taking careful aim along the bayonet lug near the muzzle. His right cheek pressed against the comb of the stock—behind his right hand. The ten-pound firelock was heavy—but not for him. Francisco was stone—steady and stalwart. "Fire!" came the order. He pulled the trigger, the spring-loaded/flint-laden hammer slammed into the steel of the frizzen. Sparks flew, touching off the powder in the flash pan. Flame shot through the touch hole igniting the compressed powder in the barrel. A thunderous boom and simultaneous kick of the musket into Peter's right shoulder launched the musket ball and three buckshot toward the British targets. A nearly synchronized clap of thunder and smoke erupted from the approximately twelve hundred muskets of the Virginia 2nd Brigade. The 46th and 64th regiments of the British 4th Brigade were lashed by the volley of musket fire from their left. Many were struck down, including a frightful number of officers who were specifically targeted by the Americans. As was common in the heat of combat, the handful of orders normally given to effect reloading (from "half cock the firelock" through priming, charging the weapon with powder and musket ball, and ramming) was quickly dispensed in favor of a single, simple command: "Prime and load!" Francisco and his fellow patriots reached back into their cartridge boxes for a fresh cartridge. They bit the pigtail end; primed the pan; poured the powder, ball, and paper down the muzzle; and rammed the firelock tight. They were ready to shower a second curtain of lead upon the British.

At the same time, Peter and the 2nd Virginia Brigade could see Muhlenberg's 1st Virginia follow with another volley into the forward ranks of the enemy. On Muhlenberg's left flank, the 1st North Carolina Regiment under Brigadier Francis Nash and remnants of Sullivan's retreating patriots dealt a stern blow into the right flank of the Crown's 1st Grenadiers. The British advance ground to a halt . . . but they did not retreat. Their officers re-formed their men, ordered "prime and load," and prepared to leverage their peerless European training and discipline to push the Americans out of Sandy Hollow Gap. The British fired, and musket shot crackled into the woods like a hard rain. Soldiers were hit. Some cried out. Men fell. Peter reloaded. He aimed and fired. Smoke filled the air and stung the eyes, and sulfur burned the soldiers' nostrils. Patriot lead now ripped into the British from three vectors. The second imperative of General Greene's mission soon became apparent. Retreating Americans began filing through the lines of Muhlenberg and Weedon's Virginians and heading to safety. Francisco and his fellow Virginians had to remain on the battlefield to guard the retreat, keep the British at bay, and avoid shooting their own patriot soldiers withdrawing in the smoke and haze. The flanking 2nd Virginia was interspersed among the forest and brush, so with their position now apparent to the enemy, fire by volleys was no longer practical. The men would likely have formed teams of two or more to fire and reload in alternative fashion—firing by files. The goal was to have a loaded firelock always ready to deliver, and not to fire until a teammate's recently discharged weapon was reloaded. Organization in the heat of battle certainly gave some soldiers cause to devolve to irregular fire—men frantically reloading and firing downrange as rapidly as possible.

That evening, the fate of Washington's army and the American Revolution hinged to a great extent on the fortitude of the 1st and 2nd Virginia brigades. The British would not retire. The Virginians would not yield. In the midst of these pendulum swings between protecting fleeing comrades and striking the pursuing British, portions of the battle lines devolved into a hand-to-hand melee. Peter Francisco engaged in ferocious fighting for forty-five minutes. His fellow soldiers, seeing bravery of their comrade in close-quarters combat, were inspired to hold their positions alongside Francisco "where his berserk fury and terrifying strength appalled both the British and his own commanders."[16] The young Virginian was baptized not only in the fire of combat but also in the blood of injury as he took a musket ball in the leg.[17] Still the Virginians fought on despite Weedon's 2nd Virginia being targeted by British artillery in the final hour of engagement.[18] Darkness began to fall, and Washington's retreating army was now safely to the east of Sandy Hollow Gap. Peter Francisco and the Virginians could finally depart the field.

Several observers confirmed that Weedon's men held their calm during the fight—deftly opening ranks and permitting retreating Americans to pass through their lines to safety and then closing ranks to deliver a hard strike on the British advance.[19] Weedon himself, in a letter to Virginia councilman John Page, recounted that his brigade "gave the Enemy such a check as produced the desired effect."[20] General Weedon was modest as the Virginians nearly destroyed the officer corps of two regiments of the British 4th Brigade—specifically the 46th and 64th regiments of foot including the commander of the 64th (Major Robert McLeroth) being taken out of action with a bullet wound.[21] It is not in dispute that Greene and his Virginia brigades were key in facilitating the Continental Army's orderly retreat and survival.[22] With a well-timed charge by Count Pulaski's cavalry in support, the Americans inflicted dreadful casualties. Greene's deft rearguard action, including the performance of the 10th Virginia, spared Washington's army annihilation and arguably preserved the colonies' fortunes in the war. The Continental forces slipped down the road to Chester, Pennsylvania, in darkness. As with Manhattan, the Americans were outflanked and beaten losing approximately thirteen hundred soldiers (killed, wounded, or captured) to Howe's six hundred.[23] Still, the "Old Fox," the British *nom de guerre* for General Washington, had again vanished into the mist, and he was still positioned between Howe and the capital.

As for Peter Francisco, he required medical treatment for the musket ball wound. The procedure was apt to be performed expeditiously at a field hospital. The sights and sounds of the medical activity would have been stirring—even to a giant. The regimental surgeons may have had an apothecary and nurses assigned; otherwise, camp followers often volunteered to assist the physicians. Given the presence of only two colonial medical colleges in America (Philadelphia and New York), rare was the presence of a formally educated physician like the venerable Benjamin Rush. Dr. Rush was present at Brandywine, and he was the equal of any physician of the day. Rush accrued stints of learning and lecturing in Edinburgh, London, and Paris before landing a prewar position as a professor of chemistry in nearby Philadelphia. Conversely, nine out of ten American doctors in this period achieved their education through apprenticeship under an established surgeon.

Ironically, combat casualties were a less common cause of death as disease claimed 70–90 percent of the lives lost in the War for Independence. For the combat casualties at Brandywine, treatment likely fell into the following categories: bullet wounds; stabbing wounds from bayonets; amputations required for joint wounds, shattered bones, or compound fractures; and finally trepanning (or primitive skull surgery) for head wounds.[24] Francisco would certainly have witnessed or heard the cries from amputations at some point during his service—perhaps at Brandywine. A skilled surgeon could perform an amputation in three minutes without anesthesia. The patient would be comforted by biting into a stick wrapped in cloth. A strap and screw tourniquet would be applied to stem blood flow, and the surgeon would target a hand's breadth above the wound for the procedure. A curved knife would be used to quickly cut into the flesh and through muscle and tendons down to the bone. A retractor would take the form of a wide leather strap with a channel cut at the midpoint leading to a circular notch in the center of the tool. The retractor would be slid onto the newly exposed bone along the channel until it reached the notch. The leather strap would be pulled back on both sides against the flesh to expose several inches of healthy bone. A saw would be utilized by the surgeon to quickly cut through the bone. The retractor would be removed to permit the healthy flesh and a skin flap to slide back and cover the freshly sawed bone. Blood vessels then would be tied off with ligatures.[25] The skin flap would be wrapped and dressed around the stump—all steps in a few minutes' time and without anesthesia. Amputations had a 50 percent mortality rate.

Musket ball wounds like that of Private Francisco's were a tricky and painful procedure owing to the unpredictable routes the round bullets might take after entering the body. The surgeon would typically make use of a long metal probe with a curved end to dig around in the wound track to find and then excavate the ball. After removal, the wound would be dressed with a prayerful hope that a deadly infection would not follow. Infection and pus discharges in wound care were quite common during this time. In fact, physicians thought the presence of the secretion was a beneficial part of the healing process, and the weeping wounds were said to have "laudable pus."[26] In Peter Francisco's case, he would have the musket ball removed from his thigh, and he would convalesce from his wound in the Moravian village of Bethlehem—fifty miles north of Philadelphia. On September 21, the Marquis de Lafayette (also wounded at Brandywine) arrived in Bethlehem for hospitalization where he became acquainted with the American behemoth named Peter. Both the noble Frenchman and the "Virginia Giant" would be sheltered and under the nursing care of a local woman—Madam Gilbert.[27] From this chance meeting, a great friendship between comrades was born that would last throughout the war and decades beyond. As a testament to Peter Francisco's youth and superior physical condition, he returned to duty in time for an impending clash at Germantown—a mere twenty-three days after taking the musket shot to his leg at Brandywine.[28]

THE FALL OF PHILADELPHIA

Washington's army dealt with the defeat at Brandywine and maintained morale. Subsequently, he issued a call for reinforcements and received approximately three thousand Continentals and militia over the next two weeks. The Americans continued the practice of maneuvering and blocking British forces from Philadelphia with skirmishes occurring along the way. One of the Americans shadowing the British was Brigadier General "Mad" Anthony Wayne and his Pennsylvanians. His nickname was derived from his fiery aggressiveness and tactical innovation. But at Paoli, Wayne's troops were set upon by British Major General Lord Charles Grey. The stealth attack occurred at 1:00 a.m. on September 21 with Grey's men ordered to remove the flints from their muskets and wield only bayonets. Insufficient pickets meant Wayne's Americans were caught sleeping, and three hundred were lost to the blade—many in their bedding. Another one hundred were captured, and General Wayne only narrowly escaped. British General Charles "No-Flint" Grey lost only eight men. A stunned General Washington cautiously continued to shadow Howe the next day. The British commanding general, however, deftly lured the Americans out of position, doubled back across Flatland Ford, and entered Philadelphia on September 26, 1777. The capital was lost, and the Congress was forced to evacuate west to York. The Americans were bolstered only by the news that British

General Burgoyne was bogging down in his Hudson Valley campaign to the north. As for Washington, he would remain in the area and seek an opportunity to dislodge the British from the former capital. To that end, the Continental Army established camp twenty-five miles west of Philadelphia near Skippack Creek.[29]

Chapter 5

THE FOG OF WAR

Philadelphia Campaign
Germantown

General William Howe had a conundrum. He had just captured the capital of the rebellion—Philadelphia. Still, his was an occupying force in a city that was less than hospitable. Moreover, supplies presented a problem. Ideally, he should have been able to have British ships transport provisions up the Delaware River to his position at Philadelphia, but the Americans had fortified the shoreline of the tributary to include Fort Mifflin on Mud Island and Fort Mercer across the river on the New Jersey shore. Howe was forced to maintain and protect a fifty-mile overland supply route from Philadelphia to his point of debarkation in August—Head of Elk, Maryland. As a measure of force protection, Howe chose to garrison some nine thousand of his men including Hessians at Germantown, which lay five miles north of Philadelphia and on the east side of the Schuylkill River. Upon learning this, General Washington decided to attack the encamped British and Hessians.

General Washington and his leadership conceived a complex battle plan for Germantown. The patriot army would march over fifteen miles through the night and launch a four-pronged attack from the north at dawn utilizing the four separate roads leading into the town. Major General John Sullivan's column—two brigades of Marylanders—would lead the main attack southward down the center along Skippack Road. Sullivan would be joined by Brigadier General Anthony Wayne's division consisting of two brigades of Pennsylvanians. A third brigade from the Keystone State under the command of Brigadier General Conway would follow Wayne. Washington commanded from this center force. Generals William Maxwell and William

Alexander were in reserve to the rear on Skippack Road. To Sullivan's left (and to the east) was Major General Nathanael Greene's column consisting of his Brandywine division (the 1st and 2nd Virginia brigades to which the 10th Virginia Regiment and Peter Francisco were assigned). Brigadier Peter Muhlenberg was placed in tactical command of Greene's entire division of Virginians. Greene's column would proceed down Limekiln Road and was joined by Major General Adam Stephen's division (made up of the 3rd and 4th Virginia brigades) as well as Brigadier General Alexander McDougall's Connecticut Brigade and Count Casimir Pulaski's cavalry. The final columns would be militia brigades under generals John Armstrong and William Smallwood. They would take the outer two prongs on the patriots' extreme right and left flanks along Manatawney Road to the west and York Road to the east, respectively.[1]

The complexity of Washington's plan along with an early morning mist contributed literally to a *fog of war* that would be factors in the Americans undoing in this battle.[2] On the evening of October 3, 1777, the commanders leading the four vectors of attack were to march the fifteen miles to their staging points. Major General Greene's column had a longer route to their rally point, and the extended march would result in a delay of deployment of troops along Limekiln Road.[3] General Washington was with Major General John Sullivan's column on Skippack Road, and Sullivan commenced the attack as planned at dawn against the enemy center.

Through the fog, Sullivan's men immediately overran the British light infantry pickets at Mount Airy, and what British General Howe thought was only a rebel scouting party turned out to be Washington's main body wielding the initiative and moving south toward Germantown.[4]

Major General Sullivan's advance was paced by Brigadier Anthony Wayne's men who were still smarting from being caught off guard by "No-Flint" Grey's men at Paoli the previous month. Sullivan and Wayne put the picketing 2nd Light Infantry Battalion on the run and charged past an impressive stone structure called *Chew House* (or *Cliveden*). This was the summer home of the Chief Justice of the Pennsylvania Supreme Court, Benjamin Chew. In the chaos and fog, another redcoat picketing detail from the 40th Regiment of Foot was now cut off from General Howe's forces in Germantown. The stranded British detachment was led by forty-year-old Lieutenant Colonel Thomas Musgrave. Adapting to the situation, Musgrave ordered his men numbering approximately 120 to seize, fortify, and defend themselves from Chew House. Musgrave left a detail of men on the bottom floor to barricade doors and bayonet any patriot intruders. He ascended to the second floor with the remainder of his men to position themselves

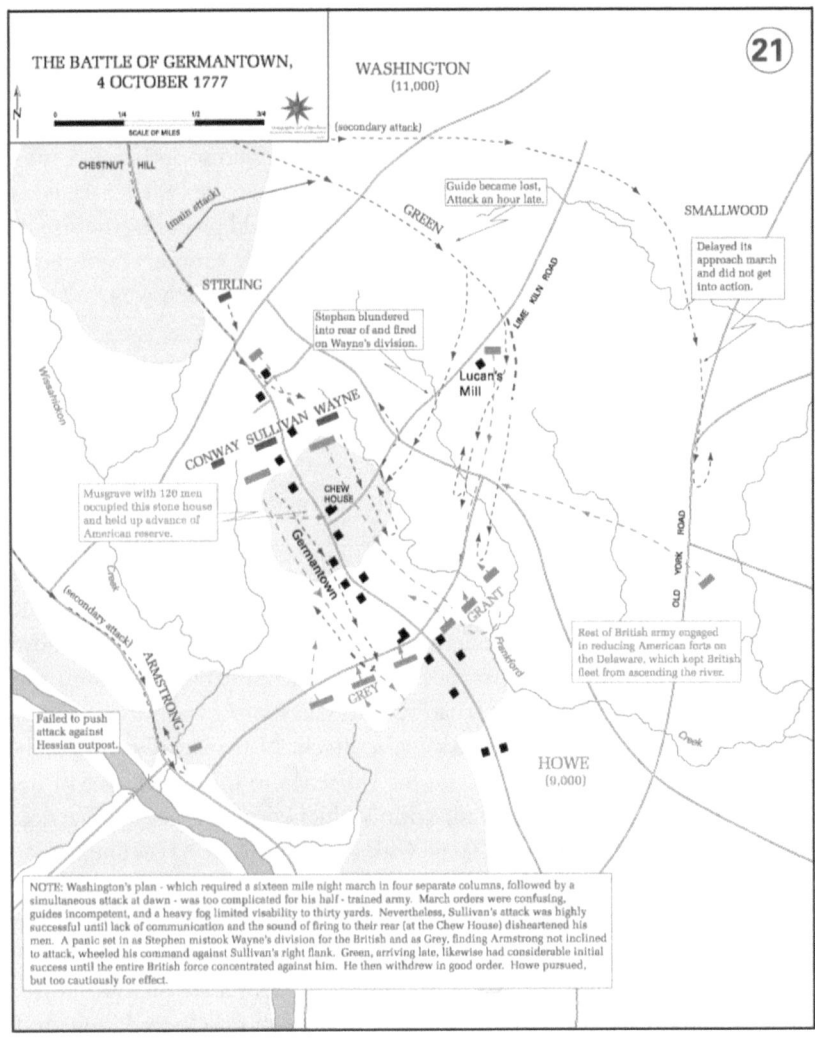

The Battle of Germantown.
United States Military Academy History Department

to defend the house with musket fire from elevated positions through the upstairs windows.

Washington received word of the British holdouts and faced a dilemma. Should he bypass Chew House or attack the enemy contained within? He took quick counsel and received conflicting advice from his adjutant—Massachusetts attorney Colonel Timothy Pickering and former book purveyor—now Brigadier General Henry Knox. Knox was assigned as part of Lord Stirling's reserve and had already established his reputation as an able artillery commander. Pickering advised the American commanding general to isolate Chew House by assigning a regiment to keep the enemy bottled up. Knox countered by advising against leaving *a castle* to the rear of the lead elements. Washington sided with Knox who soon began a cannonade with his 3-pounders. General Knox's cannons were called *3-pounders* owing to the custom of categorizing revolutionary field pieces by the size of projectile launched from the gun. As such, 3-pounder cannons fired metal projectiles weighing three pounds even though the guns each weighed several hundred pounds in total.

The stone walls of Chew House proved impervious to Knox's artillery, so two of Brigadier William Maxwell's reserve New Jersey regiments attempted a direct assault. The assault consumed an hour of valuable time and ammunition, and it resulted in fifty Americans dead. The British suffered only two killed in the engagement. In the aftermath, the ground floor and adjacent steps of Cliveden would be compared to a slaughterhouse.[5] During the unsuccessful siege of Chew House, Sullivan and Wayne's divisions began to run low on ammunition. Moreover, upon hearing the Cliveden assault to their rear, the American generals presumed the British were somehow encircling them. They began to retrace their path northward through the smoke and mist—up Skippack Road toward Cliveden.[6]

To the left (east) of Sullivan's main attack, Nathanael Greene's column went into action for better and for worse. As to the better, two of his Virginia brigades (the 1st and 2nd) with Muhlenberg and George Weedon slammed into the British right flank with the 9th Virginia Regiment taking more than one hundred enemy prisoners by way of a bayonet advance. Conversely, Brigadier General Alexander McDougall's Connecticut Brigade got lost and never saw action. Worse, Major General Adam Stephen had yielded to his fondness for the drink and was inebriated on the morning of the attack. He heard the sounds of the assault on Chew House and ordered his 3rd and 4th Virginia brigades to diverge from the planned line of attack down Limekiln Road and drive southwest through the fog and smoke toward the sounds of the clash. As the center force of Sullivan and Wayne were backtracking northward up Skippack Road, Greene's drunk and errant General Stephen mistook General Wayne's troops as British and fired through the haze into Wayne's men. Wayne returned fire into Stephen's column, and both divisions engaged in a confused melee before mutually breaking off their respective attacks.[7]

The time spent addressing the threat at Cliveden gave the British commander, General Howe, the opportunity to seize the initiative. Howe moved up from Germantown and mounted a counterattack, breaking up Washington and Sullivan's primary effort on Skippack Road. Meanwhile, General Greene was undermanned with only his two Virginia brigades engaged according to plan and the other units under Stephen and McDougall either lost or interlocked in self-destructive friendly fire. With the backtracking by Sullivan and Wayne's main body, Greene's Virginians were now dangerously overextended as the British pressed north. In fact, the entire 9th Virginia Regiment that had previously led Greene's column and captured British prisoners were themselves surrounded and compelled to surrender. As such, Greene had no choice but to disengage and leave the field to the British.[8] The plight of the center prongs' flagging fortunes was compounded by generals Armstrong and Smallwood's outer columns failing to engage in the fight as planned.

With their flanks seemingly unthreatened, the British could press a vigorous counterattack against Sullivan and Greene's center columns. Sensing victory, Howe put his redcoats in hot pursuit of the retreating Americans. For nine miles, the Crown forces dogged the patriots. Greene once again turned to his Virginians to check the enemy and facilitate the escape of their fellow comrades. Greene's men, including Peter Francisco, wheeled, formed, and faced the pursuing British. In action reminiscent of Brandywine, the Virginians covered the retreat by holding off the pursuing redcoats and deftly opening lines for retreating Continentals to make their

American attack on Chew House at the Battle of Germantown. By Edward Lamson Henry.
Art Institute of Chicago
Upper right insert: Chew House today.
Photo by J. T. Palmer

way to safety. Here again was Peter Francisco, aged seventeen years and still recovering from a Brandywine musket ball wound three weeks earlier, standing firm to preserve Washington's army.[9]

Beyond the macro sequence of occurrences at Germantown, a detailed micro-examination reveals an arduous chain of events in and around Germantown for Peter Francisco and his fellow Virginia patriots on October 3–4, 1777. The Americans had begun their fifteen-mile approach at dusk on the night before the battle. The four columns made their way in the dark taking great pains to keep silent to conceal their movements. The goal was to make it to their destination by 5:00 a.m. to start simultaneously the four-pronged assault. Understandably, some men were late to their appointed stations, including Nathanael Greene and his Virginia brigades. No doubt, Muhlenberg, Weedon, Francisco, and their fellow Virginians heard the report of Sullivan's main thrust down Skipjack Road. Knowing they were behind their time, these men must have felt the pressure to move into final position rapidly to do their part and engage the British down Limekiln Road. Within Greene's column, only the Virginia brigades under Muhlenberg and Weedon would make it to their commander's rally point at Market Square. Darkness would have given way to morning twilight, but the combined mist and smoke obscured vision beyond a few dozen yards. Confusion, chaos, and fear of the unknown in the fog would have been palpable among the companies. Major General Greene likely experienced conflicting emotions of joy and outrage as his Virginia brigades showed their mettle while Brigadier Alexander McDougall was lost in the woods, and the inebriated General Adam Stephen veered to the west and ultimately caused a friendly fire dust-up with "Mad" Anthony Wayne's units.

The Virginians' initial progress would have proved thrilling as Greene's lead elements dispatched the British pickets at Lukens Mill and the 9th Virginia Regiment captured one hundred of the enemy. The anticipation of victory would soon disappear with the fading sounds of musket and artillery to the west as the main body on Skipjack Road retreated north toward Cliveden. Greene's order to retreat must have been soul crushing to the Muhlenberg division. Representing only half of their column's strength, brigadiers Muhlenberg and Weedon had done their part and pushed back the British. Where had Sullivan's column gone? What about the outer columns under Armstrong and Smallwood? The British were now everywhere, and the 9th Virginia Regiment disappeared in the sea of Howe's reconstituted redcoats closing fast on Francisco and the rest of Weedon's brigade. The Virginians were facing the Crown's 25th and 27th regiments of foot and had to move out straightaway.[10]

Across all retreating American columns, the balance teetered between undisciplined chaos and a semi-orderly withdrawal as soldiers fired while retreating. Francisco and his comrades would alternate facing and firing at the oncoming enemy while their patriot cohorts would simultaneously retreat and prepare for their turn to check the redcoat pursuit. The British harried their quarry on the run. For the Americans, it was a maddening process of *retreat, halt, turn, fire,* and *reload* while resuming the *retreat*. Over the nine-mile pursuit, the British formations became understandably unwieldy, and this gave the Virginians time to re-form and present a credible obstacle for the redcoats. Now finding some semblance of organization, the Virginians repeated their Brandywine exploits and alternatively fired at the British and shepherded their compatriots through their lines northward to safety. At the end of the day, Washington's retreat would cover sixteen miles. Peter Francisco and his patriot cohorts marched, attacked, fought, retreated, executed rearguard action, and finally found safety after maneuvering an astonishing forty-three miles over the previous twenty-four hours—only to snatch defeat from the jaws of victory—a bitter cup for the Americans. As stated by Brigadier General Anthony Wayne: "we ran away from the arms of victory open to receive us."[11] The conclusion of Brandywine and Germantown were eerily similar. Francisco and the 1st and 2nd Virginia brigades had again done their part to prevent the annihilation of Washington's army and facilitated an escape so that the Americans might live to fight another day.

On a more lighthearted subject, the day after the battle, some American soldiers remanded a small terrier to Washington that had been found on the battlefield. The tag on the dog indicated that he was the property of his British antagonist— General Sir William Howe. On October 6, Washington dispatched the canine under guard and a flag of truce with a letter stating: "General Washington's compliments to General Howe. He does himself the pleasure to return him a dog, which accidentally fell into his hands, and by the inscription on the Collar appears to belong to General Howe."[12]

Notwithstanding the loss, the historical impact at this point in the Philadelphia campaign was profound. This is evident both in the strategic prospects of victory for the Continental Army and fledgling United States as well as the tactical performance of Greene's column—specifically Muhlenberg and Weedon's Virginia brigades. From a strategic perspective, the British decision to employ their armies in two far-flung campaigns (Hudson Valley and Philadelphia) contributed to an undermanned General John Burgoyne being forced to surrender at Saratoga on October 17 to Major General Horatio Gates and the unheralded Brigadier Benedict

Arnold.[13] The French subsequently commenced active support of the American endeavor based partly on the Saratoga victory—but only partly. After defeat at Brandywine and the daring attack at Germantown, enemy leaders and potential allies alike were impressed with the actions of the Continentals in September and October 1777. General Howe conceded surprise that Washington would mount such an aggressive attack at Germantown so soon after defeats at Brandywine and Paoli. The French foreign minister, Count de Vergennes, hailed Germantown as an inspired effort by the Americans where raw recruits traded blows with such composure against the British and Hessians.[14] It would seem that where Saratoga opened the eyes of the French, Germantown, albeit a loss, closed the deal.

In a tactical sense, Major General Greene established himself as a proficient field general and his Virginia brigades as highly competent subordinate units when under fire. Greene proudly acknowledged the prowess of his Virginians—especially the 1st and 2nd Virginia brigades (inclusive of Francisco's 10th Regiment) as he bestowed high praise for their conduct in the Philadelphia campaign—particularly stemming British attacks in rearguard action and covering the retreats of American units. On Brandywine specifically, Nathanael Greene later stated boldly: "In the action of Brandywine last campaign, where I think both the general and the public were as much indebted to me for saving the army from ruin as they have ever been to any one officer in the course of the war." General Greene lamented Washington's lack of mention of his Virginia brigades in his after-action reports. Greene could only surmise that the commander in chief did not want to appear to favor units from his home state of Virginia.[15] Still, Greene was immodest but not inaccurate. His 1st and 2nd Virginia brigades were conspicuous silver linings in the dark cloud that hovered over the initial losses around Philadelphia.

Moreover, there was a glaring opportunity cost with the loss at Germantown. Perhaps French assistance may not have been required in North America had Chew House been isolated and bypassed instead of assaulted by the patriot reserve forces. There is a narrative by some historians that posits what might have happened had Washington taken Colonel Pickering's advice to post a regiment to watch Cliveden and rejected Knox's counsel to attack the structure. In this alternative scenario, the American reserves that were diverted and expended against Cliveden could have marched south down Skipjack Road and carried on the advances made initially by Sullivan and Wayne. Moreover, Greene's Virginia brigades (including Francisco) were deep into the British encampment at this point. There is a reasonable contention that Howe may have been forced to retreat to

Philadelphia—a city bound to the east, west, and south by the Delaware and Schuylkill Rivers. The Delaware River was in the possession of the patriots by way of Forts Mifflin and Mercer at this time, so supply and reinforcement (or evacuation) by sea were untenable. In a similar fashion to Yorktown in 1781, Washington might have potentially bottled up Howe's army in Philadelphia and compelled capitulation through siege as the redcoats were without logistics support nor an escape route.[16] Although we cannot be certain, a victory at Germantown so close on the heels of Saratoga may have precipitated an end to the War of Independence in 1777.

Regardless of historical theory, this British victory would be a *last huzzah* for General Howe. Tactically, he stemmed a surprise attack at Germantown and displayed excellence on the battlefield by outmaneuvering Washington at Brandywine—as he had done previously at places such as Long Island, White Plains, and Short Hills.[17] Nevertheless, as commander in chief of British land forces, he was strategically undone by the Burgoyne loss at Saratoga and the benign effect of capturing Philadelphia. As a result, the French were now committed to the patriot cause in North America. Howe would tender his resignation as land forces commander in late October 1777 followed by a departure from North America in the spring. General Washington lost Brandywine and Germantown but held onto the strategic imperative of the Continental Army—to survive to fight future battles. Washington received his share of criticism and had to fend off a vocal minority headed by Horatio Gates calling for his replacement. The patriot's commander in chief from Virginia, however, was emboldened by the performance of many of his troops against the world-class army and mercenaries commanded by the British.[18] The drunk and blundering Major General Stephen who had fired upon the friendly brigades under Brigadier Anthony Wayne was cashiered, and his division was assigned to French Major General Lafayette.[19]

As for Peter Francisco, he faced the crucible of combat and demonstrated bravery in the face of the enemy. He led by example holding the line although wounded at Brandywine. Moreover, he returned to the battlefield three weeks later and served admirably through forty miles of marching and fighting at Germantown. He metamorphosized from raw recruit to a battle-tested veteran soldier. In the coming winter, he would defend a siege at a place called Mud Island and bivouac at Valley Forge where he would be drilled to Prussian standards by a wayward baron. Francisco would emerge from the coming winter ready to make his mark in the annals of warfare.

Chapter 6

TO THE LAST EXTREMITY

*Philadelphia Campaign
Fort Mifflin*

THE SIEGE OF FORT MIFFLIN

Despite the series of initial victories in the Philadelphia campaign, British General William Howe was still plagued with the problem of resupply of his forces. Ideally, the victory at Germantown would have been followed immediately by pursuit of the American rebels before winter set in. However, Howe was relegated to addressing concerns of basic care and feeding of his troops in Philadelphia owing to the patriots' control of the river access to the city. Downriver, a fleet of 250 ships of the Royal Navy loitered in Delaware Bay with men and materiel to reinforce and feed Howe's operations. The commander in chief of the Continental Army needed time to establish winter quarters, and the oncoming seasonal cold would halt the British maneuvers to corner and crush the rebellion. General George Washington's orders to the armed garrisons on the Delaware River were to "hold to the last extremity" as supplies to the Crown forces were vital to any British hopes of seeking and engaging the patriots before winter.[1] The American fortifications along the river prevented resupply by the tributary, and the greatest thorn in the side of the British was Fort Mifflin on Mud Island—positioned several miles downstream from Philadelphia. Fort Mifflin was a small fortification boasting triangular stone ramparts toward the river augmented by wooden palisades, earthworks, and barracks within. Even before the fight at Germantown, the British had begun their siege of Fort Mifflin beginning on September 26, 1777. The Crown forces employed the combined elements of one of Admiral Lord Richard Howe's naval squadrons led by Captain Francis Reynolds and ground forces commanded by Captain John Montresor. Captain Montresor was well acquainted with Fort Mifflin's construction, strengths, and weaknesses as he had designed the stronghold on Mud Island in 1771.

After the loss and retreat from Germantown, Private Peter Francisco reported to Fort Mifflin on October 22, 1777, along with other reinforcements ordered to the site by General Washington.[2] The garrison now numbered around five hundred and was under the command of a sickly Prussian officer—Colonel Baron Henry Leonard d'Arendt. With d'Arendt indisposed, the ranking officer was American Lieutenant Colonel Samuel Smith of the 4th Maryland Regiment. Across the river to the east lay a second American stronghold—Fort Mercer on the New Jersey bank of the Delaware. Fort Mercer was commanded by Colonel Christopher Greene and his 1st Rhode Island Regiment—the first all-black unit in the Continental Army. They were to be augmented by the 2nd Rhode Island Regiment. Fort Mifflin and Fort Mercer were supported by the Pennsylvania River Flotilla led by Commodore John Hazelwood.

Peter Francisco would not have long to wait for action on Mud Island. On the very day he arrived at Fort Mifflin, the British attacked Fort Mercer on the New Jersey side of the river by land with a Hessian force commanded by Colonel Carl von Donop. The disciplined Rhode Islanders held fire until the last possible seconds before delivering devastating fire onto the Hessians. The Americans at Fort Mercer had only thirty-five killed, wounded, or captured while inflicting more than ten times the casualties upon the Hessians. Von Donop was mortally wounded. Hours later, the British turned their attention to Fort Mifflin. They attacked by sea with their five-ship naval squadron and an assault force of two hundred grenadiers at the ready. The ships were to bombard the garrison putting the defenders' artillery out of action. Once the artillery was neutralized, the grenadiers were to storm the fort.

During the bombardment, pre-placed littoral obstructions and patriot cannon fire drove aground the sixty-four-gun ship of the line HMS *Augusta* and twenty-gun sloop HMS *Merlin*.[3] On the morning of October 23, the American forts trained their guns on the two ships, and the *Augusta* caught fire and exploded that same afternoon—a discharge that shattered windows in nearby Philadelphia and was heard more than thirty miles away. Vulnerable to cannonade from Forts Mifflin and Mercer, the crew of Merlin put their vessel to the torch and abandoned ship. Fort Mifflin was safe—for now.[4]

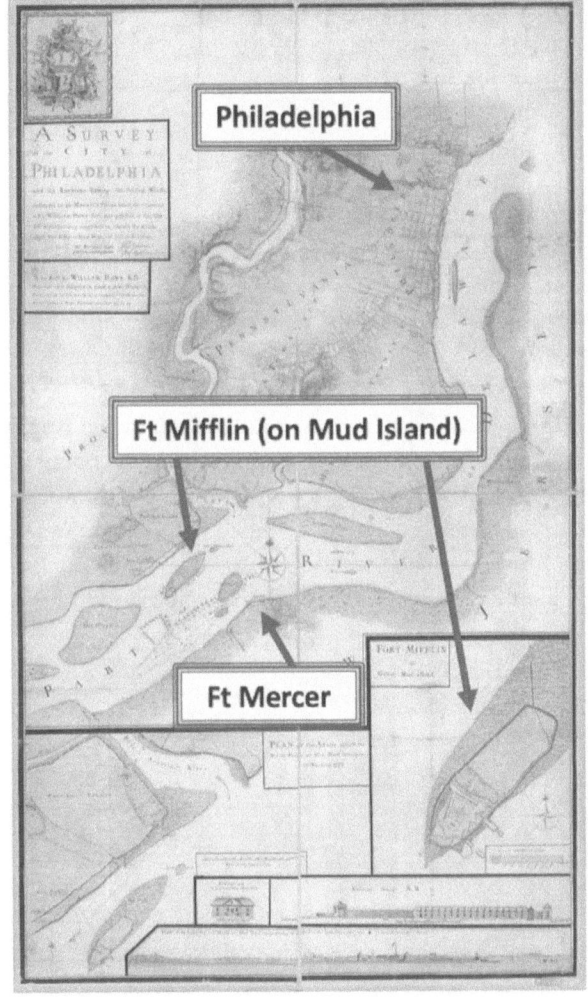

Map of Philadelphia and surrounding Delaware River area drafted by British troops, 1777.
Library of Congress; textboxes and arrows added by J. T. Palmer

On October 26, a violent nor'easter saturated the area and left much of Mud Island under water. Three days later, Washington placed responsibility for defense of the Delaware forts under the command of Brigadier General James Mitchell Varnum of Massachusetts, and he reinforced Mifflin with two Connecticut regiments. By early November, the British ground commander and former Fort Mifflin designer, Captain Montresor, formulated a plan to have guns placed and ready to pummel the Americans into submission. To augment the Royal Navy gunboats, Montresor placed fourteen cannons and mortars five hundred yards away at Province Island—a spit of land at the mouth of the Schuylkill River—to the northwest of Fort Mifflin and to the rear of the fort's most stalwart defenses. Montresor and his afloat comrades were about to embark on what would be the largest bombardment of the war.

On November 10, the British began a continuous four-day fusillade. The American defenders trudged along in knee-deep water, with scant food rations, and no sleep owing to the round-the-clock British cannon fire. Mifflin's soldiers could muster only ten pieces of artillery and were short on ammunition—so much so that the American commander offered extra rum rations to Continental soldiers brave enough to dart out into the field of fire and recover newly arrived British cannonballs for reuse by American gunners. The Americans suffered obscene casualties but persisted in restoring wooden palisades and earthworks at night to shore up defenses. The fort's nightly efforts in repair and refortification were under the superlative direction of French engineer Major François Louis Teissèdre de Fleury.[5]

On November 11, Fort Mifflin's commander—Lieutenant Colonel Smith—was stuck by a cannonball, severely wounded, and evacuated from the fort. Command transferred to Major Simeon Thayer of Rhode Island. It should not be interpreted that the American defenders simply took

Mud Island: Fort Mifflin with the Delaware River and New Jersey in the background.
Wikimedia Commons

cover during the siege. Deft troop rotation and resupply at night fueled active resistance. Of the patriot gunnery action from Fort Mifflin, British Lieutenant Francis Downman noted the Americans delivered grape shot "so thick that we could not stand to on our guns."[6] On November 14, the patriots silenced a floating British battery by concentrating sustained deadly fire that forced royal gunners to seek safety by leaping into the dark and frigid waters of the Delaware.[7] The defensive equilibrium achieved by the American patriots would be tilted in favor of the British owing to the weather and the Royal Navy's initiative. November 14 also brought unusually high tides that, along with recent rain storms, permitted eight Royal Navy gunboats armed with a total of 228 cannons to navigate the narrow western channel separating Mud Island and the Pennsylvania shore. The forlorn defenders of Fort Mifflin were now completely encircled. In addition, the British East India vessel *Empress of Russia* pulled alongside Mud Island close enough for British marines to scale the mast to the crow's nest and lob dozens of grenades directly into the fort as the cannonade from Province Island and the afloat gunboats continued. With the combined land and naval forces, the British were prepared to deliver as many as a thousand cannonballs per hour into the fort.[8] The prospects for long-term defense faded. Everyone knew it, yet Washington's orders to hold the fort echoed in the hearts and minds of the freezing, mud-soaked defenders. With their very lives, they had to buy time for the American army ashore to find safe winter quarters. They would hold to the last extremity.

It is difficult to relate to the plight of an American soldier charged with defending Fort Mifflin. Likely Peter Francisco would have preferred the cover and combat of Sandy Hollow Gap at Brandywine or the smoke and fog while attacking the British right flank at Germantown to the helplessness of a hopeless, waterlogged siege defense. For the "Virginia Giant" and the individuals charged with the defense of Mud Island, their courage was an exhibition of unflagging fortitude. Shelter during the British barrage was a dubious challenge. The November rains had made a cold muddy slop out of the interior grounds. The luxuries of food and heat gave way to the exigencies of self-preservation during the deafening, murderous offensive. November in Philadelphia is cold and doubly so along the Delaware. The ability to ignite and maintain fire for warmth would have been a nearly impossible task. The defenders' drive to survive would demand hours of crouched and cramped sheltering in small pockets of the fort where Royal Navy cannons, musketeers, and grenadiers could not direct fire. From their cold and wet existence, the American soldiers' bones would ache and muscles would stiffen and cramp. Rations were certainly sparse, cold, and likely consumed on the go in the mud and standing water. The sheltering would be interrupted by orders from the American officers to man guns, aim the cannons, and give an account to the British that the fort was still manned by men—by soldiers—by warriors. Under the cover of darkness, the demands of defense would be combined with the engineering brilliance of Major Fleury as he ordered and supervised the soldiers' reconstruction of palisades and shoring of walls and earthworks. Day by day, the enemy fusillade intensified as the defenders' resources diminished.

In the final days of the siege, a murderous barrage was planned. The Crown's gunners were allotted powder and ball sufficient to shoot in concert eighty rounds per cannon crew upon coordinated commands. The onslaught resulted in an average of more than sixteen cannonballs per minute impacting the fort during the final cannonade. Upon a projectile's impact, mud would often soar into the gray skies and then fall like heavy rain splattering as it returned to the mire. Some of the fort's interior buildings were subject to direct fire from the British cannoneers as they stood higher than the exterior stone walls, earthen embankments, and wooden palisades. Peter and his fellow defenders were actually safer when taking shelter against the lower surfaces of the fortress walls and inside the associated excavated tunnels and cavities.[9]

By November 14, an occasional flash could be seen and a report heard from one of the remaining serviceable patriot cannons, but it was not enough. No doubt, scuttlebutt abounded that the American ammunition was nearing depletion. The shower of British projectiles continued to slam into the muddy turf, and the ground shook. Some rounds would skip along the muck. Injured men caught out in the fort's center would have been devilishly hard to recover, and corpses were left unattended. A cohort of Francisco, diarist Joseph Plumb Martin, was also an American defending Fort Mifflin against all odds. He documented the action in his memoirs: "I have seen the enemy's shells fall upon it and sink so low (into the mud) that their report could not be heard when they burst, and I could only feel a tremulous motion of the earth at the time. . . . At other times, when they burst near the surface of the ground, they would throw mud fifty feet into the air." He further described numerous dead comrades as "split like fish to be broiled." Martin depicted the lot of the defenders as they "endured hardships, sufficient to kill a half a dozen horses."[10] Young Joseph Martin was just seventeen years of age—the same as Peter Francisco. The American prospects of holding Mifflin were now hopeless.

Major Thayer took inventory of the situation on the evening of November 14. Days of cold, rain, mud, and ceaseless cannonade from the

British had smashed the fort's defenses and shelters. The wooden palisades and barracks were wrecked. The fort's interior grounds were reduced to muddy cannonball ruts analogous to the furrows in a plowed field from the British gunboats' point-blank gun blasts. The American defenders had seen their ranks reduced by half. Mifflin had only two serviceable cannons and no ammunition remaining. Thayer would yield to the manifest demands of humanity. He ordered an evacuation across the river to Red Bank, New Jersey, near Fort Mercer. The withdrawal would take place by small boats with oars muffled by burlap for silent passage through the net of British gunships. In the last hours of November 15, the surviving contingent of more than two hundred American soldiers—including Peter Francisco—commenced their escape in silence under the cover of darkness.[11] The American commander stayed behind to spike cannons and torch any materiel of value to the enemy. As appropriate, Major Simeon Thayer was the last patriot to depart the fort, and he ordered the distinctive Mifflin battle flag of thirteen horizontal red, white, and blue stripes to remain aloft. At first light on November 16, all was silent. Officers of the Royal Navy observed the American banner was still on the flagstaff, but no activity was apparent. Had the rebels prepared an ambush within? The British entered cautiously, occupied the abandoned ruin, and struck the colors of the departed American defenders. As such, Fort Mifflin was defeated but never surrendered. The fall of Mud Island was followed precipitously by General Charles Cornwallis marshalling a force of five thousand on the New Jersey shore of the Delaware. The Americans at Fort Mercer had no choice but to evacuate on November 20.

The Royal Navy now controlled the Delaware River, and British maritime lines of logistics to Philadelphia were established. Howe's final victory in the Philadelphia campaign was hollow, however, given the recent surrender of Burgoyne at Saratoga and near-term Franco-American alliance that would bring French forces to North America. Worse, Howe's grip on the city was tenuous and slipping day by day. The British occupation of Philadelphia would last less than one year. Howe's resignation was already tendered; he would remove himself from the theater by spring 1778. For now, Washington would escape. A British observer described the extended American defense of Mud Island as "the costliest weeks of the war."[12] The delay enabled the rebel commander to maneuver and retire his army to winter quarters where they could rest, recover, retrain, and transform into a potent fighting force seeking action the following summer.

In retrospect, Private Francisco's brief tour of duty at Fort Mifflin spanned only twenty-four days. Still, these three weeks may have been the most harrowing and hazardous of his entire service in the American Revolution. Ambrose Serle, Secretary to General Howe, would recall, "The Americans defended ... Fort Mifflin with a spirit they have shown nowhere else to an equal degree during the Revolutionary war."[13] The artillery assault on Mifflin was the largest fusillade of the war. The defense—especially the final six-day resistance under the brutal British barrage—has been described "as heroic as any in history."[14] The valiant defenders were reduced to repairing damage, delivering insufficient fire, and taking cover in the frigid November mud as the enemy mercilessly raked them with shot and shell day and night. Nonetheless, Peter and the Mud Island defenders had held to the last extremity to make possible Washington's untrammeled establishment of a winter bivouac the following month. This was another desperate effort to preserve the cause for independence in which Francisco served bravely. At Mud Island, he was among the fortunate 50 percent to survive, but there would be little comfort for the weary soldier. After a multifarious display of courage under fire thus far in the Philadelphia campaign, he was unwell and required medical care and convalescence during the initial weeks of the upcoming encampment. To that end, Peter Francisco would descend into the most austere and consequential six months of the war. He would winter at Valley Forge.

FORT MIFFLIN POSTSCRIPT

Since the fall of Fort Mifflin, advocates and historians have differed on the causes of the destruction of HMS *Augusta* and HMS *Merlin* on October 23, 1777. Moreover, the historic understanding of the events has evolved over time. Understandably, American and British camps initially formed opposing positions. For most Americans, the ships were destroyed by fusillade from the patriot forts. For the British, the ships were torched by conscientious members of the Royal Navy who did not want the grounded ships to fall into the hands of the enemy. The historical truth may be somewhere in the middle.

Given her larger size, *Augusta* was the priority for American artillerymen and fell under concentrated assault as a result. The ship caught fire, and her magazine exploded shortly thereafter. The concussion shook Philadelphia, and the report was heard beyond the horizon. Many historians concede that the fire on board *Augusta* was likely started by the cannonade. The question remains why the officers and men of the Royal Navy would ignite the magazine of a ship that was already aflame? Perhaps they were abandoning ship and they wanted to *ensure* the vessel and contents would not be salvageable by the Americans at a later date. We may never know with certainty. As for *Merlin*, she blew up later in the afternoon. Most historians believe with fair conviction that *Merlin*, although fired upon by the Americans, was torched by her own men. In reality, the source of the fatal flames is immaterial. The two ships were both helplessly aground, unable to free themselves, and under enemy guns from two vectors. Whether the ships' final ignition was by American cannon fire or Royal Navy torches, these two men-of-war were destroyed because of their immobility and the presence of the patriot artillerymen.[15]

Chapter 7

THE CHRYSALIS

A Baron at Valley Forge

Valley Forge, Pennsylvania, was a loosely constituted industrial community located eighteen miles northwest of Philadelphia at the convergence of Valley Creek and the Schuylkill River. The village's collection of ironworks, machine shops, and mills was surrounded by Quaker farmland. The previous year, the Continental Army had periodically stockpiled ammunition and stores there, so the locality was familiar to the army staff. By setting his camp at Valley Forge, Washington could keep in close proximity to the British occupiers in Philadelphia and simultaneously check royal foraging excursions that ravaged the locals and their property.[1] South of the Schuylkill, on plateaued heights and east of Mount Joy is where the Continentals would make their encampment. Ideally, they would receive logistics support from stores maintained in the township of Reading—fifty miles northwest. The Continental Congress's adjustments made to the army's supply processes in mid-1777 were delayed in execution owing to the fall of Philadelphia and the evacuation of the capital. As a result, supply to the twelve thousand troops wintering in Valley Forge would be lacking.

The encampment commenced on December 19, 1777. General Washington had assigned specifications for two thousand wooden huts to be constructed as a superior option to sheltering in tents. The huts were constructed of notched logs that were weatherproofed by adding clay in the gaps with wood plank roofing. The dimensions of length and width were ordered to be sixteen feet by twelve feet with walls six feet in height. At one end of the hut was to be a fireplace with an oak door at the other end facing a pathway. Each hut would accommodate twelve soldiers. In actuality, all the huts were constructed in less than one month—so quickly that the dimensions and effectiveness of the shelters varied widely. Fireplaces were often ineffective as they channeled smoke into the huts. For the most part, only green wood was available for fuel, making the starting and maintaining of fires difficult. Latrines were built, but placement and use were suboptimal. As such, the huts and surrounding areas became filthy. Disease ran rampant, and three thousand American soldiers would ultimately die of disease and the elements at Valley Forge.[2]

More than one-third of the twelve thousand soldiers were not properly clothed and suffering from sickness, hunger, and exposure. Peter Francisco reported to Valley Forge on the heels of his service in the cold, mud, and blood of Fort Mifflin in ill health. He recuperated in hospital care during the first two months at Valley Forge.[3] He and the army faced stark privation during the months of December, January, and February.[4] His celebrated brigade commander, General George Weedon, stated the wintering effort could best be described as a hospital rather than an encampment and that the men were "destitute of every comfort," lacking shoes, clothing, and blankets.[5] General George Washington himself described the army as starving and in a state of famine in February. He lamented supply problems across all commodities to include the lack of footwear as he observed the Pennsylvania snow stained with the blood of his shoeless soldiers.[6] The camp received a January 1778 visit from a congressional delegation consisting of Gouverneur Morris of New York, Francis Dana of Massachusetts, John Harvie of Virginia, Nathaniel Folsom of New Hampshire, and Joseph Reed of Pennsylvania. The five-man delegation was instrumental in driving improvements in the commissary processes.[7] Still, changes in logistics fortunes were slow to develop. Washington wrote to the newly installed President of the Continental Congress (Henry Laurens of South Carolina), stating that the lack of logistics, not the British, might reduce his army as his soldiers were on a path to "starve—dissolve—or disperse."[8] To that end, Washington appointed Major General Nathanael Greene as Quartermaster General on March 2, 1777, to shore up his lines of logistics. Although hesitant to vacate his field command, Greene enthusiastically used his good offices as quartermaster to improve supply challenges dramatically during the second half of the winter encampment.[9]

Aside from the upgrade in logistics, Washington made the best use of the wintering to improve training, standards, order, and discipline within his army. The chasm between the British professional soldiers and the American patriot volunteers was profound. The redcoats trained daily under *The Manual Exercise* published in 1764. Each hand, finger, and foot movement was meticulously prescribed. There were no less than two dozen functions focused solely on loading, firing, and handling a musket, ammunition, and bayonet. Firing and reloading a musket, for example, demanded twelve intricate steps, including Poise Firelocks, Cock Firelocks, Present, Fire, Half Cock Firelocks, Handle Cartridge, Prime, Shut Pans, Charge with Cartridge, Draw Rammers, Ram Down Cartridge, and Return Rammers. Repeated drill and muscle memory were key to the British achieving a peerless level of close-order battlefield efficiency and effectiveness.[10]

Washington's catalyst for rapid improvement on the battlefield was a wayward Prussian officer styled as Friedrich Wilhelm August Heinrich Ferdinand von Steuben—known to history as Baron von Steuben. The baron was a war-wounded veteran of the battles of Prague and Kunersdorf and had reportedly served as aide-de-camp to Frederick the Great.[11] Arriving in North America in December 1777, he carried a glowing letter of introduction from Benjamin Franklin outlining a resume with a sprinkling of embellishments to include former service as a Prussian general officer. Von Steuben made a brief appearance before the Continental Congress in York before presenting himself to General Washington at Valley Forge on February 23, 1778. He immediately captured the attention of the commander in chief, his officers, and the rank-and-file soldiers. He was an impressive sight on horseback with blue coat and cloak adorned with the oversized, golden eight-point star of the Baden-Durlach Chivalric Order of Fidelity. He wore a black bicorn French hat and carried a silver-headed swagger stick. Knee-high boots, a sword, and pistols made him the image of a noble general officer clamoring to support a fledgling republic on foreign shores. Although his previous European military rank had been exaggerated, he was, in fact, a Prussian *Freiherr* or free lord. This title of nobility was honorary and not inherited, so von Steuben was essentially an unlanded baron.[12]

The baron was not a one-dimensional bully of a drillmaster; rather, he was also an enlightened European. He was socially and politically astute. Witty and engaging, he could disarm and charm senior officials and peers. He was an immediate hit with Washington's multilingual staff officers. French-speaking lieutenant colonels Alexander Hamilton and John Laurens could communicate directly with him without an interpreter.[13] Officers' wives swooned at his continental European grace, and he was an adept dancer. To the soldiers, von Steuben paid them a unique and important sign of respect by engaging them directly albeit with interpreters. He detected immediately the change in leadership methods he had to employ in the New World. Previously he had led land-bound serfs pressed into service in European armies. At Valley Forge, he was introduced to America's citizen-soldiers—free men fighting for freedom as volunteers. His American charges demanded to know *why* their orders were issued and not simply when and how to comply, but in balance the patriots proved resilient and able to adapt to difficult challenges.[14] Through his energy and theatrics, he could compliment, criticize, upbraid, and intimidate as necessary. In mere days after his arrival, von Steuben enjoyed the complete confidence of General Washington.

The baron was assigned the duties of Inspector General and given the rank of major general.[15] As Inspector General, he held sway over drill and training, discipline within the ranks, articulating logistics requirements, holding supply officers accountable, and tracking the size and state of the army.[16] Von Steuben instituted logistics records-keeping for supplies and dramatically improved accountability. As for the camp itself, he went straight to work. He inspected huts, latrines, cooking areas, and fortifications. Huts were realigned, and latrines and cooking areas were separated on opposite sides of the encampment to stem disease. Soldiers might suffer the lash for breaking von Steuben's hygiene regulations.

Beyond health and comfort for the encamped troops, von Steuben focused his attention on drill and discipline. He spoke scant English, so he communicated in French to his secretary and various bilingual officers who would serve as interpreters for the soldiers. Ironically, his penchant for profanity spanned multiple languages and was received as an endearing trait by the enlisted American soldiers.[17] He selected one hundred representatives from the various regiments, including Washington's honor guard, to form a model company. In one of the first American train-the-trainer programs, the baron instructed the members of the model company who would return and drill their individual regiments. Von Steuben infused a European-level of standardization and discipline in marching, formations, firearms, and bayonet combat.

He had no single foundation from which to work. Before von Steuben's arrival, each regiment instituted their own methods of drill and maneuver. As such, the baron was compelled to begin with the basic instruction on the *position of the soldier* or what military members today would call "standing at the position of attention." Facing movements followed. Marching at the *quick-step* (120 paces per minute) was established as opposed to a common British marching pace of 60 paces per minute which had been emulated by many American units. At a higher level of difficulty, he would teach his soldiers to rapidly wheel from columns on the march into long ranks of musketeers ready to deliver volleys toward an enemy in the field.[18] The baron had much to do and very little time to complete the transformation of his American citizen-soldiers. It would not be easy to match the British.

The baron's training began on March 24, 1778. Once the model company was sufficiently drilled, the representatives returned to their regiments for the training of their cohorts—all while under the critical eye of the impeccable Prussian drillmaster who one American private described as a mortal manifestation of a mythical "God of War."[19] Major General von Steuben would later codify his camp and soldiering standards by creating the *Blue Book* known officially as *Regulations for the Order and Discipline of the Troops of the United States*.[20] The baron's blue book would be the army standard throughout the next century, and his regulations and procedures impact U.S. land forces to this day.

At Valley Forge, the Americans had the luxury of a relatively secure environment over several months to focus all efforts on combat efficiency. A firelock may take from fifteen to thirty seconds to reload. The difference between two rounds of directed fire per minute and three or more rounds could be vital as rate of fire trumped accuracy with musket combat. This was especially true when facing the British as the Crown forces were somewhat unique in their live-fire drilling or the actual shooting of musket balls while in training. Americans were more likely to fire their muskets with powder but not musket balls ("firing blanks" in modern parlance). This was to conserve the precious projectiles while still ensuring their soldiers could develop the tactile skills necessary to rapidly reload and discharge their weapons with an audible report from the gunpowder as proof of process and proficiency.

As introduced earlier, accuracy was secondary to rate of reload and fire owing to the random, knuckle-ball flight of musket balls. A rank or section of musket-armed soldiers provided a shotgun-scatter of lead balls downrange that would indiscriminately strike the mass of enemy soldiers closing one's position. America's famed Continental sharpshooters trained in a different fashion. For soldiers bearing long guns with rifled barrels, these weapons discharged spinning projectiles, and accurate shots were expected. Rate of fire was less important as riflemen could target an individual enemy soldier at long range and, with practice, hit their targets with great frequency. Sharpshooters also employed stealth and cover, and they sought to make every shot count. The British officer corps wearing prominent epaulets suffered frightful losses from eagle-eyed backwoodsmen carrying long rifles. As such, riflemen were expected to engage in target practice sufficient to develop the precious and perishable skill of long-range accuracy.[21]

The Americans would learn that the discipline of delivering musket fire was multidimensional. Units might fire by Volley, Sections, Ranks, Files, through Street Firing tactics, or while Firing while Advancing/Retiring from the field. The most common was *fire by volley* where one or two ranks of standing soldiers might fire simultaneously with one or two ranks of kneeling soldiers directly in front of them. When two ranks of standing or kneeling soldiers were employed, the second rank of musket-men would position themselves offset by half of a shoulder's width to permit all ranks to fire in unison. Through simultaneous firing, accidents caused by reloading were mitigated as all soldiers would execute the function at the same time. The entire unit was also exposed to danger, however, as they would be unable to reload, make ready, aim, and fire for fifteen to thirty seconds.

A mitigating tactic was to *fire by sections*, and a section could be a platoon or company of men. The positioning of men within each section would be similar to volley firing (standing and kneeling ranks). The difference was that each section would take turns firing one after the other permitting safe reloading within each section while other sections trained nearly constant fire downrange. Some eighteenth-century armies trained their soldiers in *firing by ranks*, but the use of this tactic was actually somewhat rare. Firing by ranks involved the alternating fire of the standing ranks while kneeling ranks reloaded (and vice versa). This is sometimes seen in cinematic depictions of eighteenth-century warfare. This tactic was seldom used because it was dangerous to have one rank of soldiers maneuvering their weapons during the reloading process of priming, loading, and ramming while another rank of soldiers (standing or kneeling) was attempting to take aim and fire downrange.

A more common method was *firing by files*. As addressed previously, this was often a light infantry tactic involving collections of small teams of two or three men. Working as a team, shooters and reloading soldiers would rotate to deliver fire downrange (or weapons were swapped back and forth between shooters and reloaders) to increase the rate of fire and to have at least one loaded weapon at the ready at all times. *Street firing* and *firing while advancing / retiring* were sometimes utilized. These formations involved multiple ranks. There were small numbers in each rank in narrow streets, and potentially large numbers in each rank for an expansive battlefield. Regardless, both the *street firing* and *firing while advancing* or *retiring* employed the idea of front ranks firing and then retiring in an orderly fashion to the rear of a small column to reload while forward ranks delivered volleys. This ensured a reloaded rank that was ready to fire was always facing the enemy, and it protected the reloading soldiers in the ranks to the rear.[22]

Baron von Steuben instituted a hyper-efficient *Continental Manual Exercise* or *manual of arms* in today's military vernacular. Similar in some degree to the British 1764 *Manual Exercise*, the baron sought to standardize the soldiers' every motion with their firelocks from the position of a soldier under arms (the position of attention) to the loading, firing, reloading, fixing and charging bayonets, laying down, shouldering, and saluting with muskets. Given the close order (compressed, shoulder-to-shoulder formations), the units within the Continental Army must act as one with their firelocks. To have extraneous actions or movements out of synchronization could cause clashing and banging of weapons, rammers, or cartridges and potentially the accidental discharge of a musket. Moreover, the Americans were taught economies of movement in pursuit of their readiness to fire more rapidly than their royal counterparts. Efficient rate of fire over a harrowing three or four minutes at close range was the life-or-death prospect for the opposing armies on the battlefield. Von Steuben brought the Continental regulars to equal standing with the Crown forces in a very short time at Valley Forge.[23]

In summary, the baron standardized the bivouac, optimized the handling of firearms, and accelerated the marching methods for the patriots. The end game was to speed the maneuver and alignment of soldiers on the battlefield with Prussian precision so that Americans could win in conventional eighteenth-century warfare. The army's remarkable metamorphosis took less than three months. Under the tutelage of Baron von Steuben, Peter Francisco and his comrades underwent a second transformation—this time from a collection of armed farmers and tradesmen who had showed courage under fire to an army of well-trained, highly disciplined soldiers ready to trade blows with the British and their Hessian mercenaries on open ground. On June 19, 1778, after a spring with upgraded supplies, improved sanitation, and focused training, the Americans broke camp at Valley Forge spoiling for a fight. One of their first opportunities proved to be the last chapter in the Philadelphia campaign—nine days later at Monmouth Courthouse in New Jersey.

Chapter 8

COLONEL DANIEL MORGAN

Philadelphia Campaign
Monmouth Courthouse

June 1778: The Franco-American Treaty of Alliance was signed the previous February, and the agreement changed the calculus in North America for the British. Lieutenant General Sir Henry Clinton was now in charge of the British forces as General William Howe had resigned and subsequently departed North America. There was concern that British soldiers in Philadelphia could be cut off by America's land forces in concert with the ships of their new French allies. To that end, Clinton was under direction to coalesce his forces in New York, and he departed Philadelphia on June 18. One day later, George Washington moved his forces out of Valley Forge in pursuit. After six months in encampment and fresh off Friedrich von Steuben's accelerated course in eighteenth-century warfare, the American general was eager to prove his army the equal of his British adversary. Washington's officers and men were correspondingly enthusiastic, and Clinton's redeployment to New York was opportune. As for Peter Francisco, the patriot muster rolls from April–August 1778 still held him as assigned to the 10th Virginia Regiment; however, during this time his company command had shifted to Captain John Mountjoy, and the regiment was now under the leadership of Colonel John Green.[1] Born in 1742, Captain Mountjoy was from Stafford, Virginia, and served only from January to September 1778.[2] Colonel John Green was born in 1730 in Culpepper County, Virginia. Colonel Green would perform a total of eight years' service during the Revolution, and he commanded the 10th Virginia from January to September 1778.[3]

While on the march, General Clinton determined the best route to New York was to move his force of soldiers, mercenaries, and loyalists ninety miles to Sandy Hook, New Jersey, where they would be ferried by the Royal Navy over the final twelve miles to New York City. He immediately crossed the Delaware River into New Jersey and moved northeast. His division commanders were generals Charles Cornwallis and Wilhelm von Knyphausen leading ten thousand and seventy-five hundred soldiers, respectively. When possible, the divisions marched in parallel to permit mutual screening and support should the Americans harass or attack the evacuation. The June heat was stifling at well above 90 degrees Fahrenheit, and progress was slow. The two divisions passed through the New Jersey towns of Haddonfield and Mount Holly and then divided arriving on June 24 at Allentown and Imlaystown—nearly halfway to Sandy Hook.

Washington had a dilemma. Although he was happy to observe the redcoats depart Philadelphia, Clinton's army was a deadly and sizable force capable of doing great damage to the Americans if the British seized initiative and advantage. Still, he could not let the British march through New Jersey unchallenged. The Steuben-trained Americans wanted to test their newfound battlefield proficiency. Perhaps Nathanael Greene described most aptly the urgency of the situation as he advised his commander in chief: "If we suffer the enemy to pass through the Jerseys without attempting anything upon them, I think we shall ever regret it . . . people expect something from us and our strength demands it." The British march had to be contested. Along the route, Washington would convene a council of war. He determined he would apply a strategy of calculated risk and limited engagement by attacking the enemy's rear guard and potentially drawing a significant portion of the British Army into an exchange favorable to the Americans.[4]

Speed was crucial. Peter Francisco and Washington's army moved more swiftly than the British as they marched north of the Delaware River and through Pennsylvania crossing into New Jersey at Coryell's Ferry. Washington's force of 14,500 was divided into two wings commanded by Major General William Alexander (Lord Stirling) and Major General Charles Lee with French Major General Gilbert du Motier, Marquis de Lafayette, commanding a reserve. General Lee was an English-born (and one-time British) officer who was released recently from captivity in April during a prisoner exchange. Lee had suffered ignominious capture by Banastre Tarleton's men while visiting a New Jersey tavern in December 1776. Washington's army was bolstered by 1,200 New Jersey and Pennsylvania militia already in the field commanded by Major General Philemon Dickinson. Irish-born Brigadier William Maxwell's New Jersey

Brigade had been dispatched previously by Washington to join Dickinson and harass the British while on the march. By June 23, Washington positioned his main army at Hopewell, New Jersey—twenty-five miles north of Cornwallis's camp at Allentown. On the same date, Washington detached Colonel Daniel Morgan and 600 light infantrymen south to assist the New Jersey militia in harassing and slowing the British. Peter Francisco would be a *picked man*—a by-name assignment to Colonel Morgan's advance force of light infantry for the upcoming battle. Morgan was the renowned leader of Virginia sharpshooters known as Morgan's Riflemen, who were some of the most proficient and feared marksmen in the Revolution. It was said that each of Morgan's men could "cleave with his rifle ball a squirrel at three hundred yards" while on the run (double-quick time).[5] Morgan's Riflemen famously killed British General Simon Fraser at long range and helped tip the scales toward American victory at Saratoga. Morgan was subsequently captured by the British at Quebec, released through an exchange, and placed in command of the 11th Virginia Regiment.

Colonel Daniel Morgan was a tough leader forged from a tough life. Born around 1735 in New Jersey, he was on his own at age seventeen owing to friction with his father. After moving to Virginia's Shenandoah Valley, he made his fortune as a teamster. As a civilian, he served as a wagoner transporting equipment and supplies in the French and Indian War. His animus toward the British sprang from a fight he had with a royal officer, which drew him a punishment of five hundred lashes—delivered in a single

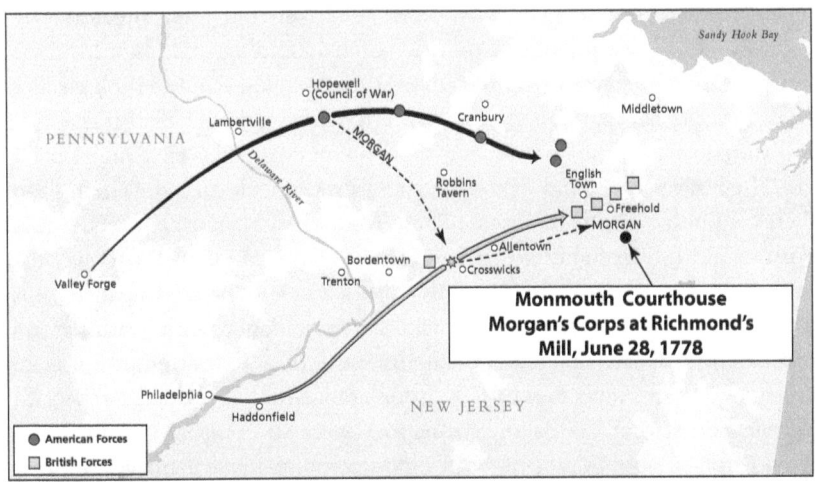

American and British troop movement to Monmouth Courthouse.

session.⁶ By comparison, the fledgling United States would limit flogging to no more than one hundred lashes during the American Revolution, and five hundred lashes would have been considered by many to be a death sentence.⁷ Morgan survived but never forgot. Throughout his life, Morgan maintained he counted the lashes, and the British miscounted and administered only 499; therefore, they owed him one more. He later served as a rifleman and received a harrowing injury from a French and Indian ambush near Fort Edwards, Virginia. He took a musket ball through the back of the neck that exited through his left cheek; the projectile dislodged many of his teeth in the process.⁸ He was scarred but unbowed. In Daniel Morgan, Peter Francisco had a rare kindred spirit in the officer class. As with Francisco, Morgan was a man of renowned physical stature, strength, and endurance. Morgan was also an adopted son of Virginia. Though not formally educated, he was highly intelligent and dedicated to the mission of American independence. Francisco would identify easily with this rugged individual who practiced leadership by example in the most austere environments.⁹

To harass Clinton's march, Colonel Morgan's corps of six hundred consisted of six regiments—two from Pennsylvania and four from Virginia. This was in addition to some of Washington's personal guards and other picked men to include Private Francisco.¹⁰ General Washington's orders to Morgan were to depart the main Continental Army at Hopewell and "take the most effectual means for gaining the enemys [sic] right flank, and giving them as much annoyance as possible in that quarter."¹¹ Morgan and his men struck out before dawn on June 24 reaching Allentown on June 25 where the British rear guard had recently broken camp the previous day. Clinton had placed his troops on the march intending to realign his divisions and march toward Monmouth Courthouse and Sandy Hook twenty miles beyond. Morgan's men would race to the rear of the British column, and they lost no time announcing their presence as they exchanged brisk fire. They traveled fast and light—advancing, probing, hitting the enemy, and then disappearing into the brush. These were classic harassment techniques born of old Indian fighting that had brought fame to colonial backwoodsmen since the Seven Years' War. After the firing subsided, Morgan led his men around to the enemy right flank in accordance with Washington's orders. The redcoats retained tight alignment in their formations to mitigate the risk to their columns while on the march. Morgan penned a report to Washington stating the enemy formations were so compact that he likely would not be able to isolate small units to inflict much damage. Morgan and his corps proceeded to shadow Clinton's right flank, reconnoitering the enemy strength, harassing periodically, and seeking advantage.

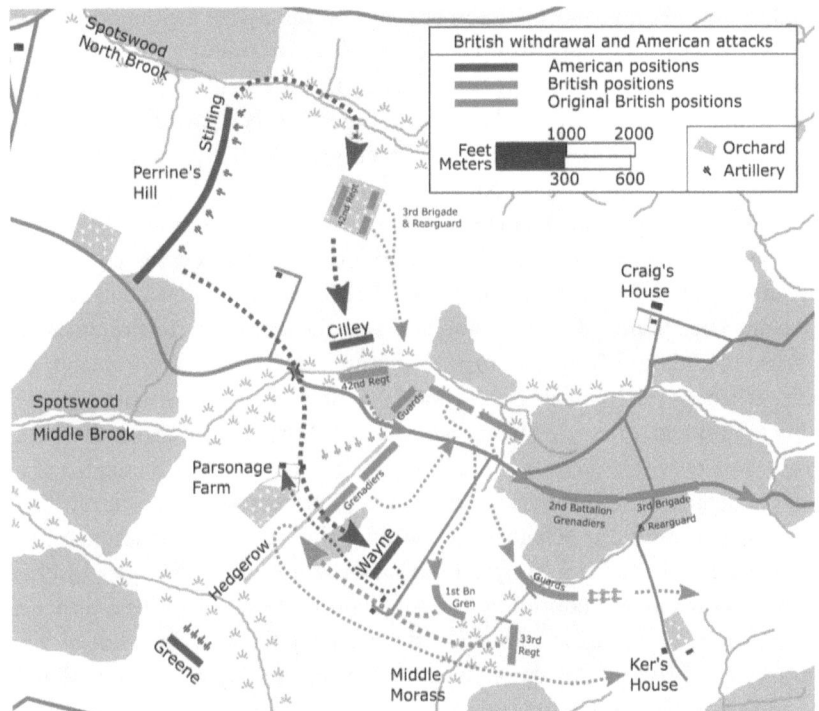

British withdrawal and American attacks during the Battle of Monmouth, June 28, 1778.
Lender and Stone (2016), Wikimedia Commons

Washington needed to do more than harass the columns of enemy soldiers to slow Clinton's march. He decided to detach a four-thousand-man vanguard of troops to speed ahead to the British, attack their rear guard, and force Clinton to halt and defend his rear while Washington could catch up with the main army. Command of the vanguard was offered to Major General Lee. He initially declined, purporting that the unit was too small for his rank and station as second in command. General Lafayette enthusiastically volunteered for the command, and he was to also take tactical control of the advanced forces in the field including Morgan's corps, Dickinson's militia, and Maxwell's New Jersey brigade. Under Lafayette's leadership, the vanguard raced ahead to Robin's Tavern—only three miles from the combined British rear guard. Washington was concerned that Lafayette had outpaced his supply lines and the protection of the main army. On June 26, Washington ordered Lafayette to assign Colonel Morgan's unit to screen the movement of his vanguard and for the French general to meet him at

Englishtown—a position in close proximity to the main Continental Army and six miles to the northwest of the British at Monmouth.[12] Meanwhile, Morgan's men maintained intense harassment of the British on June 26–27, placing all of the enemy's pickets under fire.[13] Moreover, one of Morgan's regiments, the 6th Virginia, captured fifteen grenadiers who were on laundry detail in a creek south of Monmouth Courthouse.[14]

Upon Lafayette's vanguard arriving in Englishtown, General Lee reversed himself and requested command of the advance forces for the upcoming clash of armies. On June 27, Washington agreed and placed General Lee in charge of the vanguard and the amalgamation of advance forces, including Morgan's corps. Lafayette was assigned command of reserve troops in support. Meanwhile, Major General Nathanael Greene took command of Lee's former wing, Lord Stirling still maintained his command over the other wing, and General Friedrich von Steuben led a reserve detachment in the main army. The Americans would attack on June 28 in sweltering heat—General Lee leading the way with his vanguard to be followed by the main army. Unfortunately for Colonel Morgan and his corps, command and control by the vanguard leadership had been difficult owing to the perpetual movement of the harassing forces and unclear orders from general officers. In the early morning on the day of battle, Colonel Morgan's unit was at Richmond's Moll—three miles southeast of the British encampment at Monmouth Courthouse.[15] Morgan received written orders from General Lee's staff dated 1:00 a.m. on June 28 to hold his position and to be prepared to attack *tomorrow morning*. General Lee intended *tomorrow* to mean June 28; Colonel Morgan interpreted *tomorrow* to mean June 29.[16] As such, Morgan and his corps held their position and did not participate in the main battle on June 28.

General Lee could have used Daniel Morgan's assistance on the day of battle. Lee's vanguard attacked what he believed to be only a few hundred rearguard enemy. In actuality, British commander Clinton had responded quickly by recalling Lord Cornwallis to double back and join the conflict. Clinton's most trusted general had reversed the march of two brigades that were soon moving southwest and bearing down on the American vanguard's left flank led by Brigadier "Mad" Anthony Wayne. Major General Lee's vanguard, seeing the enemy's superior numbers, began a hasty retreat to the west. Again, communications were tenuous, and Lee did not inform Washington of this turn of events.

At Richmond Mills, Colonel Morgan heard the exchange of fire to his north, and he sent messengers asking for clarification and orders. Morgan's messenger arrived at General Wayne's location. General Wayne did not

Colonel Daniel Morgan. By Alonzo Chappel.
Historica, US Congress (House Of Representatives)

Private, 6th Virginia Regiment.
Monmouth Battlefield State Park

forward Morgan's messenger to their mutual commander, General Lee. Rather, he simply relayed that, as the Americans were in retreat, Morgan should hold his position. Upon receipt of Wayne's instructions, Morgan did not advance. Meanwhile, General Washington, oblivious to Lee's retreat, rode forward of his main army and was stunned to encounter confused Continentals running to the rear with no apparent orders to re-form. He found General Lee and demanded to know the reason for retreat. Lee's answer was insufficient, and Washington upbraided his subordinate, relieved him on the spot, and sent him to the rear. Washington then took charge of the vanguard. With the help of Lafayette, he spirited his horse back and forth along the lines stopping the retreating soldiers and re-forming them near the heights on Perrine's Hill. Once organized, Washington stemmed the British advance sufficiently to permit Major General Alexander/Lord Stirling's wing (and, most important, the artillery) to form on Perrine's Hill. From the heights, Stirling could direct fire upon the British maneuvering to his southeast. Later, Major General Nathanael Greene's wing took their position on Comb's Hill to the south of Lord Stirling. With four pieces of artillery, Greene could sight and fire upon the British who had repositioned to his northeast in a low-lying area in between two creeks—Wemrock

Brook and Spotswood Middle Brook. Now, the American forces—and, most important, the Yankee artillery—had command of the battlefield from elevated positions along crossing vectors.[17] The Crown forces' situation would soon prove unsound. The American cannonade was so fierce that the patriots' female camp followers assisted gun crews by carrying water to them. The water was not only for drinking but also to clear sparks and prepare cannon between the firing of rounds. One soldier's wife, Mary Hays Ludwig, became the legendary *Molly Pitcher* as she reportedly took over for wounded soldiers and participated in the loading and firing of the artillery throughout the barrage.[18] Now drawing fire from the Americans' elevated artillery positions, the British began a tactical retreat.

General Wayne's brigade, now re-formed in the American center, was ordered to drive east and sweep the British from the battlefield. After some success, the disciplined British held off Wayne's troops to facilitate an orderly departure. Washington recalled Wayne's brigade that had fought all day in the punishing heat. Evening approached, and the American commander intended to reengage the following morning. General Clinton, however, slipped away to the north and continued his march to Sandy Hook. The advance forces, including Morgan's corps, shadowed and harassed the British column along the way. The last of Clinton's troops were returned to New York on July 6—just five days before the French fleet appeared off of Sandy Hook.

The aftermath of the battle was manifold. History records Monmouth Courthouse as a tactical draw with each side losing between three hundred and four hundred people. Although the British got away, their northern Crown forces found themselves isolated in New York City for the long term. In a shift of fortune, the Americans had taken and held the field in a battle against elite British units on open ground. Von Steuben's training had proven effective. As stated by Henry Knox: "The effects of the battle of Monmouth will be great and lasting. It will convince the enemy and the world that nothing but a good constitution is wanting."[19] Washington was vindicated, but little did he know, he would not exercise command in a major battle again until Yorktown three years later. Major General Charles Lee blamed Washington for his difficulties at Monmouth and demanded a court-martial to clear his name. Lee was granted the proceeding; he was convicted, and then he was suspended from military service for one year. Charles Lee essentially disappeared from history after Monmouth. Daniel Morgan's men, including Private Francisco, bothered, baited, and clashed with the enemy throughout New Jersey during the latter half of June 1778, but Morgan's corps was absent on the day of battle. Colonel Morgan suffered no injury to his reputation.[20] His service before Monmouth at Saratoga and after at Cowpens would seal his legacy as a great American combat leader. Peter Francisco participated fiercely with the advance forces harassing the British. He was, for the second of many occasions, wounded in action, taking a musket ball to the right thigh—an injury that would plague him for the rest of his life. Despite this injury, he ignored the painful wound and continued his agitation of the enemy. Francisco killed two grenadiers as the British made their escape to New York.[21] The "Virginia Giant" validated the wisdom of his generals' decision to select him for Morgan's advance force of *picked men*. After some minor skirmishes in the coming months, he would be picked again for a special mission. In summer 1779, Peter Francisco would transition from an honorable warrior to a hero for the ages at a place called Stony Point in New York.

Chapter 9

COMMANDO ASSAULT

Stony Point

With the Philadelphia campaign concluded, the capital was now back in the hands of the Americans, and Washington found himself monitoring the Crown forces in the north in the vicinity of Manhattan Island. Peter Francisco skirmished at Paoli and other locations in the late summer of 1778. Fall would find the "Virginia Giant" transferred from the 10th to the 6th Virginia Regiment under Colonel John Green. The 6th Virginia was stationed at Middlebrook, New Jersey, until the spring of 1779.[1]

To the north in New York, a critical landmark called Stony Point projected out into the Hudson River—twelve miles south of West Point and thirty miles north of Manhattan Island. The point extended from the west bank and into the Hudson to constrain the river through a one-mile narrow channel across from another small fortified peninsula on the east bank called Verplanck's Point. As of June 1779, both Stony Point and Verplanck's Point were in the hands of the British, which meant the relatively short river crossing in between, called King's Ferry, was under the control of the Crown forces as well.[2] A critical line of logistics, King's Ferry was an imperative for both belligerent armies. In short, the narrows between Stony and Verplanck's points represented the most viable and secure Hudson River crossing north of British-held New York City. That summer, British forces commander Lieutenant General Sir Henry Clinton not only seized the King's Ferry fortifications but also conducted raids in Connecticut in an effort to draw Washington out of the highlands and into a decisive battle.[3] Short of a decisive encounter, the Americans believed Clinton sought to capture the American garrison at West Point to break Washington's grip in the Hudson Valley.[4]

It was the heights of Stony Point that commanded the entire area—specifically, the Hudson across the narrows of King's Ferry as well as Verplanck's Point on the opposite side. It spanned ninety acres with a steep incline rising from the river to a pinnacle of 150 feet. Forming a peninsula extending from west to east, the fortification protruded into the Hudson with water bordering to the north, south, and east. Along the western edge of the heights existed a tidal marshland that converted the peninsula into an island at high tide. During low tide, the marshes could be forded by infantry theoretically. A west-to-east causeway provided access to Stony Point over the marshland.

Upon seizing the fort, the British immediately commenced bolstering defenses by cutting trees for clear defensive firing and constructing two north-to-south *abatis* consisting of sharpened logs and pikes from felled trees down the width of the peninsula. The lines of obstructions lay astride the marshland on the west side of the heights, and they extended all the way to the Hudson—water-to-water from the northwestern edge to the southwestern edge of the peninsula.[5] On the heights, an expansive first plateau existed where the British had hastily constructed temporary *lower works* to guard the fort while they built more permanent *upper works* on the summit within. The lower works were marked by pointed, arrow-shaped wooden bulwarks called fleches that both shielded the redcoats and permitted several vectors of protected fire by troops and artillery.[6] The fleches and associated pieces of artillery faced west—the assumed direction of attack should the Americans be so bold as to assault the ominous fortress. The lower and upper works boasted fifteen guns including heavy ship's cannons on trucks as well as mortars. The river side inclines were protected by a Royal Navy ship named *Vulture* and a subordinate gunboat. The British forces at Stony Point totaled 567 soldiers comprising eight companies from the 17th Regiment of Foot, two companies of grenadiers from the 71st Regiment, artillerymen, and loyalists, along with a small number of women and children.[7] The garrison was commanded by Lieutenant Colonel Henry Johnson of the 17th who was a subordinate to the senior officer based across the river at Verplanck's Point—Lieutenant Colonel James Webster. The British considered a fortified Stony Point to be more than formidable—a "Little Gibraltar."[8]

Clinton was clearly baiting Washington with his outposts on the Hudson. His indifference to Stony Point's close proximity to the American stronghold at West Point (and farther away from his protection of New York City) was an affront to his rebellious enemy.[9] Washington would respond. Stony Point was reconnoitered by the commander in chief from nearby Buckberg Mountain in July 1779. An assault was planned by General Washington and Brigadier General "Mad" Anthony Wayne who commanded a Corps of Light Infantry.[10] Wayne was a tanner, surveyor, and past French and Indian War soldier from Pennsylvania. He was a skilled troop commander and a veteran of Fort Ticonderoga, Germantown, Brandywine, and Monmouth Courthouse where he displayed courageous leadership under fire. Wayne burned at his one notorious setback at Paoli in the days following Brandywine where British General Charles "No-Flint" Grey had surprised the Americans with a nighttime bayonet attack killing many in their bunks. The two American generals conspired to utilize the silent bayonet strategy in a retaking of Stony Point. Wayne and Washington, also a former surveyor, both possessed a keen eye for discerning the lay of the land and fortifications when conceiving operations.[11]

A standard siege would have proven futile given the British efforts to fortify Stony Point. Washington's perception from Buckberg Mountain was augmented by the report of Captain Allan McLane. The captain learned of a rebel-sympathizing mother of a loyalist soldier assigned to Stony Point. Under a flag of truce, Captain McLane escorted the woman during a visit to her son in the fort. He brought back key information about incomplete upper abatis and the inability of some of the heavier artillery to slew at an angle low enough to train fire down the steep approaches to the defensive works.[12] The elements of surprise and deception would be integral to American success. Washington devised a plan to demonstrate a conventional attack from west of Stony Point along the causeway. The flash and report of musketry and artillery would draw Crown infantry out of the fort and occupy the attention of the gunners manning the cannons. Meanwhile, two teams of silent commandos would skirt along the northern and southern shorelines bordering the peninsula. They would navigate the abatis and scale the steep north and south slopes of the fort and take the citadel while much of the British were addressing the noisy threat from the west. Washington directed Wayne to conduct the assault at the midnight hour as pickets and watch-standers were typically more vigilant as dawn approached.[13]

Wayne drew picked men from more than forty battalions commanded by Washington. The assault force numbered four regiments composed of 1,360 combat-experienced veterans including Peter Francisco. Each regiment was made up of two battalions, and each battalion had four companies assigned.[14] The 1st Light Infantry Regiment was commanded by the Dane veteran of Bunker Hill and Quebec—Lieutenant Colonel Christian Febiger. Notably, one of his battalion commanders was Lieutenant Colonel

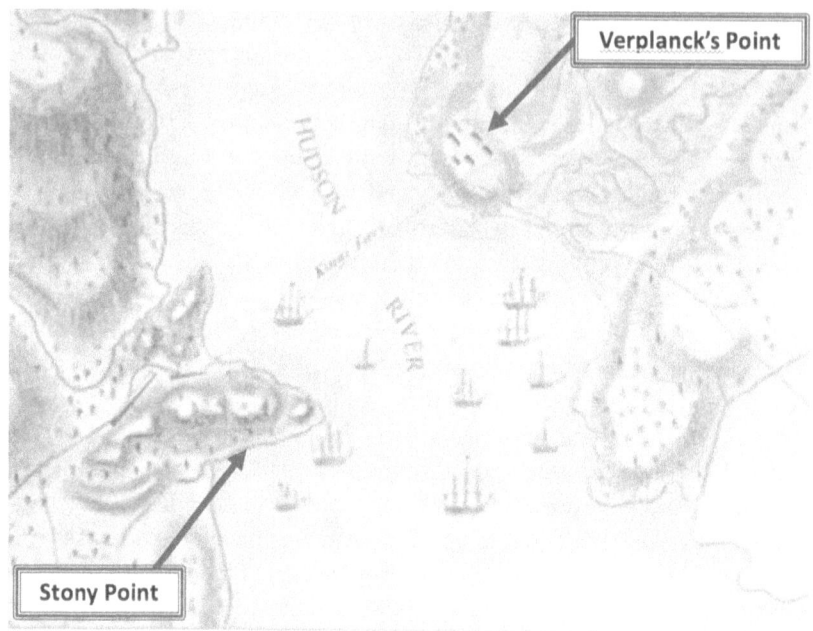

King's Ferry between Stony Point and Verplanck's Point. By John Wright.
Stony Point Battlefield State Historic Site; inserts and arrows added by J. T. Palmer

Brigadier "Mad" Anthony Wayne. By Edward Savage.
New York Historical Society

Lieutenant Colonel Richard Butler. By John Trumbull.
Yale University Art Gallery

George Washington at Verplanck's Point. By John Trumbull.
Winterthur Museum, Wikimedia Commons

François Teissèdre de Fleury—the famed French engineer who had served with Peter Francisco at Fort Mifflin and directed the nightly repair of fortifications on Mud Island. The 2nd Regiment was commanded by Irish-born Lieutenant Colonel Richard Butler—a relentless leader who eschewed dueling in favor of fisticuffs to settle differences and enforce discipline in the ranks. The 3rd Regiment was led by Connecticut Colonel Jonathan Meigs—veteran of Lexington, Concord, Quebec, and Sag Harbor. Colonel Rufus Putnam commanded the 4th Light Infantry Regiment.[15]

On the night of July 15, the rally point for the assault force was at Springsteel farm—one-and-a-half miles west of Stony Point. Wayne inspected his men personally to ensure they were shaved, powdered, and provisioned appropriately.[16] To preserve the element of surprise, all barking dogs were to be silenced along the way, and any wayward civilians would be taken into custody until after the fighting was over. All troops affixed white pieces of paper to their caps to distinguish them from other combatants in the fray. General Wayne incentivized the troops with a $500 bounty to the first soldier to enter the upper works, followed by smaller payments for the next four to breach the enemy fortifications.[17] The American right column of seven hundred men was the primary assault force that was to attack from south to north up the slopes. This column was largely Lieutenant Colonel Febiger's regiment, and he would be joined by the on-scene commander, General Wayne. The smaller force making up the left column was from Lieutenant Colonel Butler's regiment totaling three hundred soldiers, including Peter Francisco. Butler was to proceed east/parallel to the northern shoreline to cut through a line of abatis. After navigating the obstruction, Butler was to turn south to climb up the steep north-facing incline and breech the fort's lower works before climbing the earthen and stone walls guarding the upper works. Febiger and Butler's columns represented silent pincers, and their men were ordered to advance with unloaded weapons. Febiger and Butler would each select twenty brave soldiers to serve as *forlorn hope* pathfinders to cut through abatis with axes and facilitate their respective pincer assaults on the British works.

The men of forlorn hope were so called because their assignment was thought to be practically suicidal. Each band of twenty axmen would be followed by vanguards of 100 under Butler and 150 under Febiger.[18] The remaining men of the pincer regiments would trail the vanguards. For colonels Febiger and Butler and their men, the fight would be hand to hand, and the battle would be won or lost with soldiers' bayonets as well as axes that might be carried by any surviving forlorn troops.[19] The forlorn axes would likely be a wide variety among the forty men charged with chopping through the abatis. British felling axes were common in North America, and they might be single- or double-bladed forged metal with heads that could weigh between two and four pounds and span from five to eight inches in width. The heads were made of *cast steel*, which in the eighteenth century meant that steel ingots were cast and then later forged into the shape of an axe. Crude, provincial, one-off, home-forged axes were also common. Oak wood was typically the axe handle of choice, and the length of the handle could be from eighteen inches to two and a half feet—potentially longer. Large and long lumberjack axes were rare as they were unwieldy for soldiers to pack and carry. Some felling and saddle axes were small by comparison and might be more analogous to large hatchets than the type of tool one might imagine for a timberman in the hills.[20] The "Virginia Giant"—Peter Francisco—would be assigned forlorn duty from Butler's column.[21] The officer in charge of Butler's twenty-man forlorn unit was Lieutenant John Gibbon, and the leader of Febiger's forlorn detachment was Lieutenant George Knox—both from Pennsylvania.[22]

A veteran of Brandywine and Monmouth Courthouse, Major Hardy Murfree led the center thrust for demonstration from the west. Murfree's men included two companies of North Carolinians equipped with loaded weapons to carry out a noisy west-to-east feint along the causeway to distract and occupy the British infantry and artillery. To achieve victory, the silent and speedy forlorn detachments, vanguards, and troops under Febiger and Butler would charge the heights, scale the works, vault over the bulwarks, suppress the Crown forces, and compel capitulation. Upon breaching the interior upper works, the Americans were to shout the announcement "The fort's our own!" to signal all within earshot that the moment of truth was at hand.[23] On this particular night, the British defensive efforts would be hampered by high winds that forced the Royal Navy ship *Vulture* and assigned gunboat farther south to better water to ride out the blustery weather.[24] No naval gun fire support would come from the Hudson for the British defenders.

With all columns in position, the battle was to commence at midnight; however, Febiger and Butler's men were delayed owing to the level of the tide remaining in the marshes. Soon after, the silent pincer columns launched the assault at 12:20 a.m. on July 16. From positions north and south, Lieutenant Gibbon's and Lieutenant Knox's forlorn detachments slung their muskets and waded into the dark marsh with axes at the ready. They faced two hundred yards of waist-deep marsh. Silence and speed were vital. Meanwhile, Murfree's North Carolinians provided "a galling fire" from the west achieving the effect of distracting and drawing British attention toward the report of American musketry.[25] Still, the activity of the silent American pincer forces did not go unnoticed. This was especially true for Francisco's unit as Lieutenant Colonel Butler commenced his column's advance from a starting point directly to the north and in close proximity to Murfree's artillery and musket demonstration.[26]

Lieutenant Gibbon, commanding Francisco and his forlorn comrades, led the way by moving due east along the water's edge hoping to find a low-tide passage around the northern end of the abatis. Gibbon's men were soon spotted, and some of the British artillery pieces were capable of directing rounds down the hill. In concert with the musket-armed foot soldiers, the defenders opened fire. The American forlorn detachment and vanguard pressed onward but began to take casualties. At the base of this northern slope, Butler's troops were barraged with sixty-nine cannon rounds from the British 3-pounders.[27] No longer concerned with silently slipping through the marsh, the men quickened the pace. Three-pound artillery rounds slammed into the dark marshland among the Americans. The popping of flint-lock fire showered sporadic volleys of .75-caliber Brown Bess musket balls upon the patriots. Reaching the abatis, Lieutenant Colonel Butler's entire column came to a halt. Now were the critical moments. Every second of delay gave the redcoat gunners time to find their range with the 3-pound cannons. British infantry could more easily target stationary patriots below with their muskets. To keep moving was to have a chance. To be immobile was to die, and Americans were dying. They had to breach the abatis and get back on the move. The forlorn hope tore into the obstructions with axes and brute strength. The tell-tale chopping of the forlorn axes into the felled tree abatis signaled to the British that the northern slope to the lower works was Gibbon's aim. Peter Francisco gripped the oak handle of his ax tightly and swung furiously at the abatis near the water's edge. With every blow, wood chips flew into the air. The forlorn axmen were pouring sweat and short of breath, but they kept hammering away at the obstructions.

Finally, a log was severed ... then another. Some vanguard troops would sling their muskets and lend a hand to apply leverage to the freshly chopped logs. They heaved the pieces of timber to the side. Gaps began to emerge. At last, sizable pathways were achieved, and the forlorn and vanguard patriots charged through the abatis. They were on the move again. They continued due east for about 150 yards along the Hudson River's edge. This maneuver would permit them to skirt a partially completed second line of abatis along the edge of the first plateau that formed the lower works.[28]

Finally, they reached a point where the officers ordered a right turn—due south and straight up the heights of Stony Point. The slopes were daunting and rose nearly immediately out of the Hudson. The first plateau and lower works were a good one hundred feet in elevation at a dreadfully steep incline. To navigate the grade was a challenge for a daytime hiker in peacetime . . . it was treacherous under fire in the dark. Gibbon led the way; Francisco followed with the surviving forlorn and vanguard troops in their wake.

To the south, General Wayne and lieutenant colonels Febiger and Fleury, along with Lieutenant Knox's forlorn detachment, benefited greatly from Major Hardy Murfree's demonstration. Lieutenant William Horndon, the British officer commanding a 12-pound cannon crew at the southernmost fleche, returned fire in Murfree's direction as Febiger's southern pincer quietly flanked the British by stealing along the southern shoreline bordering Haverstraw Bay.[29] Their forlorn team also cut through the abatis, and the southern column began to scale the southern slopes of Stony Point. Febiger's men began to take fire. General Wayne himself took a grazing wound to the head from a musket ball. Brigadier Wayne refused to depart the battle; rather, he remained on station and continued to exercise command and control through his aides.[30] Febiger, Fleury, and Knox continued the advance. As with Francisco's northern slopes, the southern incline was equally challenging. Still, they pressed on and reached the plateau and lower works. Now, another fifty feet of steep incline and earthworks separated the pincer columns from the upper works.

Along the north slope, Gibbon and Francisco paused only briefly at the lower works plateau before courageously racing up the vertical incline. No one knew what awaited the patriots inside the upper works. There were foreboding Royal Navy cannons placed in left and right batteries at the heights, but they were made useless as they could not achieve a low enough angle to deliver fire upon the two pincer columns.[31] Dodging sporadic musket fire, both vanguard detachments breached the upper works nearly simultaneously. Lieutenant Colonel Fleury had advanced with Lieutenant Knox's forlorn unit, and they were the first to breach the upper works from the southern pincer followed by sergeants William Baker and William Spencer of Virginia and Sergeant George Donlop of Pennsylvania.[32] From the northern pincer, Lieutenant Gibbon was first over the upper works with Private Peter Francisco immediately following.[33] An unknown voice shouted: "The fort's our own!" Combat was as expected—hand to hand and brutal. Peter Francisco swapped his short axe for a longer musket and bayonet, and the former blacksmith went to work. The clash of musket stocks and bayonets could be heard in the darkness as redcoats and patriots hurled themselves at each other. Grunts, screams of rage, and cries from injury pierced the shadowy night air. Francisco alternated his handiwork—a thrusting and slashing bayonet with the clubbing of the enemy with the butt of his musket. His bayonet drew British blood several times. Fighting alongside other patriots like Ansolem Bailey, the "Virginia Giant" dispatched three grenadiers despite suffering a horrific bayonet wound to the abdomen and exposing a nine-inch gash.[34] Francisco ignored the wound as he hacked his way toward the flagstaff and the enemy ensign.[35] The battle lasted twenty minutes and concluded with the surviving British defenders calling for "Quarter!" The enemy flag was captured. Shortly after the British capitulation, the American artillerymen commandeered some of the enemy's guns, spun them eastward, and began a cannonade of Verplanck's Point across the river.[36] After the battle abated, 15 Americans and 20 British lay dead with 144 wounded. Seventeen of the 20 members of Francisco's northern forlorn hope axmen were either killed or wounded.[37] A total of 543 British would be taken prisoner.[38]

Soon after, Washington visited Stony Point and determined he would neither fortify nor garrison the heights against British counterattack. The Americans destroyed the works and abatis and departed with the British

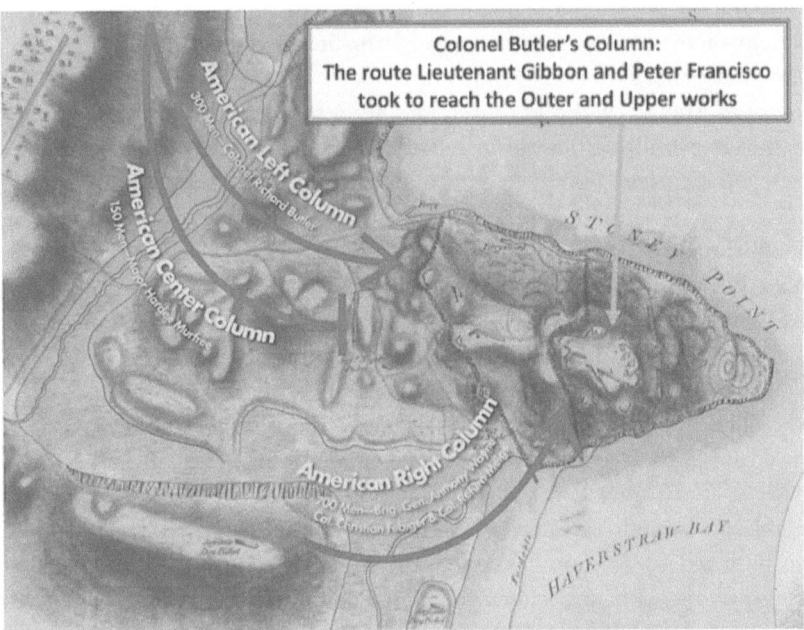

American strategy: demonstration west to east along the causeway with pincers from the north. By John Wright.
Stony Point Battlefield State Historic Site; textbox and arrow added by J. T. Palmer

artillery, supplies, and prisoners.[39] The British reoccupied Stony Point, but only for a few months. They determined that exigencies of facing a new French enemy on the continent plus their strategy to take the fight to the south meant there were no available troops to hold Stony Point. The British departed King's Ferry in October 1779.[40] The Americans positioned a small caretaker detachment on the heights to observe, guard the ferry passage, and facilitate lines of logistics across the Hudson for the remainder of the war.

So, the obvious question is this: What did the Americans gain by their assault and taking of Stony Point? The answer? It was a demonstration of will. Once fortified, Stony Point was seen to be virtually impregnable by the British and many Americans. Yet, Washington and Wayne hand-picked several light infantry regiments, and from this collection of combat veterans, they determined a vanguard and designated forty men as the forlorn hope to conquer the unconquerable. This was an eighteenth-century American commando raid that was both an unqualified success and an exhibition to the British that there was no safe haven from the ever-improving rebel military. Peter Francisco suffered a serious injury by British bayonet, and he was fortunate to survive what was typically a fatal wound beyond the capacity of physicians of the day.[41] He did, however, recuperate from his abdominal laceration at Fishkill, New York, and he was now celebrated as a hero of the Revolution—a bigger-than-life picture of frontier strength, fury, and courage.[42]

On August 19, though barely one month beyond his gruesome injury, Francisco would participate in a battle at Paulus Hook, now modern-day Jersey City, New Jersey. Peter was detailed under Major "Light Horse" Harry Lee of Virginia. The Americans marched from New Bridge to spring a night attack on the British fort. Lee and his troops failed to take the stronghold, but they captured 158 British soldiers. In the action, Francisco killed two enemy soldiers.[43] The young, thrice-wounded veteran of Brandywine, Germantown, Fort Mifflin, Monmouth Courthouse, Stony Point, and Paulus Hook was developing a reputation for ferocity and valor under fire.

The northern sector of the American Revolution would grind to a stalemate with George Washington positioned outside the British stronghold at New York City. As major fighting in the north subsided, Peter Francisco's Continental Army enlistment expired in December 1779, and he returned to Virginia.[44] As the Crown forces turned their attention to the southern states, the veteran Francisco could not stand idly by while his countrymen continued the struggle for independence. He volunteered for service in a regiment in the Virginia militia under his former colonel—now Brigadier General Edward Stevens. As a battle-tested soldier under Stevens in the Continental Army, the "Virginia Giant" was undoubtedly a welcome addition to the militia unit where he would serve famously with Captain (later Colonel) John Mayo of Powhatan.[45] The fight moved south and so would Mayo and Francisco to South Carolina and a place called Camden.

STONY POINT POSTSCRIPT

Often, the hard historical record is less than clear about the exploits of men in combat in centuries past. Such is the case with Peter Francisco in a few engagements, including Stony Point. The muster rolls for the soldiers assigned light infantry duty under Major General Wayne are incomplete, and Peter Francisco does not appear in the rolls known to exist. One historian has gone so far as to question Private Francisco's very presence at Stony Point.[46] Still, the stories of Francisco's heroic service and injury at Stony Point were so numerous, this author is inclined to believe he not only participated but also fought bravely.[47] Secondarily, the nature of his brave exploits is also debated. After-action reports credit Lieutenant Colonel Febiger's southern pincer as being first in the fort and Major Fleury as capturing the enemy colors. Many of the descriptions surrounding Francisco's acts, however, state Lieutenant Gibbon was first in the upper works with the "Virginia Giant" entering immediately thereafter.

Moreover, there exists a recounting that Peter Francisco fought hand to hand, received the gruesome bayonet slash to the abdomen, and persevered to kill three enemy on his way to being the first to lay hands on the flagstaff—enemy colors that he later passed to the French officer Fleury. Francisco himself claimed in a pension affidavit that he "volunteered himself under Colo [François Louis de] Fleury to storm Stony point fort on the North river, he was the second man who scaled the walls at the enemies fort on the right wing, & recieved [sic] a wound slaunting through the belly nine inches long."[48]

Indirect evidence supporting Francisco's participation begins with Ansolem Bailey. In his book *Washington's Immortals*, author Patrick O'Donnell highlights that Bailey stated Francisco was at Stony Point and other battles. Moreover, Bailey made postwar claims of service at Stony Point, and he accepted and submitted Francisco's sworn affidavit attesting to his participation in the forlorn hope.[49] An oft-cited source in support of Francisco is Captain William Evans—also of the 6th Virginia Regiment. Evans outlined the private's exploits at Stony Point in an 1828 affidavit supporting the issuance of a pension. The captain stated in a detailed account that Francisco "was the second man who entered the Fort and distinguished himself by numerous acts of bravery and intrepidity. In a charge which was ordered to be made around the flag staff, he killed three British grenadiers and was the first man who laid hold of the flag staff and being badly wounded laid on it that night and in the morning delivered it to Col. Fleury. Those circumstances brought Mr. Francisco into great notice and his name was reiterated throughout the whole army."[50] The only problem is that the existing muster reports, although incomplete, do not list Evans as a combatant at Stony Point. As such, his credibility as a firsthand source in the battle is undermined.[51]

On balance, there is the possibility that there is some truth to the multiple accounts that include or ignore Francisco's service. First, it was a night attack where visibility was diminished. The upper works plateau was expansive and contained stark undulations, further obscuring clear lines of sight from one side to the other. As such, the two forlorn and vanguard pincers likely did not observe their counterparts on opposite ends of the fort entering the upper works. It is entirely possible both Gibbon and Fleury believed they entered the works first. In addition, the senior officer breaching the works was Fleury, and he made after-action reports through his chain of command that outlined prominently the soldiers in his proximity (southern pincer). Finally, there was a monetary bonus offered by Brigadier General Wayne for the first men in the upper works. This bonus system created a financial incentive for soldiers to assert their actions (and the actions of their charges close by) to the exclusion of soldiers serving under other officers.

Peter Francisco was a fierce warrior and a giant of a man, but he was still an orphaned immigrant with no familial or societal connections in the New World. Conversely, the noble French officers and landed continental gentry that made up much of the American officer corps would not be blamed for overlooking the exploits of a penniless, illiterate young volunteer—making his way alone and holding only the rank of private. Some valorous service was clearly performed by Francisco as the Battle of Stony Point proved to be his introduction throughout the Continental Army and public lore as a prolific fighting man. To be clear, repugnance to stolen valor is not a new phenomenon. Historically, comrades in arms act as meticulous gatekeepers over gallantry on the battlefield. Warriors monitor and administer judiciously the honors to be bestowed upon heroes and denied to charlatans. It is not in dispute that Stony Point sealed Private Francisco's reputation as an oft-wounded and ferocious fighter—in the thick of America's toughest battles. At this point in the war, he was renowned as a twice-selected "picked man" for hazardous duty, yet he never yielded to injury, hardship, or foe. If the stories of his courageous service bore no truth, this author—with three decades of military service—finds it incredulous that a brand of counterfeit-fame of Peter Francisco's Stony Point exploits could spread throughout town and country without overt challenges by senior officers who were present at the battle. No such eighteenth-century opposition to the famed exploits of the "Virginia Giant" is known to exist. Therefore, I hold Private Peter Francisco as a gallant member of Colonel Butler's forlorn hope. He braved shot and shell while climbing the heights, and after entering the upper works, suffered injury under the British blade—all while dispatching several of the enemy.

Chapter 10

AMERICAN HERCULES

Camden

Summer 1780: The British had taken the fight to the south. They perceived a greater concentration of loyalists might fuel their strategy to resecure the colonies by sweeping northward and ultimately isolating and then destroying rebel strongholds in the northeast.[1] In rural South Carolina, friction between patriot and loyalist devolved into murderous terror campaigns resembling civil war. Armed bands of men settled old scores by raiding each other's farms, destroying crops, stealing livestock, and putting homes to the torch. Civil order was shattered in the Carolinas. Lieutenant General Sir Henry Clinton, commander of British forces in North America, led the siege and capture of Charleston, South Carolina, on May 12, 1780, where five thousand Continentals were taken prisoner. A small band of four hundred Virginians led by Colonel Abraham Buford had been marching toward Charleston to assist in its defense when word of the city's fall reached the patriot unit's commander. Buford subsequently received orders to depart South Carolina and redeploy his troops to Hillsboro, North Carolina. He proceeded north with Lieutenant Colonel Banastre Tarleton's dragoons in pursuit. The British horsemen numbered approximately 150. On May 29, Tarleton overtook the Americans at a place called Waxhaws—just south of the North Carolina border and ten miles east of the Catawba River. Buford stood and fought but was quickly outmaneuvered by Tarleton's swift mounted forces. Seeing a hopeless situation, Buford ordered a surrender; however, the British ignored the white flag, and the patriots received what came to be known as *Tarleton's quarter*—or no quarter at all. *Buford's massacre* at Waxhaws ensued as many Americans were bayoneted, hacked, and shot after laying down their arms. The Americans suffered more than three hundred killed, wounded, or captured compared to British casualties numbering less than two dozen. Word of "Bloody" Banastre's indecent treatment of the Americans under the white flag spread throughout the south, and passions were further inflamed.[2] Tarleton was not reprimanded for his conduct at Waxhaws.

Immediately after the siege of Charleston and in conjunction with Buford's massacre, the British sought to fortify outposts in the northern and western parts of their colony to protect Charleston and project power in the Carolinas. Georgetown on the coast, Camden in the center, and Ninety-Six to the west constituted a defensive arc from which the Crown forces could solicit loyalist support and subdue rebels in the backcountry.[3]

With Charleston conquered and ostensibly protected by the northern line of fortified towns, Clinton desired to shift the location of his command of all North American forces back to his former headquarters in New York. In June, he turned over the southern campaign to Lieutenant General Lord Charles Cornwallis. The new commander of British forces in the south had recently returned to the North American continent after burying his departed wife back in London.

General Washington responded to the Crown advances in South Carolina. While Charleston was under siege, he coordinated with Congress and ordered fifteen hundred seasoned regulars from Maryland and Delaware southward under the command of a Bavarian-born officer in French service—Major General Johann von Robais, Baron de Kalb. Similar to Baron von Steuben, de Kalb was a veteran of European conflicts who had earned his title *baron* for his military service and not inherited peerage. A friend and mentor to Lafayette, Baron de Kalb arrived in America in 1777.[4]

Simultaneous to de Kalb's deployment, Congress—over Washington's objections—assigned the "Hero of Saratoga," General Horatio Gates, command of Continental forces in the south. Gates was charged with expelling or at least checking the northward movements of the enemy. This was an aggravation for the American commander in chief as Gates had been actively pursuing congressional support to supplant Washington.

Camden, in the state's midlands on the Wateree River, was the center outpost that would soon become a priority for British defense and a target for an American attack. The British at Camden numbered one thousand and were commanded by Irish nobleman Colonel Lord Francis Rawdon. General Gates assumed command of de Kalb's experienced but undersupplied professional soldiers at Hillsboro, North Carolina, on July 24, 1780. Three days later, Gates initiated a forced-march 120 miles south on a direct course through barren country toward the British garrison at Camden. Along the march, the hungry and fatigued patriot soldiers subsisted on green corn and green peaches causing stomach ailments, diarrhea, and dehydration. On August 7, General Gates was augmented by eighteen hundred militia from North Carolina led by Brigadier General Richard Caswell—a Maryland transplant and attorney by trade. On August 13, Gates and his troops arrived thirteen miles northeast of Camden at Rugeley's Mills. The next day, Brigadier Edward Stevens and seven hundred Virginia militia arrived to join Gates's forces.[5] Marching with the Virginia militia was Peter Francisco as well as Captain John Mayo.

On the evening of August 15, Gates began the final approach south with the intention of attacking Camden the next morning. Unknown to Gates, General Cornwallis was now at Camden. The British commander had sped north from Charleston with troops to augment the outpost along with reinforcements that had arrived from the western outpost at Ninety-Six. Simultaneously on August 15, Cornwallis began a march north from Camden to meet the Americans.[6] In the early morning hours of August 16, the opposing forces' cavalrymen stumbled upon each other at Saunders Creek—about seven miles north of the British garrison. After a brief exchange of fire, the two belligerents withdrew to organize for what would be the Battle of Camden a few hours later at daybreak.

Horatio Gates. By Gilbert Stuart.
Metropolitan Museum of Art

Lieutenant General Charles Earl Cornwallis. By Thomas Gainsborough.
National Portrait Gallery, London, Wikimedia Commons

The Gates versus Cornwallis struggle would prove to be a glaring mismatch. Cornwallis, facing north, formed his redcoats in traditional British fashion with his best brigade holding the honored position of the right side. These crack units were the 23rd and 33rd regiments of foot under Lieutenant Colonel James Webster. The lieutenant colonel was also assigned artillery support in the form of two guns. To the left, a brigade made up of provincial units included the 2nd American Regiment, British Legion, Royal North Carolina Regiment, and a complement of two guns was under the command of Lord Rawdon. In reserve, Lieutenant Colonel Alexander McDonald commanded the 71st Regiment of Foot along with the venerable Lieutenant Colonel Tarleton's British Legion cavalry—mounted dragoons clad notoriously in green.[7]

America's commanding general, facing south, also fought *righthanded*. A former British officer, Gates positioned himself in keeping with Crown tradition with the seasoned regulars from the 2nd Maryland and 1st Delaware regiments to his right shielded on the flank by a western swamp. Baron de Kalb commanded this brigade assisted by Brigadier Mordecai Gist of Maryland. The right brigade also possessed artillery—namely, three guns. The patriot center was commanded by Brigadier Richard Caswell who was assigned an amalgamation of North Carolina militia. Caswell also possessed two cannons. To the American left was the brigade of Virginia militia (including Peter Francisco) under the direction of Brigadier Stevens. Stevens also was assigned Armand's Legion of foreign fighters under the direction of Colonel Charles Armand Tuffin of France. As a reserve force, General Gates assigned Brigadier William Smallwood and his 1st Maryland Regiment with a complement of two guns. Baron de Kalb was positioned to the right so that he could lead his American regulars from Maryland and Delaware.

In summary, Gates had a force approaching four thousand, and the Americans enjoyed a numerical advantage approaching two to one. Under the oversight of Baron de Kalb were the fifteen hundred hardened regulars clad in blue coats from Maryland and Delaware. They were joined by approximately twenty-five hundred unpredictable militia outfitted in a motley array of uniforms and homespun garments led by brigadiers Caswell and Stevens. The key problem for General Gates was the recent compilation of regulars and militia meant he had no time to train, drill, or assess his units nor the occasion to forge them into a cohesive force. As both armies' commanders were fighting righthanded, the Battle of Camden would hinge upon which army's elite regular troops could more rapidly dominate their weaker militia and provincial counterparts across the battlefield. Shortly after assembling on the field, General Gates received a report from the

American left that the British positioned across the battlefield were showing signs of confusion. The patriot commander attempted to seize the initiative and ordered the militia on his left to advance and attack—directly into the teeth of the best redcoats on the field. If Horatio Gates expected the militia to be a match for the Crown's best soldiers at Camden, he would be sorely disappointed. They were not. The order to advance would be Gates's first and final orders of the day.[8]

The battle began as the Virginia militia moved forward. The crack troops of the 23rd Regiment of Foot on the British right fired a volley and then, in keeping with their custom, shouted out three *huzzahs* and advanced with bayonets charged—bladed muskets parallel to the ground.[9] The Virginians attempted to stem the advance with musket fire, but it was apparent the redcoats were closing too quickly for volleys to blunt the attack. As the bayonet-wielding redcoats closed the distance, the Virginia militia took flight . . . but not Peter Francisco nor Captain Mayo. In domino fashion, most of the North Carolina volunteers broke immediately there-after. Gates, unable to re-form his left flank, was swept away in the deluge of retreating militia. The American commander did not return to the battlefield; rather, he passed the fleeing militia and did not rein his horse until midnight in Charlotte, North Carolina. Meanwhile on the American right flank, Baron de Kalb's regulars were advancing and finding good success against the Crown's provincial units. Unaware of the collapse of their comrades to their left, the remaining fifteen hundred American regulars from Maryland and Delaware continued to press the British loyalists nearly collapsing the enemy left. After breaking up and dispersing the militia on the American left, however, British Lieutenant Colonel James Webster eschewed chasing the retreating soldiers farther north. Instead, he wheeled his regulars to the west in good order and smashed into the patriots' left flank. The American regulars and remnants of militia were now in trouble. Banastre Tarleton spirited his mounted troops through a gap in the Maryland brigades, and the British cavalry fell upon the American rear. One of the worst battlefield defeats of Continental forces in the Revolution was in the making.

There would be neither flight nor surrender for Private Peter Francisco and Captain John Mayo. Both remained on the battlefield—Mayo to try and regroup fleeing militia and Francisco to fight and support the brave officer from Virginia. Captain Mayo's efforts to halt and re-form the troops were futile, and he and Francisco were left with one alternative. They were forced to fall back while fighting for their lives to closer proximity to the patriot regulars from Maryland and Delaware—still locked in deadly combat against the British left. Overrun, Mayo was at the mercy of a British grenadier preparing to bayonet the captain when Francisco quickly elevated, aimed, and discharged his musket—killing the soldier. Shortly thereafter, Tarleton's dragoons roared into the fray, and Francisco and Mayo were separated. Grasping his unloaded musket with attached bayonet, Private Francisco faced two galloping horsemen—a nearly impossible challenge for a lone infantryman on foot. They thundered toward the giant militia man, and the ground shook as they approached. As they reined their horses, the first demanded the American's surrender. Peter realized he could not survive an encounter with mounted dragoons without creating some sort of advantage. Thinking quickly, the American private feigned capitulation by holding his musket upside down—by the barrel with the butt toward the sky. As the first horseman approached nearer, Peter tightened his grip on the muzzle end of the firelock with his massive hands, and shifting his weight, he spun around and swung the weapon at the dragoon as a lumberjack might swing his axe to notch a tree. With 280 pounds to his frame and superhuman strength, the butt of the musket slammed into the head of the surprised horseman with tremendous centrifugal force. Knocked unconscious, the dragoon was at the mercy of gravity as his wilted frame fell from his horse.[10]

Francisco's ruse of surrender was now exposed. The second saber-wielding cavalryman would not make the same mistake. He charged Francisco at a gallop. The "Virginia Giant" spun his musket and bayonet around to assume a fighting position as he gripped tightly the small of the stock with his right hand and the long stock and barrel with his left. Francisco was still shamefully outmatched taking on a mounted adversary from the ground with an unloaded musket. The horseman closed the distance. Peter steeled himself for what might have been his last living act on this battlefield. The cavalryman and steed were now nearly on top of Francisco with the dragoon's saber flashing. Suddenly, the giant parried the dragoon's blade strike with his musket and side-stepped the enemy steed to a position opposite the sword hand of the rider. The dragoon could not effectively slash his dismounted quarry with Francisco on the left side of his horse. The horseman yanked the reins to the left to wheel his horse into Francisco to knock him off balance. He could then deliver a coup de grace to the colossal infantryman with a deadly stroke of the saber. With agility that defied his enormous physique, Francisco maintained his position inside the turn of the horse and lunged forward with his bayonet, striking home in the enemy's ribs. Peter then stepped forward alongside the horse. As though he were a farmer pitching hay, his powerful arms and shoulders elevated the impaled trooper with the bayonet and musket and unhorsed him. The wounded dragoon was tossed over Francisco's shoulders to the turf behind him.[11]

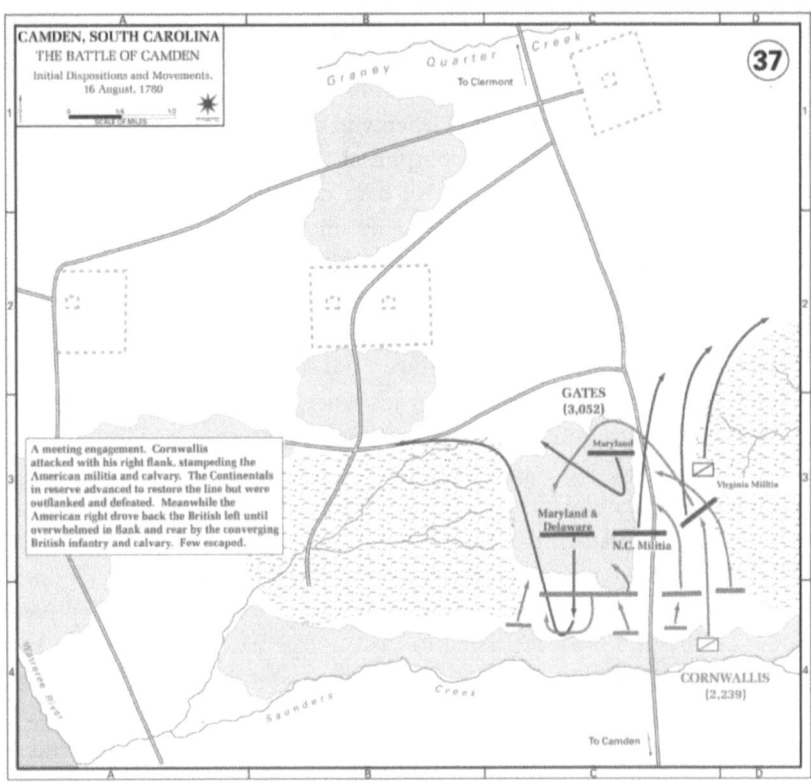

The Battle of Camden.
United States Military Academy History Department

Peter Francisco impales the British dragoon. Artist unknown.
Porter and Albertson (1929)

Peter Francisco transfers his mount to Captain Mayo. Artist unknown.
Porter and Albertson (1929)

Francisco saw no value in continuing this fight from the ground. Seizing one of the enemy's cavalry sabers and jumping astride the dragoon's horse, he cantered his new mount in the direction where he last saw Captain Mayo. Encountering more enemy in the melee, the quick-thinking Virginian dressed as a provincial purported to be a loyalist horseman and shouted, "Huzzah, my brave boys, we have conquered the rebels!"[12] With that, Peter thundered through the enemy lines as the British yielded the right of way. Francisco galloped on toward the noise of battle and his American compatriots. In the distance, he saw that Captain Mayo had been taken prisoner in the midst of the chaos. The captain was in the custody of two dismounted redcoats—an officer and an enlisted guard. Francisco approached at the gallop and, raising his saber, cut down the two enemy soldiers who had captured the militia officer.[13] Next, he reined his horse to a halt, dismounted, and implored Captain Mayo to use the steed to make his escape. After a momentary exchange, Mayo relented, mounted, and sped away on the captured British charger.

The battle still raged, and Francisco fought his way to the patriot lines. A short time later, he spied an American artillery piece about to be captured by the enemy. The horses tethered to the carriage had been killed. He ran to the scene. Suddenly, he observed a nearby wagon that might be used to carry the gun to safety. The "Virginia Giant" detached the carriage moorings. Crouching beneath a 6-pounder cannon, he placed his hands and a shoulder on the underside of the artillery barrel. Next, he slowly stood up and pressed one end of the load skyward with his enormous arms. As he elevated one end of the cannon, he tilted the field piece on edge—nearly vertical. He then found the fulcrum (or balancing point) on the cannon and leaned his shoulder in against the upright metal field piece. Summoning herculean strength, he rotated the cannon horizontally and shouldered the gun. Extending his legs, he carefully balanced it on his massive frame. He used his hands to stabilize the cylinder as he began his move toward the wagon. Slowly he took a step ... then another. The stress on his shoulders, the compression of his spine, and the strain on his legs were nearly unbearable. He persevered—one slow step after another. In a scene reminiscent of a mythological demigod, the "Virginia Giant" made his way toward the wagon carrying an 1,100-pound load—step by step in the midst of combat. Upon arrival at the wagon, he deposited the gun safely onto the conveyance.[14] He now returned his attention to the fight. He observed the men from Maryland and Delaware breaking up and making a dash for the safety of the woods. The British were all around, and some had begun to cheer "*Huzzah!*" to celebrate their impending victory. The battle was lost. Peter

Francisco took flight on foot, evading capture as he fought his way to safety. He and other surviving patriots made their escape through a swamp to the west of the battlefield. He would later be reunited with Captain Mayo.

The Americans had nearly 1,900 killed, wounded, or captured at Camden. The British suffered only 320 casualties/missing soldiers.[15] Baron de Kalb would give his last full measure in the waning moments of the battle. He had endeavored to lead his men from Delaware and Maryland as British forces converged. The baron was unhorsed, received three wounds by musket, and was bayonetted eight times. British General Cornwallis reportedly attended to de Kalb expressing sorrow for his wounds and assigning his surgeon to the task of triage. The redcoat doctor's efforts were to no avail, and three days later, de Kalb died at Camden after remarking to a British officer, "I die the death I always prayed for: the death of a soldier fighting for the rights of man."[16] Throughout the United States, Baron de Kalb would be memorialized appropriately for his valor. His name adorns numerous towns, counties, and roadways.

Conversely, General Gates, the "Hero of Saratoga," was disgraced and would not command in the field again. While de Kalb suffered from his wounds at Camden, Horatio Gates continued his extended flight for 120 miles back to Hillsborough, North Carolina. He paused only to pen his reports to General Washington and Samuel Huntington, President of the Continental Congress, stating in part: "In the deepest Distress of Anxiety of Mind, I am obliged to acquaint your Excellency with the Total Defeat of the Troops under my Command."[17] The defeat was the low water mark for the patriot fortunes in the south and might have been crushing if not for the resolve of the commander in chief. General Washington received word of the catastrophe at Camden and immediately nominated his old warhorse, Major General Nathanael Greene, to the task of rescuing American interests in the south.[18] Under General Greene, the trajectory of the Americans in the Carolinas would be reversed.

WAXHAWS POSTSCRIPT

The opening passages of this chapter described *Buford's Massacre* at Waxhaws much as it was portrayed shortly after the event throughout the Carolinas. To borrow a popular military leadership maxim, "The First Story Is Never the Story."[19] As with the *Boston Massacre* in the north, Buford's Massacre at Waxhaws served to inflame patriot passions and stoke hatred for the British in the southern colonies. Equally so, careful study over time reveals that both events were less British massacres and more patriot opportunities to engender revolutionary furor against the Crown forces and associated loyalists.

To be clear, Tarleton's victory was a one-sided affair with galling losses for the Americans. Historians, however, have made a compelling case to absolve the British dragoon commander of intentional and gratuitous cruelty. In his book *War at Saber Point*, historian John Knight highlights several reasons for the appalling losses by the patriots at Waxhaws. Poor tactics by the American commander (Colonel Abraham Buford) was a primary cause—especially his orders for his infantry to hold fire until Lieutenant Colonel Tarleton's British Legion cavalry was within ten paces of their position. This tactic resulted in the patriot foot soldiers being overrun by enemy horsemen. Moreover, Buford departed the field shortly thereafter, leaving his troops leaderless. This situation was exacerbated when Tarleton's horse was struck and fell—pinning the British commander beneath his mount for a period of time. With both senior commanders either out of range or out of commission, the soldiers in the field were left to their own devices. Some Americans tried to surrender by laying down their arms while others continued to fight. As a result of the uncoordinated American actions, some helpless patriots "calling for quarter" were treated as armed combatants and shot or bayonetted by the British. Most compelling, Knight's research shows that in the postwar pension applications of fifty American veterans, none charged the British Legion with untoward actions.

In short, Colonel Buford, having departed the field before the battle concluded, could not have witnessed the massacre that he claimed took place. Tarleton's men were far from perfect, and he acknowledged some of his soldiers continued the attack after many of the patriots called for quarter. Still, stories of the British executing Buford's soldier bearing his white flag of surrender and fallen patriot bodies being skewered and tossed aside by bayonet-wielding grenadiers appear to be significant exaggerations of the events that day on the battlefield. As with the Boston Massacre, the historical truth of the battle at Waxhaws was immaterial. The patriot narrative about *Buford's Massacre* and *Tarleton's Quarter* took root, and an entire region of patriot-leaning citizenry was energized to exact revenge from the king's men-at-arms in the Carolinas.[20]

CAMDEN POSTSCRIPT

Multiple tales, stories, and biographies document the activities of Peter Francisco at Camden. They maintain that Captain Mayo (later promoted to colonel) did not forget the gallant deeds of the "Virginia Giant" that day. Mayo bestowed upon Francisco a ceremonial sword and promised him a thousand acres of land along Richland Creek in Kentucky.[21] The bequest of acreage did not occur at Mayo's death owing to the objections of the colonel's surviving family.[22] In their 1929 biography titled *The Romantic Record of Peter Francisco*, Nannie Francisco Porter and Catherine Fauntleroy Albertson reported that the cannon Peter removed from the caisson was a 6-pounder weighing 1,100 pounds.[23] This feat sounds impossible, yet other reports of Francisco's superhuman strength would seem to align with this assertion. Francisco's courage and strength at Camden were soon the talk of the war and were later memorialized by the U.S. Postal Service in 1975 with the issuance of an eighteen-cent stamp showing Francisco shouldering a large cannon.[24]

Some historians, however, such as Karl G. Elsea, contend the cannon may have been smaller. Recent discoveries of British hand receipts of captured artillery from Camden confirmed the Crown forces ultimately seized all patriot artillery deployed that day. The Virginia militia entered the battle with two, 2-pounder amusettes weighing approximately three hundred pounds each. Elsea surmises the Virginia militia's cannon were closest to Francisco and likely the subject of his transfer to a wagon—although larger 3-pounder and 6-pounder pieces were also utilized by other American units at Camden.[25] It is hard to say definitively which cannon Peter Francisco carried. Some biographical material indicates Francisco's removal of cannon was conducted after encountering Tarleton's horsemen. We know Lieutenant Colonel Tarleton's dragoons engaged the regular Maryland brigades on the American right primarily (opposite of the Virginians on the extreme patriot left), and Karl Elsea himself highlights that the Marylanders had 6-pounders assigned (weighing more than one thousand pounds each). Elsea's argument of smaller cannon owing to proximity to Virginia militia artillery early in the battle may be tempered somewhat by Francisco's reported hand-to-hand combat against Tarleton's cavalry on the American right (near the heavier Maryland guns) just prior to his removal of the field piece.

In 2019, a team of four championship-level strongmen attempted to replicate Peter Francisco's accomplishment by lifting and carrying various sizes of cannon. Each man could barely shoulder a bulky 250-pound period cannon. In the second round with a heftier 350-pound field piece, three of the men could barely elevate the barrel waist high, and only one was able to shoulder and walk a short distance with the larger-sized cannon. The strongmen left the experiment convinced that the movement of an 1,100-pound cannon was not humanly possible.[26] Still, it is a nonunique fact that many examples exist documenting exhibitions of superhuman strength when emergencies arise. In 2012, a Virginia woman reportedly elevated a BMW 525i automobile to free her father when a jack failed. Seven years earlier an Arizona man raised a Chevy Camaro to save a trapped cyclist. Automobiles such as these can weigh as much as 4,000 pounds. These feats are impossible to replicate for scientific study, yet they represent documented incidents of humans moving thousands of pounds when facing imminent danger.[27] Perhaps Peter Francisco's feats of strength are not so farfetched.

In 1936, a Richmond physician named J. K. Hall addressed Francisco's superhuman strength through his entry in the *Annals of Medical History*, titled "Peter Francisco—Hyperpituitary Patriot." Dr. Hall found the 1,100-pound cannon story plausible given the reports of similar acts by the Virginian— even late in life. The postwar chapter of this book addresses many of these actions in detail, and they include the raising of grown bovine livestock off the ground with only one arm, the lifting and transporting of a grown horse, and the freeing of a loaded tobacco wagon from a muddy bog. The doctor recounts a specific claim by Francisco's postwar tutor named McGraw who stated the "Virginia Giant" could balance his entire 190-pound frame on a single outstretched arm as though he were holding an apple. Dr. Hall theorized that Francisco possessed an overactive pituitary gland that was responsible for his gigantic stature, energy, endurance, physical prowess, and

Peter Francisco carries a cannon from Camden Battlefield.
U.S. Postal Service

indomitable courage. Hall cited as further indirect evidence the reports of Francisco's penchant for constant physical activity—ostensibly to drain his pituitary-fueled, unnatural accumulation of energy.[28] We will never know with certainty the size of the cannon Peter Francisco lifted and carried away from capture—300 pounds, 1,100 pounds, or some load within that range. Still, even if Mr. Elsea's hypothesis is correct, the struggles highlighted in the modern strongman challenge demonstrated that the shouldering and moving of a 300-pound cannon in the midst of combat would still be a tremendous feat of courage and strength and worthy of high admiration.

Chapter 11

CAVALRYMAN FRANCISCO!

Scott's Lake

THE HORSE

Although stinging from the loss of Camden, the Americans achieved a small victory at Musgrove Mill in the upstate two days later. On October 7, 1780, the patriots regained the initiative when British Major Patrick Ferguson and his eleven hundred loyalists were annihilated at King's Mountain, South Carolina, by nine hundred patriot militiamen that included the overmountain men from Appalachia. On October 14, Major General Nathanael Greene was appointed as Horatio Gates's successor.

Nathanael Greene was born to a Quaker family in Rhode Island. The Greene family was hardworking, successful, and well connected in the community. Young Nathanael bucked against the Quaker prohibition on education and reading beyond the scriptures.[1] Moreover, long-standing rumor held that he was cast out from the Quaker religion for his martial proclivities in the years preceding the Revolution. Whether his disaffection with his father's faith stemmed from the parade field, the library, or the ale house is unclear.[2] What is clear is that the estranged Quaker would fashion himself a determined officer and one of America's ableist commanding generals in the field.

In December, he arrived in the Carolinas to take command of the southern army—a force that was in decline. Although 2,300 soldiers were on the rolls, no more than 1,500 were present and otherwise fit for duty. Only 950 were regulars, and Continental soldiers such as these were to be the core of his forces and key to victory in the south. Greene looked immediately to the lax discipline in the ranks—especially desertion. He published his intent to deal firmly with deserters, and in December, one of the first defectors to be captured was tried quickly and hanged. The execution was witnessed by his entire army. There was a new American commander in the south.[3] Deliverance for Greene arrived in the form of Daniel Morgan who had retired to Virginia years earlier after being passed over for selection to command a large light infantry unit in favor of "Mad" Anthony Wayne. Losses in the south drew Morgan back into service, and he headed toward the Carolinas with 600 veteran Maryland Continentals and a contingent of cavalry. Now a brigadier, the battle-scarred and hard-scrabble "Old Wagoner" sped south and immediately reversed the crisis in morale within the southern army. Upon arrival, Brigadier General Morgan was also tasked with raising greater numbers of local militia.[4] Morgan and Greene would have to organize quickly as the patriot army was fatigued, undermanned, and undersupplied and Lord Cornwallis was on the prowl.

As for Peter Francisco, he had fought valiantly and survived the lopsided loss at Camden. The Virginia militia to which he had volunteered earlier in the year had fled the field at Camden and departed the area. As such, Francisco returned to Cumberland County, Virginia, after the battle, but he did not remain long. Captain Thomas Watkins of Prince Edward County issued a call for veteran soldiers to populate a cavalry unit to ride south and join the fight. Ultimately, Francisco's stint as a cavalryman would be a function of his Virginia unit's assignment under the direction of the commander of the 3rd Continental Light Dragoons. This cavalryman was a well-seasoned second cousin of George Washington—Lieutenant Colonel William Washington. Dragoon commander Washington was from Stafford County, Virginia, and he enjoyed the reputation as a hard fighter with combat experience going all the way back to New York's Battle of Harlem Heights in September 1776. At Trenton, he and future president James Monroe led an assault that overwhelmed Hessian pickets and seized key enemy cannons. In 1778, he was assigned leadership over a series of dragoon regiments and eventually ordered to the south. He participated in the defense of Charleston where he began an extended rivalry with enemy horse commander "Bloody" Banastre Tarleton with both cavalry leaders scoring victories in 1780. Unlike Francisco, Washington's dragoons were notably absent from Camden owing to then commanding general Gates's preference for infantry.[5]

In the eighteenth century, cavalry (often referred to simply as *horse*) was a key part of land warfare along with infantry and artillery. There were three basic types of horse: heavy cavalry, light cavalry, and dragoons. At the pinnacle, heavy cavalry sometimes had armored combatants on the finest horseflesh used to crash into adversaries—breaking up tight infantry formations or assaulting well-defended enemy positions on the battlefield. The second type of horse was the light cavalry, and they were used primarily for intelligence gathering, skirmishing, foraging, attacking enemy lines of logistics, and delivering critical messages among army leadership. Dragoons were the third type of cavalry and were originally envisioned as mounted infantry. The name harkens back to the seventeenth century when members of this class of horse carried rudimentary pistols that the French called *dragons* as the hand guns conjured images of a fire-breathing mythical reptile when discharged. Over time, the mounted infantry evolved into a hybrid of cavalry for mounted combat often accompanied by infantry units. Mounted warfare in the American Revolution was conducted largely under the dragoon model.[6]

At the commencement of the American Revolution, the British Army boasted sixteen regiments of cavalry. The Americans had none. Fortunately for the patriots, the global nature of the war with France meant the Crown could deploy only two units to North America—the 17th Light Dragoons followed by the 16th Light Dragoons. The remaining mounted units in North America were largely made up of homegrown loyalist regiments such as Tarleton's British Legion and the highly capable Queen's Rangers. The Americans were forced to create their mounted forces from scratch beginning in 1776.[7] At the outbreak, the American cavalry model followed loosely the British standard. George Washington was considered one of the premier equestrians of the day. As such, he had a keen interest and key influence on the original organization of the U.S. cavalry as well as any departures from the Crown's model. Ideally, the American cavalry regiment would have three field officers, a staff, and six subordinate units called *troops*. Each troop would be led by three officers supported by six non-commissioned officers with a trumpeter assigned. Thirty-four privates would complete the troop. Specialist soldiers would accompany each troop, and they would include a logistics sergeant and two privates responsible for duty as an armorer and a farrier. In addition to the blacksmith duties of keeping the troop's horses shod, the farrier would also double as the veterinarian. Periodically, the troops could rely upon a regimental riding instructor to hone the skills of the horsemen.[8]

Polish cavalryman Count Casimir Pulaski distinguished himself early in the war at battles such as Brandywine Creek, and he was later designated Commander of the Horse by Congress. In similar fashion to von Steuben, the count was made a general officer (brigadier) and charged with

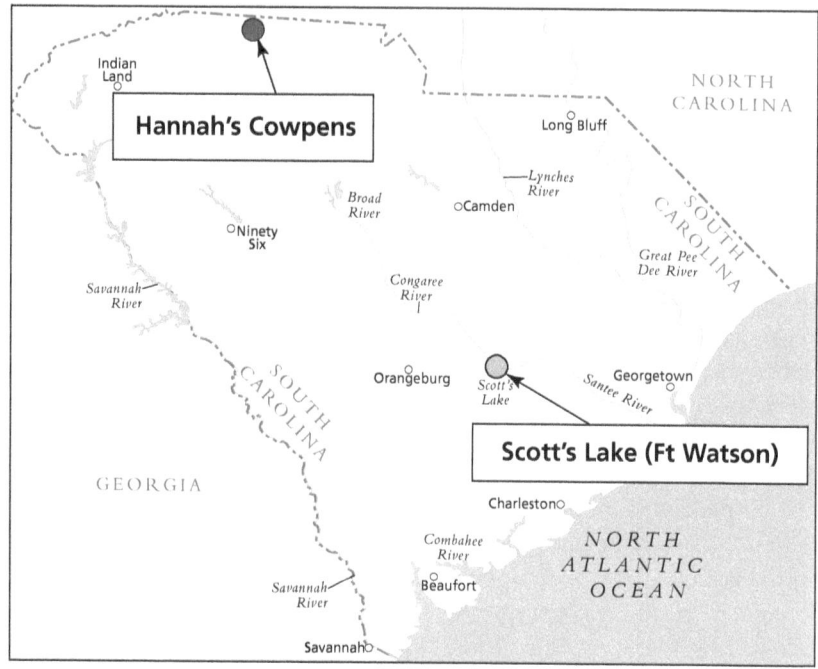

South Carolina, Scott's Lake, and Hannah's Cowpens.

establishing a corps to be the American model. Pulaski's high standards sometimes ruffled patriot feathers; still, he built and led impressive mounted units. General Pulaski served bravely throughout the conflict until he was killed leading his men in the siege of Savannah in 1779. As such, the count is known to history as the "father of the American cavalry." Throughout the war, patriots such as "Light Horse" Harry Lee and William Washington would establish themselves as the top tier of native-born patriot cavalry commanders.

As with most militia or provincial cavalrymen, Peter Francisco would be responsible for providing his own mount and tack (riding accoutrements such as saddle, bags, bridle, and blanket). In his service in the patriot horse, Francisco would procure a series of equine by various methods. Sometimes, he would purloin horseflesh during combat or raids on the British. He also purchased horses, and in one case, Francisco bartered twenty-three thousand *weight of tobacco* to acquire an appropriate mount.[9] Doubtless, his formative years as a child blacksmith gave the "Virginia Giant" keen insight into the riding, care and feeding of his horses, and the necessity of maintaining his riders' tack in good condition.

Francisco and his cavalry comrades would wield the primary weapon of the horseman—the blade. There were a variety of swords and sabers employed by dragoons—most had a blade length of around three feet. Necessity would force Americans to forge copies of British light dragoon sabers. James Potter of New York fashioned these weapons for the Loyalist horse, and many fell into the hands of patriot riders. Not to be outdone, James Hunter of Rappahannock Forge in Virginia outfitted patriot cavalry. Pistols were also a desired accoutrement, and one or two may have been secured in leather or bearskin holsters near the pommel of the saddle. Flintlock pistols were employed for close-quarters combat, and the variety included .69-caliber French 1733 and 1763 models. Domestically, the Americans would fashion the homegrown Bailey or .69-caliber Rappahannock Forge pistols, which were copies of the British Elliot version. In addition to the sword and pistols, many horsemen were also armed with a musket. Some of America's men of the horse used carbines (shortened muskets), but this was a rare luxury for the patriots. For those few cavalrymen equipped with carbines, the French contributed two types—the .69-caliber Model 1770 Dragoon Musket and the Model 1773 Cavalry Musketoon. America would produce an even shorter .70-caliber Composite Carbine. British dragoons were often outfitted with either the 1760 or 1776 model .72-caliber Royal Foresters Carbine.[10] With long leather slings attached, cavalry firelocks were either slung along a trooper's back, or the horseman rode with the weapon at his side with the firelock secured in a short thimble by the stirrup.[11]

It is hard to know if Captain Watkins's militia cavalrymen were dressed in a motley collection of plain clothes or if they were permitted to wear the uniforms known to be worn by regulars of the 3rd Continental Light Dragoons.[12] William Washington's Continental dragoons displayed a dashing ensemble that had been their tradition since 1778. Washington's troopers were outfitted in white coats with divided tails offset with blue facing on the collars, lapels, and cuffs worn over matching blue waist coats, white trousers, and black boots. The horsemen were topped off with black leather headgear—highly polished with a plume of horsehair often affixed to the top. During Washington's service near Charleston, he became acquainted and enamored with Miss Jane Riley Elliot—a woman he would marry shortly after the Revolution. The dragoon commander confessed to his intended that his regiment had no standard around which his troopers might identify and rally. Miss Elliot immediately fashioned one from a piece of red silk embroidered with a subdued floral design that had served previously as a chair backing. The gallant Washington accepted the banner with appreciation, and it was unfurled at the head of the 3rd Continental Light Dragoons for the balance of the war.[13]

SCOTT'S LAKE

In early 1781, Peter Francisco was part of a reconnaissance force along the road halfway between Camden and Charleston. Nathanael Greene had issued general orders to the cavalry to harass the enemy as they maneuvered in South Carolina. He had expressed to General Washington a plan to assemble a 240-man combined unit of cavalry and infantry to rove the Carolinas in pursuit of that end. The British had recently established a small fortification called Fort Watson on the east bank of the Santee River called Scott's Lake (referred to as "Scotch Lake" in Francisco's postwar reflections).[14] At the time Francisco's detachment arrived at Fort Watson, the patriots were able to bottle up the British inside their fortification, which was placed upon a small hill that Peter Francisco described as the shape of a "sugar loaf."[15] The fort was actually on an ancient Indian burial mound that rose dramatically roughly twenty-five feet from the level of the river topped with seven-foot wooden palisades protecting the British soldiers within.[16]

Logistics was still a crippling challenge for the patriots as the army struggled to resupply. Some *hogsheads* or barrels of British supplies had been outside the fort when the Americans arrived on the scene. In the enemy's rush to secure their supplies and return to the fort, several of the hogsheads were marooned outside the British fort, and some had rolled down hill toward Scott's Lake. Although well within firing range of the Crown's defenders, Private Francisco observed the situation and surmised the difficulty the redcoats might have training accurate fire at such a steep angle from the fort and down the hill toward the water's edge. The "Virginia Giant" courageously and deftly low-crawled along the base of the hill to a position just below a British hogshead. Brisk British musket fire either sailed over his head or was impeded by the large barrel that lay between Francisco and the fort. Slowly Francisco inched the barrel toward the edge of the lake with musket balls flying. Once in the lake, Peter Francisco carefully maneuvered the heavy barrel through the water using it as a shield from enemy fire. After he reached the patriot camp, he opened the hogshead to find a stash of trousers, shirts, and overalls, among other clothing—necessities the American soldiers desperately needed. Francisco did not remain at the camp to celebrate; rather, he acted on intelligence that was gathered while skirting Fort Watson. Previously unnoticed, Private Francisco had seen eight British

Fort Watson today, Francisco's "Sugar Loaf."
Photo by J. T. Palmer

horses tethered about one hundred yards from the fort. As his compatriots were sorting through the captured barrel, Francisco mounted his horse and put the equine to the whip. He dashed past the British fort and through musket fire to the group of redcoat horses. He quickly unlashed the beasts and nimbly led them back to the American camp. Clearly, if not for his demonstrable fighting prowess, Peter Francisco would have made an able quartermaster in the patriot army.[17]

HANNAH'S COWPENS

Meanwhile in Charlotte, Nathanael Greene hatched a plan to split his main army into two swift columns leading an eastern prong back into central South Carolina and sending Morgan to the west. This plan broke the cardinal rule of never dividing one's forces. With the split, however, the American army could more ably resupply themselves when occupying different areas of South Carolina's piedmont. Greene's goal was to keep General Charles Cornwallis in a constant state of flux between (1) the necessity of concentrating his forces to face Greene and Morgan's fledgling but growing number of regulars and (2) the temptation of disaggregating his redcoats to chase local militia and guerrilla fighters such as the "Swamp Fox" in the low country (Lieutenant Colonel Francis Marion), the midlands' "Gamecock" in Lieutenant Colonel Thomas Sumter, and the upstate's Colonel Andrew Pickens.[18] Major General Greene's orders to Brigadier Morgan: "Sir—you are appointed to command a corps of Light Infantry, a detachment of Militia, and Lt. Col. Washington's Regiment of Light Dragoons. . . . The object of this detachment is to give protection to that part of the country and spirit up the people. . . . I entrust you with this command, being persuaded you will do everything on your power to distress the enemy and afford protection to the country."[19]

Lieutenant Colonel William Washington's dragoons were assigned to General Morgan's column, which was now called a *light corps*—sometimes termed as Morgan's flying army or flying corps. As one might infer, speed was of the essence for men serving under Daniel Morgan. British General Cornwallis, positioned approximately sixty-five miles southwest in Winnsboro, South Carolina, correspondingly split his forces. The Americans played cat and mouse leading the British columns farther into the Carolina wilderness with Tarleton seeking Morgan while Cornwallis would concern himself with Greene. When Tarleton learned Morgan was west of Winnsboro, he pursued him in great haste, fatiguing his own troops. Morgan, moving north, was looking for appropriate ground upon which to make his stand. He found the spot at Hannah's Cowpens in the upstate— just south of the Broad River and near the North Carolina border. Cowpens was so named as the land was a grazing area for drovers to rest and water their herds while transporting cattle from the western Carolinas to the more populated low country around Charleston. Hannah's Cowpens were formed inside a natural corral of trees and brush, and the grazing fields had sparse numbers of pine and oak trees sprinkled throughout. The borders of the area measured five hundred yards square, and it was in these open spaces that the two fiercest leaders of the Revolution would square off—British Lieutenant Colonel "Bloody" Banastre Tarleton against American Brigadier General Daniel Morgan—the "Old Wagoner."

Daniel Morgan set the battlefield for victory. Taking a page from Hernán Cortés's burning of his ships, Morgan placed his troops facing south with the swollen Broad River to their rear. It was immediately apparent to regulars and militia alike that retreat into the North Carolina wilderness was not possible. Across the battlefield were the British. Their commander, Banastre Tarleton, was not known for granting quarter. It was a fight-or-die situation for Morgan's corps. Moreover, the American commander knew

Tarleton's tactics and proclivities. He recognized "Bloody Ban" was sometimes impulsive in battle. He crafted a strategy to use the Cowpens' undulating hills and patriot militia to bait the British commander into close-range combat with a firing line consisting mostly of American regulars. What ensued was a battle that some students of military history have described as *perfect*.

At daybreak on January 17, 1781, Tarleton pressed his soldiers north into the Cowpens rapidly as he believed that the American militia on the hill were rearguard forces covering Morgan in retreat. The British commander presumed Morgan's main force was in flight and fording the Broad River just beyond the rolling battlefield. Near the base of the first hill, the American Brigadier Daniel Morgan placed 150 sharpshooters from North Carolina and Georgia on the front line. Behind the sharpshooters were Colonel Andrew Pickens's dismounted Carolina militia numbering 300 with horses tethered to the rear. The third line at the crest of the first hill consisted of 450 regulars from Maryland and Delaware under Lieutenant Colonel John Eager Howard mixed with various state troops led by Captain Edmund Tate. To the rear, hidden along the woodland edges of Hannah's Cowpens were 125 mounted dragoons commanded by Lieutenant Colonel William Washington under whom Peter Francisco and his cohort Virginia militia men were assigned.[20]

Taking the field from the south, Lieutenant Colonel Tarleton anchored his forces on the right and left flanks with the 17th Light Dragoons. Inward from the mounted troops were battalions from the 7th Regiment of Foot (Royal Fusiliers) under Major Timothy Newmarsh on the left—opposite the British Light Infantry to the right with the British Legion infantry in the center. To the rear was a battalion of the 71st Frasier's Highlanders led by Major Archibald McArthur aligned with Tarleton's Legion dragoons. In total, Morgan had approximately twenty-one hundred men at arms while Tarleton had only thirteen hundred officers and men; however, the British lieutenant colonel enjoyed a two-to-one advantage in cavalry.[21]

For Morgan's part, he had positioned his men in the night and spent the evening and early morning moving from unit to unit to converse with his soldiers, elevate the mood with his home-spun levity, and remind them of the battle plan. He encouraged: "Just hold up your heads, boys, three fires, and you are free ... when you return to your homes, how the old folks will bless you, and the girls will kiss you, for your gallant conduct."[22] The sharpshooters in the front were to engage first by shooting two or three volleys and focusing their fire on the *epaulet-men* whose uniform accoutrements on their shoulders identified them as officers. Once their volleys were launched,

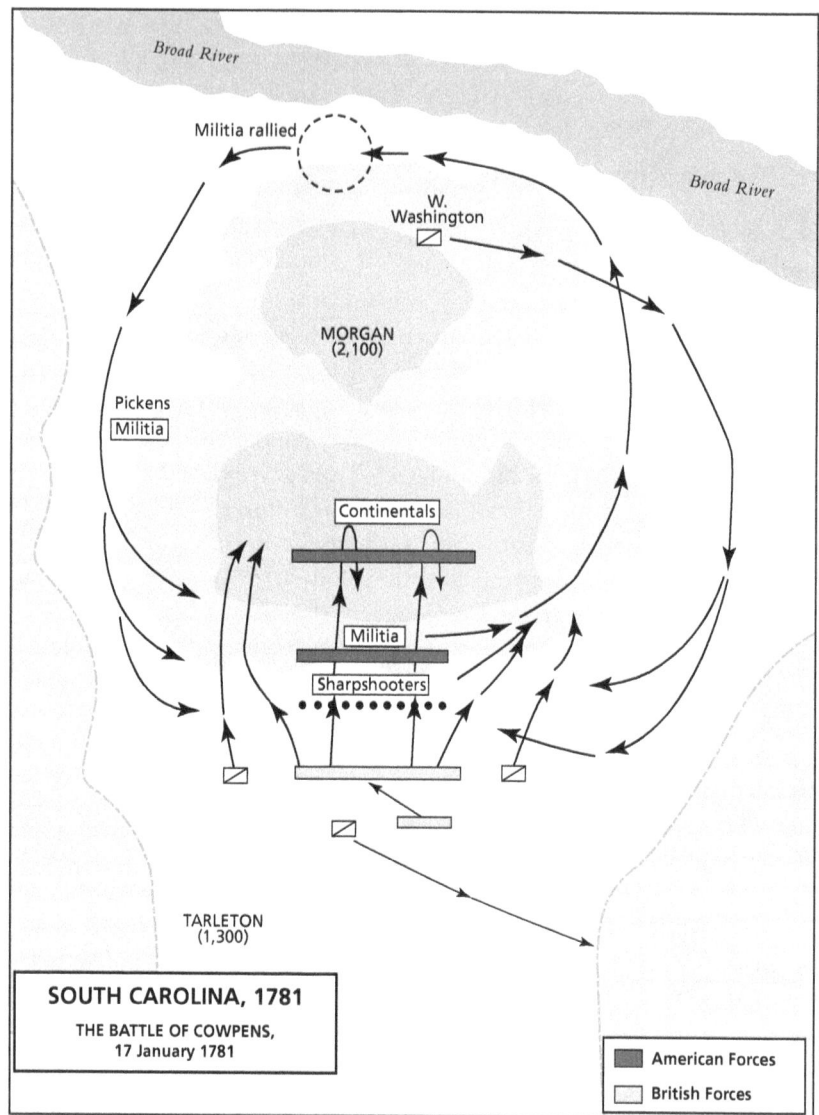

The Battle of Cowpens. By Emerson Kent.

the sharpshooters would retreat past the militia line to the third line where the Delaware and Maryland Continentals were stationed. The militia would then repeat the process with two or three volleys and a retreat to the Continental line. It was presumed the combined forces of sharpshooters, militia, and Continentals would then break up the British advance with the help of Washington's mounted cavalry. The key was Morgan's perception that Tarleton would act impulsively and charge the retreating sharpshooters and militia—dismissing the threat of the Continentals in the third rank and without knowledge of Lieutenant Colonel Washington's dragoons concealed behind the hills toward the Broad River to the north.

Morgan's plan unfolded with only minor deviations. Thinking Morgan was actually escaping with his main force across the Broad River, Tarleton imprudently advanced his troops without having his entire line of battle set. Tarleton observed the American sharpshooters and deployed the 17th Light Dragoons from the British left sweeping to the right along the line of marksmen. Patriot riflemen momentarily checked the advance of the British mounted troops. Colonel Tarleton advanced his infantry units into the American center. The sharpshooters' volleys achieved the desired effect of depleting some of the British infantry, and the retreat of the riflemen drew the attention of the Crown's mounted dragoons. At this point, the American cavalry commander—William Washington—revealed his force and pushed back the British mounted advance. Meanwhile, the American militia (second line under Andrew Pickens) fired volleys and beat a hasty retreat to the Continental line with the British infantry in hot pursuit.

British Major Archibald McArthur's 71st Highlanders advanced from the rear along Tarleton's left and threatened the American right flank. Pickens's retreating militia were re-formed, and they wheeled in good order along a north-south radius, took aim, and delivered deadly, point-blank fire into the highlanders—halting their advance. Washington's American horsemen then swept aside their mounted British counterparts and encircled the enemy by attacking from Tarleton's right. Pickens's American militia rallied and attacked the British left flank, and a lethal double envelopment ensued. Tarleton was done for. The British lost just over nine hundred soldiers—captured or killed. The Americans suffered only about seventy-five killed or wounded.[23]

Upon hearing of the loss, Lord Cornwallis reportedly leaned so heavily upon his sword he snapped the blade in two. He wrote to Lord Rawden: "The late affair has almost broke my heart.... I was never more surrounded with difficulty and distress, but practice in the school of adversity has strengthened me." Tarleton would say: "The defeat of the British must be ascribed either to the bravery or good conduct of the Americans." Of the victory, Nathanael Greene reported to General Washington: "The event is glorious.... The brilliancy and success with which it was fought does the highest honor to the American arms." With trademark brevity, the commander in the field—Brigadier General Daniel Morgan—quipped:

Brigadier Daniel Morgan. By Charles Willson Peale.
Independence National Historic Park, Wikimedia Commons

"We gave Tarleton a devil of a whipping."[24] It was a resounding American victory over their most hated adversary—"Bloody Ban." The battle lasted less than one hour. Tarleton escaped and reconstituted what was left of his forces with Cornwallis. As expected, Cornwallis gave pursuit to try and rescue the British prisoners. Morgan and Greene were already on the move and proceeded to lure the redcoats through North Carolina on a mad dash toward Virginia.

COWPENS AND SCOTT'S (SCOTCH) LAKE POSTSCRIPTS

So, where was Peter Francisco during Cowpens? The answer to this question is unclear. Biographies and attestations document Francisco's volunteering to join Captain Thomas Watkins's cavalry troop in late 1780. Captain Watkins's cavalrymen were assigned under Lieutenant Colonel William Washington. Francisco issued postwar attestations about action at Fort Watson on Scott's Lake occurring in early 1781. In his writings, Francisco indicated he was under the command of Washington at Fort Watson, and that he remanded to the dragoon commander the horses he seized from the British. Other evidence of Washington being on hand for the hogshead and horse heist is scant.[25] In mid-January at Cowpens, Washington led the horsemen who were key to Morgan's victory. Later in spring 1781, Washington and Francisco were known to serve together in North Carolina.

So, was Peter Francisco at Cowpens? He never made a claim that he was a veteran of Cowpens in his pension requests. A Virginia newspaper at the beginning of the twentieth century, however, recounted Francisco's wartime record and stated he was at Cowpens on January 17, 1781.[26] If Francisco's attestation is accurate and Lieutenant Colonel William Washington was on hand at Scott's Lake, it is reasonable to presume Francisco was with Washington shortly thereafter at Cowpens. If Washington was not commanding Francisco's actions at Scott's Lake, perhaps the two men were separated at Cowpens as well. Patrick O'Donnell, in his book *Washington's Immortals*, states that Peter Francisco had to submit multiple postwar pension requests with added statements by supporting parties because his feats of armed combat were too fantastical to believe. Perhaps Peter Francisco did not attest to service at Cowpens because he fought without distinction or he survived the battle unscathed. Many of Francisco's postwar attestations centered on battles where he was wounded as the purpose of the administrative exercise was to receive pensions as well as compensation for expenses. If not at Cowpens, where else could he have been? Did the action at Scott's Lake overlap with Cowpens? Was he detached from Washington and assigned to some other area under Major General Greene's column in the eastern part of the Carolinas? Cowpens was such a watershed victory; one doubts a soldier would intentionally fail to mention participation. Still, by the time Cowpens took place, the "Virginia Giant" was already famed for incredible battlefield bravery and achievement. Perchance he did not highlight his service at Hannah's Cowpens because, in his mind, his battlefield actions were too benign to warrant special attention. This is a mystery that, for the present, remains unclear.

As for Fort Watson, the British would repel a siege led by Thomas Sumter shortly after Cowpens in February 1781. In April, the "Swamp Fox"—Francis Marion—would pin down the redcoats with the assistance of Lieutenant Colonel "Light Horse" Harry Lee's legion. Lacking artillery, Marion faced a stalemate. He would need a novel approach. Capitulation was forced on the strength of an idea conceived by Major Hezekiah Maham where an imposing log tower was envisioned at the base of the Indian mound. Upon Francis Marion's approval, trees were felled and notched in seclusion, and the tower was constructed in a single night. With their new elevated position, American sharpshooters would lay down fire into the fort to provide safe conditions for other patriot soldiers to approach the Indian mound, eliminate abatis, and choose the time and location to scale the seven-foot palisades. The British garrison commander himself—Lieutenant James McKay—was wounded by Major Maham's sniper fire. McKay and his redcoat charges could not expose themselves to return fire as the American riflemen had command of the walls and much of the grounds inside the garrison. The American commander Francis Marion offered terms for surrender, and McKay, recognizing the futility of continued resistance, relinquished Fort Watson on April 23.[27] Fort Watson was the first of several fortifications to be wrested from the British in the wake of American victories at King's Mountain and Cowpens and an exhausting, pyrrhic British victory in North Carolina at a place called Guilford Courthouse.[28]

Chapter 12

LEFT FOR DEAD

Guilford Courthouse

After Cowpens on January 17, 1781, the remnants of Banastre Tarleton's forces fled to the safety of the British who were encamped in Winnsboro, South Carolina. Daniel Morgan's victory aside, Major General Nathanael Greene knew his Continentals were in danger of defeat while divided, and he needed to reconstitute the large patriot army to stand a chance against General Charles Cornwallis. Greene was located one hundred miles east of Hannah's Cowpens at Hicks Creek on the Pee Dee River. Cornwallis was in Winnsboro, slightly to the south but between Greene and Morgan. He needed only to move north to keep Morgan and Greene apart. Brigadier General Daniel Morgan deduced that Lord Cornwallis would depart Winnsboro and move northwest to pursue his victorious American corps with expediency. As such, he left a detail to bury the dead, and within eight hours after victory, Morgan and his flying corps crossed the Broad River and headed north into North Carolina with his weapons and British prisoners in tow. The "Old Wagoner" presumed correctly. Lord Cornwallis put his soldiers to the march in pursuit to catch and defeat the victors of Cowpens and free any of the Crown's combatants held captive.[1]

Cornwallis gave chase as Morgan sped north, and he sought to match the speed of the lighter Americans. On January 24, the British commander ordered the burning of his supply and baggage train with the exception of ammunition, hospital stores, and salt plus a collection of four wagons for ambulance duty. Gone were the slow, plodding train of wagons in the rear, including rations of rum, personal baggage, and even some of the food supplies. The British were now lighter and faster but on limited supplies.

On several occasions, Cornwallis's men skirmished with Morgan's men, and periodically the armies came within sight of one another across swollen rivers. General Nathanael Greene also moved his army northward on a course to the east and parallel to Morgan and his British pursuer. Greene's aim was to rendezvous and combine forces with Morgan to present a credible threat to Cornwallis. He took a personal interest in Morgan's escape and rode a circuitous route of one hundred miles in the company of a small cavalry detachment to meet his brigadier and direct some delaying action at river crossings. On February 7, Morgan and Greene's forces met in Guilford County, North Carolina—some thirty-five miles south of the Dan River and Virginia. Greene had constantly been surveying ground for the prospect of wheeling and facing Cornwallis.[2] He took careful observation of the terrain surrounding Guilford Courthouse, and this would prove fortuitous a few weeks later.

Upon hearing of General Cornwallis's burning of his supply train, Greene considered taking a stand, but during a council of war, his senior officers outlined the desolate state of the patriots given the recent sprint through the wilderness. Greene resolved to head for the supplies and security of southern Virginia, and the final leg of what would be known as the *Race for the Dan* was headed to a feverish climax. The significance of the Dan River and Virginia that lay beyond was threefold. First, if Greene could reach and ford the river first, the Dan River would present a barrier that could be defended from the opposite banks. Second, there were patriot units under Major General Friedrich von Steuben in Virginia that could initially protect and potentially augment Greene's fatigued army. Third, General Greene's men could rest and resupply in Virginia while a strategy for redeployment could be planned. For Lord Cornwallis, the imperative was to catch and destroy Greene before he reached sanctuary in Virginia. Moreover, if Greene's forces were eliminated, the British commander could claim North Carolina for the Crown, and he could freely draw badly needed loyalist men and supplies to refortify his army.

Greene proved a wily fox to Cornwallis's hunt. First, he wanted to make sure the British could not catch his forces nor pin his men against the river and engage them during a vulnerable crossing. Cornwallis assumed the Americans would ford the upper Dan River to the west, and Greene wanted to reinforce this belief with subterfuge. Greene assembled a special screening unit of sufficient strength to demonstrate on the British flank and purport to be Greene's main force. Ideally, this unit would serve under his most accomplished commander—Brigadier General Daniel Morgan. Morgan, however, was critically unwell. He had been fighting through painful chronic back injuries for some time. Greene recognized that his best brigadier was in agony and had likely served in his last battlefield command when he stood victorious at Cowpens. On February 9, General Greene bid farewell to his best field commander and gave him leave to return to Virginia to heal. Greene lamented: "Great generals are scarce. There are few Morgans to be found."[3]

Command of the American screening force now fell to a Marylander—Colonel Otho Holland Williams. In the force was Lieutenant Colonel William Washington's hybrid cavalry of 250 to which Peter Francisco was assigned. Maryland and Delaware Continentals numbered 280 and were led by John Eager Howard. Sixty riflemen served under the direction of Colonel William Campbell, and there were 100 members of "Light Horse" Harry Lee's legion. Colonel Williams both screened Greene's main army, and he baited Cornwallis toward the upper Dan crossings. This was incredibly dangerous duty, but Francisco and the rest of Williams's force were hardened veterans with years of experience in orienteering, maneuver, and combat. Otho Williams's men would be sorely tested, but they would meet the task admirably. The pace was so frenetic that some of the Americans under Williams were sleeping only six hours out of every forty-eight owing to the need for perpetual, strong pickets and scouting parties to fend off the British who were close behind. Williams's men were bone weary—sometimes forgoing meals to catch a few moments' sleep. Meanwhile, Greene and his main body commandeered all water craft in the area and made for the lower Dan crossings. Once Cornwallis comprehended that he had been duped, he raced for the lower Dan, making twenty-five miles per day over rain-soaked ground, but he was too late. On February 14, the patriot screening force commander—Colonel Williams—received word that Greene was safely across the Dan by way of Irwin's crossing, and he pressed his troops to the same junction. Deft rearguard action by cavalrymen under William Washington and Harry Lee bought time for Williams's infantry and riflemen to cross. Williams left enough water craft to allow Washington and Lee's troopers, including Peter Francisco, to navigate the Dan with their tethered horses swimming abreast of the boats during the final crossing. Cornwallis's men reached the Dan only to observe the cavalrymen exiting the river safely on the Virginia side. The Americans were out of harm's way in Virginia where supplies and protection by the forces under von Steuben awaited. Greene's leadership and organization during the retreat had been a master stroke of generalship reminiscent of Fabius himself.[4]

Nathanael Greene now turned his attention to making his army fit to fight. While in Virginia, General Greene reconstituted his ranks and resupplied his army with the goal of driving south to reengage Lord Cornwallis. The British commanding general had failed to capture or destroy Greene. Still, the Americans were now on the other side of the river, and Cornwallis could address the needs of his army by foraging for supplies in North Carolina and getting his troops rested and ready for a future contest. Greene saw the importance of reentering North Carolina precipitously to rally the spirits of patriotic supporters and depress the Carolina loyalists.[5] Unlike his predecessor Horatio Gates, Major General Greene recognized the essentiality of cavalry for intelligence, screening the movement of troops, and seizing the initiative on the battlefield. As such, the Americans executed the search and requisition of fresh mounts for "Light Horse" Harry Lee's legion and William Washington's dragoons—sometimes by force. Greene had the permission of Virginia's governor, Thomas Jefferson; however, the procurement of replacement horses was not without friction along the North Carolina border. On February 22—barely over a week since entering Virginia—Greene recrossed the Dan River to confront General Cornwallis.[6]

With Greene now in North Carolina, one matter of logistics was exclusive to the "Virginia Giant" as a cavalryman. A sword or saber was an essential accoutrement to mounted warfare as long guns were largely infantry tools and, beyond an initial volley, impractical from the horse while engaging the enemy. Although of greater utility from the saddle, pistols of the day were less reliable than the blade and difficult to reload in the heat of combat. As such, the sharp-edge of a cavalry unit was demonstrated literally in the saber-slashing dragoons on their thundering steeds. Swords of the day did not fit the six-foot, six-inch, 280-pound horseman that was manifested in the now fully grown Peter Francisco. The shortcomings of the toothpick blades of the day would plague him for only so long. A sword befitting a giant would be fashioned for him under the orders of the commander in chief—General George Washington. On March 13, 1781, a six-foot-long broadsword with a five-foot blade was delivered to Francisco's camp. Hardly the work of a master craftsman, the sword was described as "rough and uncouth." Still, it was unquestionably the heaviest blade in the army, and it could only be wielded in single-handed fashion from the horse by a giant—the "Virginia Giant."[7] Peter Francisco was now suitably armed to maximize his fighting prowess from the horse.[8]

On March 14, Greene moved to his choice of battleground. It was a small hamlet called Guilford Courthouse where he had bivouacked in early February—just before the final sprint north to the Dan River. Cornwallis was encamped approximately ten miles to the southwest. Greene expected him to attack the following day, and the American general was not disappointed.⁹ The British advanced from west to east along Salisbury Road. Taking a page from Morgan's successful strategy at Cowpens, Greene assembled multiple defensive lines facing west. Yet one key difference was that the distance between the American defensive lines was much greater. As such, the visibility was obscured by forests and undulating hills. The Americans could not discern visually the success or failure of their comrades. This would provide a troublesome task for Greene to maintain command and control.

The first American line was posted along a rail fence and consisted of notoriously mercurial militia troops—this time from North Carolina. Similar to Cowpens, the first line was tasked with firing several volleys before retreating three hundred yards to the second line made up of Virginia militia. The third line was located on higher ground some seven hundred yards to the east and contained fourteen hundred hardened regulars from Maryland and Virginia. Cavalry secured the American right and left flanks. To the south on the left flank was Lieutenant Colonel "Light Horse" Harry Lee. To the north on the right flank was Lieutenant Colonel William Washington with Private Peter Francisco among his mounted forces. The American cavalry on the right and left flanks were each augmented with dismounted sharpshooting riflemen from Virginia.¹⁰ Greene had approximately four thousand American troops defending against Cornwallis's two thousand soldiers. The Americans were equipped with four, 4-pounder cannons. The British Royal Artillery was under the direction of John McLeod and consisted of three, 6-pounder cannons.

On March 15, the British, short of rations, would begin the twelve-mile march to Guilford Courthouse before daybreak and without breakfast. Greene spent the morning bolstering the spirits of his skittish North Carolina militia by reminding them they needed only to shoot three well-aimed rounds at the redcoats. Simultaneously, Tarleton clashed with Lee's horsemen in the morning to no advantage. Lord Cornwallis and his infantry would arrive at noon. The British straddled Salisbury (more recently named New Garden) Road as their lines approached with precision. Major General Alexander Leslie commanded the time-honored position of the British right leading the two regiments—the 71st Highlanders and the von Bose Hessians. Leslie's regiments were augmented by Lieutenant Colonel Chapel Norton's 1st Guards Battalion. To the left, Lieutenant Colonel James Webster commanded the 33rd Regiment of Foot and 23rd Royal Welch Fusiliers. Reserves, including the 2nd Guards Battalion, were led by Brigadier Charles O'Hara. As always, Ban Tarleton prowled with his cavalry, ready to pounce when advantageous.¹¹

The front line of North Carolina militia fired their rounds early—before the British were in range. They hastily retreated toward the second line after inflicting only minimal damage. Contrary to their orders, the militia did not fall in with the second line; rather, they continued their retreat. As such, the planned combination of first- and second-line militia did not take place. The Virginia riflemen on both flanks (posted near Lee and Washington's cavalry) delivered fire, drew British attention, and held their positions well for a period of time. The Virginians disrupted the continuity of Crown forces' advance. Washington's dragoons and his dismounted riflemen fell back and took their positions on the right flank of the American second line (to the north). "Light Horse" Harry Lee and his sharpshooters maintained their positions on the left (southern) flank of the first line, delivering fire as the British approached the center of the battlefield.

The British left, led by Webster, began to gain the upper hand on the American second line at the right flank but soon overextended themselves by continuing their advance to Greene's hilltop third line. This portion of the American third line contained stalwart regular soldiers of the 1st Maryland Regiment. The Marylanders delivered scathing fire and checked the advance.[12] Webster's regiments fell back, and the reoriented British now formed to face the American third line. Cornwallis ordered his reserve forces under General O'Hara to pressure the American left. The less experienced 5th Maryland Regiment began to cave.

Colonel Washington and his horsemen observed the ongoing clash. Within the regiment of dragoons, Peter Francisco sat astride a fidgeting charger. With reins in his left hand, he stood ready with his new broadsword—sheathed safely in the scabbard. Doubtless, he and his fellow cavalrymen battled nervousness by checking their weapons—firelock long guns and pistols affixed to saddles. Sabers remained sheathed for the time being. The telltale creaking of leather saddles under the weight of riders was interrupted by an occasional low, growling harrumph from one of the many warhorses. Sensing the oncoming battle, the horses shifted to the right and left slightly . . . some pawing at the turf with front hooves. Riders gripped and tightened reins and clasped the horses forcefully with their legs to exert control over their mounts as the crackle and smoke of combat unfolded before them. Dragoons often stood in their stirrups momentarily to stretch their legs and adjust their weight in their saddles. The time to advance approached. On order, the cavalrymen ripped swords and sabers from their scabbards. All blades were free for the task at hand. To a common observer, Francisco must have appeared as a storybook warrior from medieval lore—a massive man on a correspondingly large horse with six-feet of broadsword at the ready.

Witnessing the struggles of the American 5th Maryland Regiment against the British 2nd Guards, Washington sensed the moment of truth. As the flagging Marylanders abandoned two of their cannons, Lieutenant Colonel William Washington gave the order to advance, and his cavalrymen spurred their horses into a trot—then they accelerated quickly to a canter. Francisco's lower body strength melded him to the saddled horseback and permitted him to handle the gait with ease. The British soldiers' normally tight ranks had been disrupted in the battle. To men of the horse, gaps in the infantry provided opportunity to charge into formations and hack away at the enemy. Washington and his men would do just that. Swords gleaming and pointing downrange, they thundered down toward their prey. Warhorse hooves churned the turf; soil, grass, and mud splattered the underside of the beasts and the gray and blue coats of their riders. The rhythmic beat of the *tra-da-lump, tra-da-lump, tra-da-lump* of the horses' gallop pounded the earth and seemed almost to synchronize into a drum roll. The chargers were lathered in sweat as the dragoons spurred them on. The red coats of the British soldiers of foot filled the eyes of the patriot horsemen.

Suddenly, Washington's mounted dragoons slammed into Lieutenant Colonel James Stuart's 2nd Guards Battalion on the British right and delivered what Tarleton would describe later as a great slaughter. In the fray, the American cavalry cut like a scythe into the British infantry and "the Swords of the patriot horsemen were upon the enemy . . . before they suspected danger . . . multitudes lay dead."[13] Private Francisco would dispatch at least four redcoats in the fray with his mighty sword. William Washington's biographer, Stephen Haller, asserted the "Virginia Giant" slew eleven British Guards single-handedly.[14] A noteworthy victory was over a grenadier who thrusted his bayonet at the mounted giant. Francisco parried the strike, but the deflection resulted in the bayonet finding its mark in the Virginian's thigh—the steel piercing all the way through and pinning the rider's leg to the horse. Doubtless, the redcoat thought he had bested his massive antagonist, and Francisco would be unhorsed or perhaps try to retire. Not so. The massive horseman retained his balance, disregarded the pain, reached down, and with his free hand, grasped the barrel of the musket below the bayonet. With the indomitable strength of his one free arm, he expelled the bayonet from his horse and then down the wound path in his leg until it was free from his thigh. Next, Francisco twisted and wrenched the weapon from the hands of the enemy belligerent. Mortified and now unarmed, the British soldier attempted to escape. The redcoat's flight was doomed.

Francisco spurred his horse, raised his sword, brought it down on the head of the infantryman with a crashing blow, and split his cranium in half down to his shoulders. The carnage was dreadful. Nineteenth-century biographer Reverend William Henry Foote noted:

> Francisco performed a deed of blood without a parallel. In that short recounter, he cut down eleven men with his brawny arm and terrible broadsword. One of the guards thrust his bayonet, and in spite of the parrying of Francisco's sword, pinned his leg to the horse. Francisco forbore to strike, but assisted him to extricate his bayonet. As the soldier turned and fled, he made a furious blow with his sword, and cleft the poor fellow's head down to his shoulders. The force of the blow, added to the soldier's speed, sent him on a number of steps, with his cleft head hanging upon each shoulder, before he fell. The astonished beholders shouted, "Did you ever see the like?"[15]

To the right of Washington's dragoons, the 1st Maryland, fresh from dispatching Webster's regiments, wheeled and slammed into O'Hara's troops. There was no time to prime and reload firelocks. Men with their bayonets and horsemen with their swords and sabers engaged in a frightful mob of close-quarter, hand-to-hand combat. Colonel Washington's horsemen

The Battle of Guilford Courthouse. By H. Charles McBarron.
Center of Military History

were slashing through the British infantry when he noticed a collection of British officers coalescing around a figure two hundred yards away. It was Cornwallis! Washington could not let the opportunity pass to capture or kill the enemy commander. He ordered his regiment to the charge—further into the mass of enemy before him toward the British general.[16] Though skewered through the thigh, Francisco fought on and continued to hack and rip into the determined and well-drilled redcoats. The "Virginia Giant" brought carnage and delivered a multitude of other wounds that were most certainly mortal.[17] Despite the extended lines of defense and departures from the planned order of battle, Greene's American soldiers were gaining the upper hand.

Suddenly, Francisco felt a fresh and intense pain in his leg. Looking down he saw a horrifying sight. He had taken an infantryman's bayonet strike entering above the knee and exiting at the hip socket. The steel bayonet was excruciating. Francisco wheeled his horse to facilitate the extraction of the blade, but the deed was done. Francisco's life blood was pouring out onto the field at Guilford Courthouse. He struggled to retain his mount. At the same time, Cornwallis saw the tide had turned against his men, and he did the unthinkable. He ordered a cannonade of grapeshot into the mass of British and Americans engaged on the high ground to break the patriot advantage. After first resisting, the British artillerymen executed their commander's order. A series of massive *ka-booms* shook the entire battlefield. The cannonade blasted holes into the British and Americans indiscriminately and gave pause to the 1st Maryland and Washington's dragoons. Horses jumped and reared on their hind legs. For the "Virginia Giant," the combination of his latest wound and the cannonade of grapeshot unhorsed him. His massive frame slammed into the battlefield, and he soon lost consciousness.

The Americans were stunned by Cornwallis's extreme tactics. After the grapeshot, Greene's best troops then began to falter, and rather than risk the army in total, the American commander ordered retreat. After two hours of pitched battle, Cornwallis would hold the field but at the expense of more than five hundred men or 25 percent of his army with no reserves from which to draw. Yielding the field, Greene lost the battle tactically with a total of 250 casualties, yet strategically, he still commanded an operational force in North Carolina where he could continue to draw logistics support and volunteers.[18] Greene had taken the preeminent British general's best effort and was poised for victory. Cornwallis survived the day by directing fire into his own men, and the battle was concluded.

Guilford Courthouse had numerous Quakers in the area, and some patriots saw their pacificist neutrality as loyalist support in disguise. Greene leveraged his childhood religious credentials to encourage the North Carolina Quakers to provide medical attention to his wounded soldiers. In a letter, he requested assistance from the those residing in nearby New Garden, and he alluded to the continental perception about their loyalties and the pervasive animus harbored against them by the patriots. He wrote in part, "I was born and educated in the professions and principles of your Society; and am perfectly acquainted with your religious sentiments and general good conduct as citizens. I am also sensible . . . from the misconduct of a few of your own, that you are generally considered as enemies to the independence of America. I entertain other sentiments. . . . I respect you as a people, and shall always be ready to protect you from every violence and oppression." The message was clear. The Quakers should assist the wounded Americans. Otherwise, they could find themselves subjected to the violence that patriot and loyalist marauders had visited upon their counterparts throughout the Carolinas. In conjunction with Greene's admonition, the Quakers responded by tending to the needs of the patriot casualties.[19]

Peter Francisco was one of the beneficiaries of Quaker care after Guilford Courthouse. Suffering two brutal bayonet wounds and a whiff of grapeshot, he was left for dead. His body would lie on the battlefield among four corpses. Quaker John Robinson was surveying the after-battle carnage and discovered the "Virginia Giant" alive! Private Francisco survived the battle but was badly in need of care and convalescence. He remained a recipient of the Quakers' hospitalization and hospitality for some six to eight weeks before being strong enough to depart North Carolina for Cumberland County, Virginia. His freshly burnished reputation as a superhuman warrior preceded him on his journey home.[20] In thanks for Peter Francisco's stalwart service and fortitude, Major General Greene presented Private Francisco an engraved razor case that is on display at the Guilford Courthouse Battlefield museum.[21] The emblazoned annotation praised Francisco's "moral worth and valor" and closed with the salutation: "from his comrade in arms Nathanael Greene."[22]

Ironically, Guilford Courthouse was a loss for the Americans that reverberated until the end of the war in the patriots' favor. After the battle, the venerable Cornwallis would recount: "I never saw such fighting since God made me. The Americans fought like demons."[23] British politician Charles James Fox added, "Another such victory would destroy the British Army."[24] General Nathanael Greene did not overly lament the outcome, saying of the British "except for the honor of the field they have nothing to boast of."[25] Cornwallis would retire to Wilmington, North Carolina. Major General Greene, with his numbers temporarily diminished by some expiring militia enlistments, would shadow Lord Cornwallis, and then he unsuccessfully attempted to lure the British commander southward on another wilderness chase. Cornwallis eschewed a second folly into the backwoods with Greene; rather, he proceeded on to Virginia to reconstitute and resupply his army while leaving North Carolina in patriot hands.[26]

GUILFORD COURTHOUSE POSTSCRIPT

Historical debate exists over several events before and during the battle at Guilford Courthouse. The first is the procurement or fashioning of the broadsword on the orders of George Washington. Some historians question this fact by asserting there is no historical record of the commander in

Peter Francisco Monument, Guilford Courthouse National Military Park.
Photo by J. T. Palmer

chief purchasing such a sword at his own expense. To be clear, Washington was known for keeping detailed records of his expenses. For much of his adult life, he was a reliable diarist from which his activities have often been reconstructed. In addition, the idea that General Washington would be able to ship such an implement five hundred miles on short notice strains the credulity of naysaying historians.[27]

The first element of this challenge seems to rely upon the assumption that such a sword would be bought and paid for by Washington from a commercial craftsman. As mentioned in the chapter, the sword was described in one account as *rough and uncouth*—hardly the product of a conscientious swordsmith. Perhaps the sword was ordered to be fashioned by a blacksmith in service to the patriot cause and not a renowned professional of bladework. In this scenario, orders, invoices, bills of lading, receipts, and such would not exist. Moreover, if the sword were ordered from a soldier/blacksmith, the location of manufacture could have been at any one of the patriot army forts or campsites—including one in relatively close proximity to the site of battle. Finally, Washington suspended his practice of daily personal diary entries during the war, so the absence of such documentation is in keeping with a wartime dearth of corroborating evidence. As to the actual sword, it was placed in the care of the Virginia Historical Society by Mrs. Edward Pescud, one of Peter Francisco's daughters.[28] One of the last references to its location was nearly a century later by grandson Robert Lafayette Francisco. He petitioned the governor of Virginia to release the blade to his custody from the Armory of Richmond in 1861 in conjunction with the outbreak of the Civil War.[29] Ian McDowell penned one of the handful of myth-versus-reality articles, and he conceded that the presence of a large sword was not at issue—just the source of the implement.[30] No one is certain what became of the sword of Francisco, and presently, it is lost to history.[31]

A second fact at issue with some historians is the number of enemy soldiers killed by Francisco at Guilford. Francisco himself claimed only four. Other biographical accounts and a Guilford Courthouse stone monument with an associated plaque assert as many as eleven men killed by Francisco's broadsword. The true number is difficult to ascertain given that not every wound by the blade results in immediate death before the victorious swordsman. Peter Francisco may have claimed only the four deaths that he felt were certain according to his recollection. Moreover, the McDowell examination goes on to highlight how American comrades witnessed an extraordinary level of carnage at the hands of Francisco, with Lieutenant John Woodson stating, "when leaving the Battleground [Francisco] was very bloody and also was his Sword from point to hilt."[32] This description is in keeping with a multitude of wartime attestations made on Peter's behalf. Brother in arms John Nichols, for example, said that Francisco's exploits "were individually equal to six or eight of the best soldiers of the army."[33] In summary, the sword of Francisco certainly existed. Moreover, the "Virginia Giant" wielded it in hand-to-hand combat achieving a British soldier versus Francisco *killed-or-wounded rate* of no less than four to one (possibly as much as eleven to one) at Guilford Courthouse. Not a bad day's fighting for Private Francisco.

Chapter 13

CUTTING DOWN TARLETON'S RAIDERS

Amelia, Virginia

In July 1781, Peter Francisco was in his familiar state of Virginia still recovering from the injuries he received four months earlier at Guilford Courthouse. From May through July, General Charles Cornwallis had moved north from Wilmington, North Carolina, to what was called at the time the *southside* in Virginia. The southside represented the lateral expanses from the southeastern coastal Tidewater region to the Blue Ridge Mountains to the west. North to south, this territory extended loosely from the James River down to the northern banks of the Dan River.[1] Lord Cornwallis was engaged in a give and take with Major General Gilbert du Motier, Marquis de Lafayette. The British commander was attempting to lure the young French nobleman into a trap and nearly did so on July 6 at the Battle of Green Spring Plantation in Virginia—about five miles west of Williamsburg. Spearheaded by "Mad" Anthony Wayne, a quarter of Lafayette's 4,000 patriots charged headlong into what he originally thought to be the British rear guard. In fact, it was the enemy's main body and a clever deception set by Cornwallis who had 7,000 men of the Crown forces at the ready. This included units commanded by the former American turncoat—now newly commissioned British General Benedict Arnold as well as "Bloody" Ban Tarleton's British Legion. General Wayne was caught in a pincer between two veteran redcoat regiments and had to hold the enemy at bay while effecting an orderly retreat. Lafayette, Wayne, and their

American troops fell back toward Richmond, suffering 150 casualties compared to 75 British losses.[2]

Shortly thereafter, the commanding general of the British forces in North America—Sir Henry Clinton—acted upon his fear of an attack by George Washington on his position in New York. As a result, he ordered his subordinate commander in the south, General Cornwallis, to establish a base along the navigable York River in the vicinity of Gloucester and Yorktown, Virginia. This would enable near-term redeployment of soldiers from Virginia to New York as necessary. Moreover, from this waterside base of operations, Cornwallis's forces could project power into Virginia while simultaneously receiving maritime resupply and reinforcements as the war progressed. One of Lord Cornwallis's tools of power projection was rendered through the strident efforts of Banastre Tarleton and his British Legion. The unit included the notorious green-jacketed cavalry and had been rewarded recently for their service in the Carolinas. The legion was converted from a provincial regiment to *regular establishment* within the Crown forces. This designation garnered for the legion equal station and equal standing with British regulars in all matters including pay and benefits. Since Guilford Courthouse, battle attrition had reduced the British Legion somewhat to an amalgamation of 180 dragoons and 70 mounted infantry for a total force of 250 men under arms. Cornwallis charged Tarleton with an extended raid throughout southside Virginia to destroy patriot supplies, manufacturing, and cash crops that could be converted to logistics support through trade. On July 8, Cornwallis penned the following orders to Tarleton:

> Begin your march tomorrow with the corps of cavalry and mounted infantry under your command to Prince Edward Courthouse, and from thence to New London in Bedford County, making the strictest inquiry in every part of the country through which you pass for ammunition, clothing, or stores of any kind, intended for the public; and as there is no pressing service for your corps in this province, I must desire you will be in no haste to return; but do everything in your power to destroy the supplies destined for the rebel army. All public stores of corn and provisions are to be burnt and if there should be a quantity of provisions of corn collected at a private house, I would have you destroy it, even although there should be no proof of its being intended for the public service, leaving enough for the support of the family, as there is the greatest reason to apprehend that such provisions will be ultimately appropriated by the enemy to the use of General Greene's army, which, from the present state of the Carolinas, must depend upon this province for its supplies.[3]

For his part as a militiaman, Peter Francisco was permitted independent reconnaissance duty in Virginia to trail the British and aid patriots against the raiding and plundering redcoats. Nearby, Francisco's familiar nemesis, Colonel Tarleton, was engaged in raids against suspected rebels and potential allies to the patriot cause—robbing and burning with no quarter for traitors to the Crown. This was dangerous duty for the Portuguese-born patriot. Although a seasoned soldier, he would perform this duty alone, nearly guaranteeing an adverse, perhaps deadly outcome if he encountered the enemy in any significant numbers. In addition, he was a giant, and his exploits were well known to belligerents on both sides of the conflict. As such he would have difficulty performing his duties incognito. Finally, if found out of uniform (and many American soldiers were still not outfitted in European style), he could be seen as a spy and hanged on the spot. If not a uniform, a buckskin or linen hunting shirt may have been Francisco's choice of apparel.[4]

On July 12, Francisco was reconnoitering in the vicinity of Amelia, Virginia, roughly forty-five miles southwest of Richmond. This country would have been familiar to him as it was not far from Buckingham County where he was indentured as a child. He happened upon a tavern house owned by a Mr. Ben Ward, and shortly thereafter, nine of "Bloody" Ban's plundering dragoons appeared and confronted him outside the establishment. Peter deftly recognized he was outnumbered, so he acquiesced to their pronouncement that he was their prisoner. Presenting a docile manner, the now gentle giant was seen as harmless, so eight of the green-coated raiders entered the Ward house, leaving Francisco in a one-on-one situation with a British paymaster. The paymaster began to evaluate his captured rebel and demanded that the colossal captive "give up instantly" all of his valuables, or "prepare to die." Peter responded he had nothing to give up. It was at that moment the dragoon noticed the shiny silver buckles on Francisco's shoes. Brandishing an unsheathed saber, the cavalryman demanded that his captive deliver the buckles.[5] Peter responded: "They were a present from a valued friend, and it would grieve me to part with them. Give them into your hands I will not. You have the power to take them if you think fit."[6]

The paymaster tucked the naked three-foot blade under his arm and bent down to remove the buckles from Francisco's shoes. The American soldier recognized this brief moment of advantage. In a flash, Peter Francisco grasped the hilt of the saber while simultaneously stepping back and ripping the weapon from under the dragoon's arm, gashing the opposing cavalryman. He then delivered a thundering blow to the skull of the trooper. Wounded and dazed, the now swordless cavalryman unholstered his pistol and pointed it at the American. Peter Francisco slashed the dragoon's gun hand, nearly severing it from the wrist. The pistol discharged, and the giant felt the now familiar sensation of a hot musket ball contacting his frame. Fortunately, the wound was a grazing shot to his side and not debilitating. Owing to all the commotion with the paymaster, the house emptied with the remaining eight green jackets and Ben Ward now on the scene. The troopers surveyed their comrade with fresh wounds to the head, armpit, and hand. All soon fixated upon the patriot behemoth who stood before them—now armed with their stricken cohort's cavalry saber and closing the distance on them quickly. One dragoon made for his horse, and Ben Ward handed a musket over to the horseman who, now mounted, took dead aim at Peter Francisco's head. For Peter, these precious seconds must have seemed like an eternity as he stood helpless and awaited the eruption of gunpowder, smoke, flame, ball, and buckshot from the barrel of the firelock. Was he doomed to suffer a mortal wound at close range from the blast of an enemy's long gun? Not this day. The musket misfired! Chaos ensued. With saber in hand and energized by his good fortune, the giant rushed the horseman, seized the barrel of the musket with his free hand, and in the struggle left the dragoon unhorsed, disarmed, and wounded. He leapt upon the riderless horse. The strapping American was now aboard an enemy charger and facing a handful of dragoons who were scrambling for weapons and their mounts. More important, Tarleton's entire British Legion appeared in the distance and was bearing down on the tavern. Reversing the feint tactic he employed at Camden, the ever-clever Francisco called into the woods to phantom comrades shouting: "Come on, my brave boys, now's our time; we will soon dispatch these few, and then attack the main body."

The ruse worked. The half dozen cavalrymen feared that a mounted American unit sufficient to take on the whole of Tarleton's Legion lay just beyond the wood line. Francisco was now positioned between the enemy and their horses, so the dismounted green coats dashed on foot for the safety of the oncoming hoard of friendly horsemen.

Francisco slashes the dragoon paymaster at Ward's Tavern. Artist unknown.
Virginia State Library

Engraving depicting Francisco's Fight in Amelia (now Nottoway) County, Virginia. By Augustus Kollner.
Courtesy of Peter Francisco Society member Ed Bowman

This left Peter Francisco to calm and tether the eight British horses and to deal with the owner of the tavern. With horses in tow, Francisco found and cornered Ward, and he was bent on dispatching him for his assistance to the Crown's men. The proprietor of the home pleaded for his life. Suddenly, Francisco then heard the telltale pounding of hooves in the distance. He then spun around and saw a detachment of ten fresh dragoons speeding his way and leading the remaining British Legion. With no time for recriminations, Francisco handed the reins of eight horses to Ward, and he instructed the man sternly to conceal his newly procured chargers for him to reclaim later. He then spurred his borrowed horse in the other direction—into the brush.

Francisco knew the surroundings well, and the British did not. He was able to evade the pursuing dragoons' initial foray and steal into the wilderness. Concerned they might track and overtake him, the American doubled back and spied his British pursuers resting their mounts. Once they resumed following his trail, he ensured the posse would not find him by stealthily following the rear of their column from a safe distance. The next day, he returned to Ward's place to claim his horses and address the previous actions of the proprietor. Ward had kept the horses hidden as Francisco had ordered, and now he haggled for two horses for his trouble. Incredulous, Francisco considered a measure of final vengeance against Ward, but he realized that his continued presence placed him in danger as the area was thick with enemy patrols. He acquiesced and departed Mr. Ward's property with his six horses. He could always return at a later date to exact satisfaction from Mr. Ward. The "Virginia Giant" sold all remaining horses except for one fine white thoroughbred stallion that he would retain through the war and beyond. Francisco named the white charger *Tarleton*.[7] Any desire by the giant to repay the tavern owner's treachery was superfluous. Shortly after the events at the tavern, Mr. Ward died from a broken neck after falling from one of the very horses Francisco had conveyed to him.[8]

AMELIA POSTSCRIPT

The family of Ben Ward disputed vociferously any accusation that the tavern owner aided the enemy against Peter Francisco. Ward was a captain in the local patriot militia, and he owned a nearby mill from which American units had drawn flour during the war. In 1815, the late Captain Ward's son outlined in a Richmond periodical his father's side of the events of July 12, 1781, complete with independent affidavits attesting to the patriotic disposition of Ben Ward. For the "Virginia Giant," the events of the day soon became known as *Francisco's Fight*, and some accounts credit him with killing as many as three dragoons at Ward's Tavern. Of his hand-to-hand combat facing nine-to-one odds, Francisco would later recount: "This is the last favor I ever did the British."[9]

Chapter 14

THE FINAL BLOW

Yorktown

In September and October 1781, Peter Francisco was at the tobacco trading port of Yorktown, Virginia, on the staff of his old friend and comrade—Gilbert du Motier, Marquis de Lafayette.[1] He would be on hand for the siege and surrender of Lord Charles Cornwallis to Washington. The historical record is unclear as to the combat participation of the "Virginia Giant." General Lafayette, however, commanded units that he directed to assault multiple British redoubts. As such, Francisco may have participated actively or at least been in the company of the marquis as he exercised command and control over his siege troops. Regardless, several biographers show Private Peter Francisco beside Lafayette as they witnessed the British laydown of arms.[2]

The victory at Yorktown was a long time in the making. Francisco had participated in army maneuvers and many battles throughout the Carolinas designed to exhaust and maroon Cornwallis far from his bases of supply. The general commanding the British southern army staggered to Wilmington, North Carolina, and then on to Yorktown where it was assumed the Crown forces could rest, be resupplied, and potentially redeployed or reinforced from the sea by way of the Chesapeake Bay and the Royal Navy. After all, General George Washington was mired in a long-standing stalemate outside New York City although he had been recently bolstered by six thousand French troops under Lieutenant General Jean-Baptiste Donatien de Vimeur, Comte de Rochambeau.[3] The British aimed to control Virginia and cut off the Carolinas, which would have made moot Nathanael Greene's impressive Fabian strategy earlier in the year.

Washington anticipated a decisive battle to liberate New York. However, hurricane season had slowed shipping to and from the sugar-producing islands in the Caribbean, and messages arrived that Admiral François Joseph Paul, Comte de Grasse, Marquis de Grasse-Tilly (known to history as the Comte de Grasse) intended to lead the French fleet north to Chesapeake Bay to support Franco-American forces ashore. After some advice and consideration, Washington determined he had to shift his focus to the south. He crossed the Hudson at King's Ferry adjacent to Stony Point and marched his army to Head of Elk, Maryland. Upon reaching the Chesapeake, the Americans and French boarded transport ships to move quickly down to the southern bay—to the Tidewater area of Virginia. To hide his maneuver and prevent a countermovement south by British General Henry Clinton, the American commander in chief—the "Old Fox"—left a small force behind to make the pretense of preparations to attack New York City.

Simultaneously, a French fleet of twenty-nine ships under the command of de Grasse appeared at the entrance of Chesapeake Bay off Cape Henry, Virginia, on September 2. His flagship, *Ville de Paris*, boasted a stunning 104 guns. Three days later, de Grasse turned back British Rear Admiral Thomas Graves's nineteen men-of-war in the fierce four-day Battle of the Capes. The losses on both sides were comparable, but at the end of the contest, the French fleet remained in the Chesapeake, and the British fleet was in the Atlantic and making way to New York. The calculus that included unchallenged control of the sea by the Royal Navy had changed—if only for the remainder of hurricane season.[4]

The presence of de Grasse not only prevented the Royal Navy from resupplying or evacuating Cornwallis but also the French expedition held an additional three thousand troops ready to disembark in Virginia to assist the allied forces ashore. Equally important was a French delivery of hard currency to make long overdue payments to soldiers in the American army.[5] Washington and the main Franco-American body arrived in the vicinity of Williamsburg on September 15, giving patriots a three-to-one advantage over the entrenched redcoats. Yorktown rapidly became shaky ground for the British. After taking counsel from flag and general officers, the American commander in chief settled on a siege strategy. On October 6, General Washington ceremoniously fired the first cannon to commence the Battle of Yorktown. French engineers were on hand to plan trenchworks to enable more effective cannonade and to provide protected staging points from which to launch infantry attacks on British redoubts. Baron Friedrich von Steuben commanded the center division populated by the ever-stalwart

Maryland regulars. Generals Mordecai Gist and Anthony Wayne commanded combined units of soldiers from Maryland and Delaware as well as Pennsylvania and Virginia, respectively. Analogous to falling dominoes, the British lost defensive position after defensive position. Cornwallis corresponded with his commander—General Clinton—several times, but promises of relief from New York never materialized.

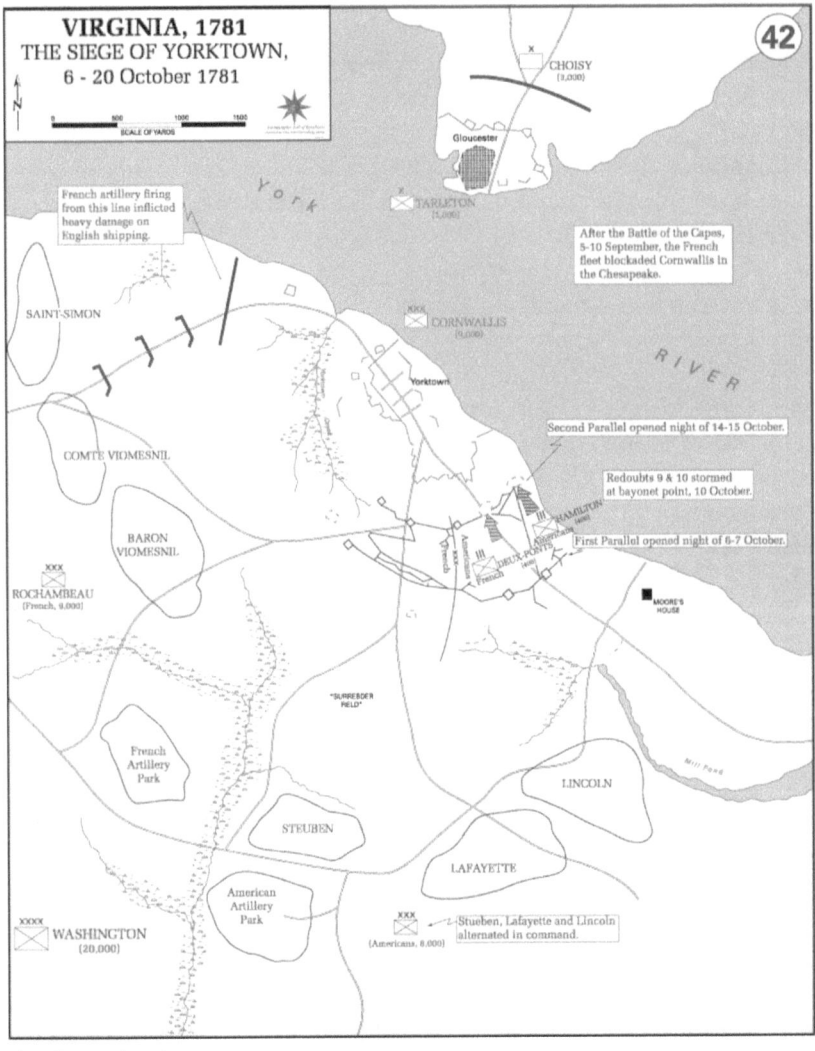

The Siege of Yorktown.
United States Military Academy History Department

October 14 would see the Franco-American trenchwork facilitating murderous bombardment of the last remaining British redoubts by cannon and mortar fire. General Lafayette would deal the final blow in the form of simultaneous attacks on redoubts 9 and 10 by the French and Americans, respectively. Redoubt 9 would face four hundred French regulars commanded by Comte de Deux-Ponts. Redoubt 10 was assaulted by four hundred light infantrymen led by Lieutenant Colonel Alexander Hamilton. After fierce fighting without and within, both redoubts were brought to heel in a single moonless night. Washington could now convert the British redoubts to friendly artillery batteries and pour fire into Yorktown from three vectors. After gallant but ineffective nighttime raids to spike American guns and an unsuccessful retreat across the river, the British had to face the reality of their situation. They could neither hold, attack, nor escape.

On October 17, Cornwallis dispatched a drummer to beat a request for parlay to discuss surrender. Washington, ever mindful of skullduggery in eighteenth-century warfare, asked for the British intent to surrender to be presented in writing. On October 19, George Washington mounted his favorite horse, Nelson, and observed the British soldiers marching out between lines of French and American forces to lay down their arms. Nearby, the Marquis de Lafayette surveyed the historic event flanked by a mountain of a man—Peter Francisco—astride his impressive white thoroughbred, Tarleton. The British betrayed their penchant for stoic professional conduct. Many had become drunk the night before the surrender affair. Some officers refused to yield their unit colors to American sergeants who had been detailed to recover the banners. An American junior officer had to be deputized to seize the flags and turn them over to the enlisted men. Some British had the audacity to mock the shoeless American ragamuffins who stood solemnly to receive their enemy's arms. Still, the victory went to the French professionals and Yankee citizen-soldiers. Reports of Lord Cornwallis being ill meant he would be absent from the ceremony.

Washington and his officers would not have the pleasure of receiving the British commander's sword directly from the general in charge of the Crown's southern army. Rather, a surrogate, Brigadier General Charles O'Hara, was appointed to stand in for the vanquished Cornwallis and lead the British through the ignominy. In a bout of confusion, O'Hara approached Rochambeau with the sword. The French general deferred to General Washington. The American commander in chief recognized he was not in the presence of his martial equal, so he consigned Brigadier O'Hara to the patriots' second in command, Major General Benjamin Lincoln of Massachusetts, who would receive the sword.[6] In his report to his commander in New York, Lord Cornwallis's letter to General Clinton began: "Sir, I have the mortification to inform your Excellency that I have been forced to give up the posts of York and Gloucester, and to surrender the troops under my command, by capitulation on the 19th inst. as prisoners of war to the combined forces of America and France."[7] In a gentlemanly tradition of the eighteenth century, General Washington and his officers hosted their vanquished British counterparts for supper and spirits. All of the royal officers were invited with one notable exception—Lieutenant Colonel Banastre Tarleton.

At Yorktown, the Americans secured as prisoners fully 25 percent of the British ground forces in North America. The British surrendered six thousand troops to include Hessian and British colors, guns, small arms, ammunition, and equipment. British casualties during the siege totaled 500. The Americans and French lost 280 killed and wounded.[8] It may not have been clear to the battle's participants that Yorktown meant sure defeat for the British and independence for the Americans, yet history confirms it represented a *fait acompli*. Yorktown was the final major battle of the American Revolution. This patriot victory ushered the beginning of a precipitous end for British interests in the thirteen United States that were formerly the

The storming of redoubt 10 at Yorktown. By H. Charles McBarron.
U.S. Army Center of Military History

Crown's colonies. Under the deft leadership of Washington, the stalwart persistence of American warriors like Peter Francisco, and some indispensable European allies, the patriot amalgamation had proven an unlikely victorious *David* to Great Britain's *Goliath*. Sporadic fighting would occur in areas near strong loyalist communities, but these hostilities would cool in the coming months as peace negotiations were contemplated. In Charleston, British General Alexander Leslie's forces as well as the Crown's army in New York were evacuated by ship. The formal conclusion to the war occurred by way of the Treaty of Paris, signed in 1783, wherein Great Britain acknowledged the independence of the United States. The longshot American army of farmers, tradesmen, and shopkeepers had won their freedom, and Peter Francisco enjoyed widespread notoriety as a titanic American warrior without equal.

Chapter 15

CITIZEN FRANCISCO

Postwar

Postwar, Peter Francisco's life was marked by three marriages (owing to the deaths of his first two wives), some celebrity, attempts at becoming a successful gentleman planter in Virginia, government service, and legal entanglements. Initially, he returned to his formative experience as a blacksmith and established a productive foundry. On land donated by Joseph Curd in Buckingham County, Peter Francisco built a smith-work that was soon surrounded and supported by shopkeepers, grocers, parsons, craftsmen, and associated families that would make up the hamlet of Curdsville, Virginia—population three hundred.

COURTING SUSANNAH ANDERSON

Susannah Anderson was a fetching daughter of Captain James Anderson from Cumberland County. The Anderson clan was a prominent family descended from Irish settlers who arrived in the New World in 1635. The Andersons made their homestead on sixteen hundred acres known as "*The Mansion*."[1] Susannah was one of Captain and Mrs. Anderson's seven children—two sons and five daughters. The first meeting for Peter and Susannah was by happenstance shortly after Yorktown at St. John's Church in Richmond. Peter Francisco was on hand in the company of his now legendary friend, Gilbert du Motier, Marquis de Lafayette. In an event approaching Shakespearian fate, Miss Anderson, a girl of only sixteen years at the time, was exiting the church and tripped down the stairs.

Chivalrous Peter Francisco was nearby and caught her in midair—sparing her from injury. After informal courtesies, Lafayette noticed that Francisco could not take his eyes off the lovely Virginia maiden. The French nobleman predicted a future nuptial, charging Peter: "Promise me that you will name one of your descendants for me, whether he have blue eyes like her or black ones like yours." Peter Francisco responded, "Yes, unless me she doth deny."[2] Days later, Peter Francisco—now aged twenty-one—made the formal acquaintance of Miss Susannah Anderson at a party for returning soldiers at the Carrington home in Richmond. The Anderson and Carrington families were quite close even though Colonel Carrington began the war as a loyalist before the British manner of warfare persuaded him to the patriot side. Peter Francisco had to outperform a friend and fellow young veteran from the Carrington family (George Carrington) to win the favor of Miss Anderson. With trademark persistence and a natural grace and charm, Susannah Anderson's giant suitor captured her affections.[3] There was only one problem. James Anderson objected to the match owing to Francisco's lack of education. Their marriage would have to wait. The love of a woman may have been, in part, the impetus for Peter Francisco to become educated.[4]

EDUCATION

The biographical data about Peter Francisco are unanimous on his inability to read in his childhood and throughout the Revolution. Nevertheless, his intellect and quick thinking were evident in his performance as a combat soldier in the field. In fact, several historical accounts assert that the prolific warrior distinguished himself well enough for consideration for a commission as an officer in the Continental Army or state militia. Yet, his illiteracy—specifically the inability to receive and issue orders in writing—made such an appointment impossible. Now, with his military duty to the fledgling United States concluded, the veteran threw himself into self-improvement in the form of reading instruction under the tutelage of Frank McGraw.[5] To be clear, Francisco desired literacy to such a degree that he attended McGraw's classes with small children. One can imagine a vision unique in elementary education—a room full of children reading and reciting prose, practicing writing, and engaging in mathematics accompanied by a grizzled adult war hero four times their size as a classmate. Giving in to his penchant for pranks, Peter once pilfered the lunches of his classmates and drew the ire of the schoolmaster. Mr. McGraw could not let the offense go unaddressed and gave the hulking veteran-student a choice—expulsion or corporal punishment. Francisco chose the latter, stating: "Lay it on."[6] At that, the wiry schoolmaster assembled the class to witness the sound whipping of their gargantuan classmate who outweighed the instructor by a hundred pounds.[7] Tomfoolery aside, the giant's brain was as formidable as his brawn. He was a quick learner, and he mastered reading and writing sufficient to understand and enjoy the classics after only three years of instruction. From there, his predilection for voracious reading represented an effective method of continuous education for the newly literate Peter Francisco.[8]

MRS. SUSANNAH ANDERSON FRANCISCO

James Anderson died in 1782. The death of the family patriarch combined with Peter's pursuit of education removed any impediments to the nuptials. Moreover, the widow Anderson had long been an admirer of the "Virginia Giant" for his physical strength tempered by his pleasant disposition. Three years after their first meeting, Francisco took Susannah as his bride in December 1784. As was the practice at the time, James Anderson's estate was distributed primarily to his sons. Still, Susannah received 60 acres, one black man named Ned, one steer, some dishes and cookware, a handful of tools, books including a bible, and a small amount of cash. Determined to be a gentleman planter and not a tradesman, Peter Francisco gave up his smith-works in Curdsville, moved to Charlotte County, and purchased 250 acres on Louse Creek around March 1785. The couple had a son named James Anderson Francisco in 1786 and a daughter (Polly) in 1788. Along with the arrival of his daughter, Peter Francisco was appointed surveyor of roads in Charlotte County in the same year. In 1789, the Franciscos sold their 250 acres with the intent of moving to 500 acres on both sides of Dry Creek in Cumberland County. Before the move, Susannah died in December 1790 leaving Peter Francisco with James (age four) and Polly (age two).[9]

CATHERINE FAUNTLEROY BROOKE

Two years after Susannah's death, Peter Francisco was visiting his mother-in-law—the mother of his deceased wife—at "The Mansion." A cousin, Catherine Brooke, was a guest at the time. Miss Brooke had been a close friend of Susannah's and came from a distinguished family descending from the Fauntleroys and Robert Brooke—a member of Governor Alexander Spotswood's Knights of the Golden Horseshoe. The Brooke family made their home at *Farmers Hall* on the Rappahannock River in Essex County, Virginia. Peter was smitten with the captivating Catherine. Moreover, he was a single father, and his experience as an orphan led him to believe that a mother's nurturing was essential to a child's well-being.[10] Francisco pursued her to Farmers Hall the following summer and proposed in the family garden. Miss Brooke applied for a marriage license on December 8, 1794.

Catherine proved to be a fine match for the famous war veteran. Her father had sent her to England as a young girl where she was presented at the court of King George III. She was beautiful, graceful, charming, and a sought-after guest at London's social events. At Peter's home at Dry Creek, Catherine established herself as a consummate hostess, and they entertained many luminaries of the time. Catherine's social graces blended well with the wartime notoriety of her husband, along with his disarming humor, remarkable singing voice, courtesy, warmth, and intellect. They were a "power couple" in today's manner of speaking. Catherine bore four children for Peter—Susan Brooke, Benjamin, Catherine Fauntleroy, and Peter Francisco II—bringing the blended family's total number of children to six.

In 1803, they sold the Dry Creek property and settled for four years on 74 acres at New Store in Buckingham County where Peter also operated a tavern. The year 1810 would find the family on 110 acres in Buckingham dubbed *Locust Grove* located approximately seventeen miles east of the courthouse. Locust Grove would become the most famous of all of the homes owned by Peter Francisco.[11] Peter enjoyed twenty-seven years with his beloved second wife. He would again try his hand as a Virginia gentleman planter, and the couple would manage farm operations, raise children to adulthood, and entertain at Locust Grove to great fanfare. The people of Virginia were keen to remember the wartime deeds of their giant of the Revolution. In nearby Richmond, the proprietor of Locust Grove would have the honor of seeing an eighty-one-ton ship christened in his name (*Peter Francisco*) in 1819.[12] Tragedy would strike two years later as Catherine would die on October 23, 1821, leaving Peter alone at Locust Grove—a widower for a second time with his adult children far-flung and raising their own families elsewhere.[13]

MRS. MARY BEVERLY GRYMES WEST

Two years later he married an attractive aristocratic widow—Mrs. Mary Beverly Grymes West. She had been wed to a wealthy Virginia planter, Colonel Robert West, who died after two years of marriage in 1817. Born in the London suburb of Brompton, England, Miss Mary Beverly Grymes immigrated to Virginia at the age of fifteen and lived at times with her two uncles: Phillip Ludwell Grymes of Middlesex County and Edmund Jennings Randolph—the first U.S. Attorney General, second U.S. Secretary of State, and seventh governor of Virginia. At their marriage in July 1823, the groom was sixty-three and his new bride was forty-one years of age. In 1825, Peter was nominated by Charles Yancey of Buckingham to be Sergeant at Arms of the Virginia House of Delegates. This placed him in Richmond where his third wife was happier than being in the country.[14] In some ways, the Richmond area suited Peter Francisco as well. He could engage many government officials and businessmen of the day with ease. They would remain in Richmond until Peter's death, and Mrs. Mary Beverly Francisco would outlive her husband by a quarter century, dying in 1859.[15]

GENTLEMAN PLANTER

Although fame and a venerated place in Virginia society had been secured, Peter Francisco never achieved the success and wealth he desired through his endeavors as a Virginia planter. His lack of accomplishment was not from a want of effort; rather, Francisco overspent in pursuit of maintenance of his large family and status as a Virginia gentleman. In short, he became indebted trying to live as an aristocrat as he outfitted himself in the finery of the day. Peter wore high hats and silk stockings along with bright waistcoats, and he could be observed in yellow trousers with black riding boots topped off by a blue coat with gold braid.[16] In addition to his apparel, the Francisco family was renowned for their predilection toward good food and drink, and Peter had a stable of fine thoroughbred horses—often white in color owing to his fondness.[17] It should be noted, his favorite horse was his prize of war, *Tarleton*, who lived for some years after the conclusion of hostilities.[18]

Peter Francisco was called to account and availed himself of the courts with great frequency—to include two actions brought by the same Winston family that took him in under indenture as a youth. Against the Winstons, charges of trespassing and petty theft were addressed, and Peter Francisco prevailed in both situations netting in one judgment an award of sixty-five hundred pounds of net crop tobacco along with compensation for the cost of the suit. In other legal matters, a finding against Francisco for assault and battery yielded only a single penny to a Mr. John Beasley as the jury believed the plaintiff's thrashing at the hands of the giant, though unlawful, was justified. Mr. Beasley had been seeking £500. Peter Francisco brought thirty-six acts to guard his interests against friends in situations where he had cosigned notes on their behalf. There were twenty-five suits against Francisco for similar acts, such as signing as security on the behalf of other parties. Twenty-one suits were filed against the "Virginia Giant" for debt with Francisco prevailing in ten of the actions. Peter Francisco's challenges with debt worsened with his marriage to his third wife—Mary Beverly Grymes West. Her vast estate was mortgaged in full to keep pace with her lavish tastes. Upon marrying the widow West, Francisco rashly assumed her prodigious debts and toiled under the weight of these obligations for the remainder of his life.[19]

Locust Grove. Artist unknown.
Courtesy of Brian Carlton of the *Farmville Herald* (Virginia)

INDENTURE AND SLAVERY

Peter Francisco's formative years as an indentured servant did not preclude him from engaging in the practice of slaveholding as he pursued a life as a Virginia planter. As mentioned earlier, his first wife's inheritance from the Anderson estate resulted in their ownership of an enslaved man named Ned. Moreover, the Winston family made a wedding gift to his young bride of a maid-servant who had in years past been charged with the personal care of Peter when he was a newly arrived orphan at Hunting Tower.[20] Still, Francisco's land holdings and associated servants working the property were small when compared to the more affluent planters of the region. Some historians place the typical level of Francisco family ownership at five to ten slaves.[21] A historical review of public records and tax filings, however, revealed a range of persons in bondage spanning from his wife's inheritance of Ned in 1787 to as many as seventeen slaves in 1807.[22]

Given the times and legality of slavery throughout America, Peter Francisco reportedly showed a level of benevolence as a master to his servants. This largess extended to the poor as well. Son Benjamin Francisco's biography records: "His prominent traits of character for temperance, good temper, and charity were no less striking. In time of peace I have seen him shell with his own hands corn for the poor and put it on their horses and something to eat with it. I have seen him rise from his table and pass through his wide field conveying to his poor old, superannuated toothless servants something suited to their appetites and condition. Then sitting in their cabin-yards in social conversation recounting the events of bygone days."[23]

Perchance, Peter Francisco's years of indenture and experience as an orphan infused into his nature the ability to identify with the poor and enslaved on an unusually personal level. Historical accounts do not indicate sadism or abject cruelty on the part of Peter Francisco beyond the palpable abhorrence of holding fellow human beings in bondage. Dr. Mervyn Williamson's research revealed a man of eighteenth- and nineteenth-century America who, bearing in mind the times, would have been considered charitable with the poor as well as affable and attentive to the needs of slaves.[24]

FEATS OF STRENGTH

The Franciscos were popular in Virginia society and invited to all manner of formal and informal events. At Red Oak Plantation near Locust Grove, Peter was a frequent guest where picnics were hosted. At one affair, chairs were provided on the lawn, but Francisco's immense size forced the chair legs into the turf down the first rungs. As a parlor trick, the giant was known to kneel, grasp two grown men by their lower legs, stand, and then raise them until their heads touched the ceiling with Peter's arms extended parallel to the floor—as though one might hold candlesticks at arms' length.[25] At parties, Peter stood ready to wrestle any friendly adversary but seldom found takers, with one war veteran stating, "though I am large I did not feel it necessary that I risk widowing my wife."[26] Aside from size and strength, Francisco was known for his good nature and social graces. His pure tenor singing voice was remarkable, and he was prevailed upon often to perform ditties of the day, including "The Battle of the Kegs" and "Old England's Downfall." Perhaps a product of his noble birth, one contemporary described Peter "as charming as those who know they are descended from England's royalty."[27]

Far into his postwar life, Peter became the target of thrill seekers and strongmen pursuing invariably to burnish their reputations at the expense of his. He was an otherwise peaceful man, but when challenged, the old warrior spirit of Camden and Guilford Courthouse could be roused with terrible effect. On one such occasion, he was set upon by two traveling toughs in a tavern in Buckingham, Virginia. They were from an adjoining county and long into their liquor this particular evening. They bragged they could whip any man in Virginia. The barkeeper countered he knew a Buckingham County man who could handle both of them with one arm tied behind his back . . . but that he was good natured and not easy to provoke.[28] The two drunkards took this as a challenge. Not long later, Peter Francisco arrived at the tavern. As Peter took his seat, one man kicked the chair out from under him. Peter fell to the ground, and both pugilists leapt upon him. The fight was on. The formidable giant quickly regained the upper hand on the bellicose duo. With each of his massive hands grasping the backs of both of their necks, he smacked their heads together. All went dark for the visiting bar patrons. The most fortunate belligerent was unconscious only for a few hours. His ill-fated accomplice did not awaken until the next day.[29]

In 1806, a western man from Kentucky by the name of Pamphlet traveled all the way to the home of Peter and Catherine Francisco at a time when the Portuguese strongman was running a tavern nearby at New Store in Buckingham County. Mr. Pamphlet presented himself to Peter Francisco with the intent to whip the famous veteran. Taking the high road and showing his inclination for humor, Francisco sent a servant to cut switches from a willow tree and subsequently invited Mr. Pamphlet to commence with the lashing. The bold visitor did not appreciate Peter's wit, and the

Peter Francisco throws Mr. Pamphlet over the fence. Artist unknown.
Library of Virginia

engagement took a more serious character when Mr. Pamphlet rode his horse into Mrs. Francisco's flower garden. Francisco rose to his feet as Mr. Pamphlet dismounted his horse. The giant presented himself calmly to his uninvited and ill-mannered guest. In keeping with a pugilistic courtesy of the day, Mr. Pamphlet first requested of Peter to *feel his weight* or lift him from the ground. Francisco acceded to the pre-fisticuff practice. Wrapping his arms around Peter, Mr. Pamphlet was able to raise him slightly off the ground. When it was Francisco's turn, he lifted Mr. Pamphlet three times and then spun and hurled the big Kentuckian like a sack of livestock feed over a four-foot fence and halfway into the road on the other side. Collecting himself, Mr. Pamphlet thought better of pressing the issue further and stated he would be on his way. He sarcastically remarked that he would be obliged if Mr. Francisco might toss his horse over the fence as well. At that, Peter captured the horse's reins, moved to the rear of the steed, crouched down, placed his right hand behind the rump and the left under the animal's belly. Through the power of his legs and back, he stood and lifted the mount up and then over the fence.[30] Mr. Pamphlet's folly and embarrassment were complete as he remarked, "I am satisfied." As Pamphlet departed for parts west, Peter bid him farewell, calling out, "Good bye Sir, Call again if you are passing."[31] Pamphlet would not return. Years later a similar incident occurred. Francisco's micromanagement of a hired man charged with repairing a barn at Locust Grove escalated into a fierce argument. The maintenance man descended from the barn roof spoiling for a fight because of the giant's persistent oversight and criticism of the repair work. As the enraged man approached Francisco, the giant simply clasped the smaller man in his enormous hands, spun around, and hurled him back onto the barn rooftop. From the safety of the gable, the hired man could only say that he might have been whipped by his gigantic employer, but he was not scared of him.[32]

In a more jovial demonstration, Peter pranked two chums while returning from a fishing trip. While on the return hike from the fishing hole, they passed a springhouse owned by one of Francisco's neighbors. The entry to the structure was locked, but through the small window of the springhouse, the men could see crocks of milk being cooled by the stream that ran under the building. Parched with thirst, the fishing party began to lay in a strategy to obtain the milk. Peter, knowing that many springhouses were without floors or securing foundations, forced his hands under the structure's exterior wall, and with a great heave, elevated the corner of the outbuilding. His fishing partners entered by scampering under the wall, at which time Francisco lowered the springhouse to the turf—making prisoners of his two mischievous cohorts. As rats in a trap, they tried in vain to escape but lacked the strength to force a door nor raise the springhouse walls. The "Virginia Giant" then sprinted toward the landowner's farmhouse over the hill and alerted the proprietor that there were thieves trapped in his springhouse. The property owner was an old friend of Francisco unbeknownst to the trapped and panicked fishermen. Once on site, the farmer angrily addressed the men as though he had captured nomadic bandits. Peter revealed the ruse to his neighbor and the fishermen, and Francisco's fishing companions were released to a good laugh by all parties.[33]

As a farm owner, Peter had ample opportunity to leverage his herculean strength. At the behest of his wife Catherine, he promised to free a calf from a bog at Locust Grove. Moreover, a young female cow that would not abandon her offspring had also become stuck herself.[34] Catherine advised her husband of the situation and implored him to save the pair. Francisco responded: "Well if nothing else will do her ladyship, I will carry her out." After failing to coax the pair from the swamp, Peter muttered mockingly to the cow, "Your ladyship—all right I'll bring you out."[35] He first laid rails down in the mire for firm footing. Second, he grasped the calf under one arm and elevated it from the muck. This was a noteworthy exercise in physical vigor, but not surprising given Francisco's size and strength. To the astonishment of onlookers, he stepped upon the rails, leaned over, wrapped his free arm around the cow, pinned her to his hip, and then stood tall to elevate the bovine's feet from the bog. Slowly, Peter emerged from the marsh with the calf in one arm and the cow under the other—thrashing her feet and shaking her head and horns.[36] Another report recounts Francisco single-handedly freeing a wagonload of tobacco from a muddy mire after six horses had pulled against the load unsuccessfully.[37] While traveling, Peter happened upon the wayward tobacco farmer with his valuable harvest stuck in the muck. Knowing that the tobacco on the wagon represented a year's work and the farmer's livelihood, he offered to assist. Francisco examined the situation and ordered the farmer to unhitch and move the exhausted horses. Once the beasts were safely trussed out of the way, the farmer reentered the sludge and elevated the tongue at the front of the wheeled dray out of the mud. Entering the bog, the giant first secured his footing and found the best area to apply force. He then coiled his massive body, and finally he threw his shoulder against the rear of the wagon. With a mighty heave, his piston-like legs combined with his mammoth back and shoulders strained against the tobacco laden vehicle. The wagon began to shift slowly in the muck. In short work, Francisco pushed the tobacco wagon up and out of the swamp to firm ground so the farmer could re-hitch his horses and depart.[38]

PEACETIME HERO

Peter Francisco's courage and strength were not limited to wartime service. During the Christmas season in 1811, the "Virginia Giant" was in Richmond attending a play at the local theater.[39] A fire erupted causing great panic to those within. After making his way out of the building, Peter paused to observe that many attendees were still inside, including women and children. A local woman named Nelson bore witness to Peter's actions as he entered the flames repeatedly and carried from the inferno more than thirty people, including Mrs. Nelson herself. In the aftermath, Francisco sought no credit for his participation in the conflagration as he believed his actions to be expected of any man on the scene and far from heroic. In fact, his modesty gave him cause to request that his name be omitted from the roster of individuals who rendered aid that evening.[40] In the days leading up to the War of 1812, Peter Francisco enlisted in the 5th Regiment just before his fifty-second birthday. There is no record of combat service from this second struggle with Great Britain.[41]

LAFAYETTE'S RETURN TOUR

One year after his third marriage, news carried through the states that the French Lieutenant General Marquis de Lafayette had received and accepted an invitation from the U.S. government. He would return to North America to tour the new nation that he had helped liberate. In Virginia, a committee was established to invite veteran officers to receive the French general. Sixty-seven names were considered with only four privates on the list—one being Peter Francisco. Francisco went on horseback to greet the marquis. Dr. Benjamin Francisco recorded: "In 1824, my father rode from Buckingham to Yorktown to see General Lafayette. On his arrival . . . he was invited under the marquee to see him. An aisle was formed for them to meet where they made a most affectionate embrace. He escorted General Lafayette from Yorktown to Richmond and from Richmond to Petersburg, where by his request he was formally introduced to myself, brother (Dr. Peter Johnson Francisco), and two sisters—Mrs. Catherine Spotswood and Mrs. Edward Pescud."[42] At a ball in Petersburg, Virginia, General Lafayette was introduced to Catherine Brooke Francisco—the beautiful daughter of Peter and his late second wife. Upon learning of the young Miss Francisco's parentage, the marquis invited the maiden to join him in opening the ball. Also, while on the tour, Lafayette and his host, Peter Francisco, were received at the home of the Chief Justice of the U.S. Supreme Court—John Marshall.[43]

The "Virginia Giant" attended a ceremony at William & Mary College where the marquis was made an honorary man of letters. Later he bid farewell to Lafayette as he boarded the ship *Brandywine* to return to his home. Before boarding the ship, Peter reminded his friend of a vow made thirty years prior when Francisco rescued Miss Susannah Anderson from her fall down the church stairs in Richmond. He reiterated his pledge that a product of that first marriage would bear the name Lafayette.[44] True to his promise, the union of Peter Francisco and Susannah Anderson did produce a namesake of the marquis—only one generation removed. This occurred through Peter's son, James Anderson Francisco, who had wed Judith Woodson Michaux.[45] Shortly after the marquis returned from his American tour to France, he received a letter announcing the birth of Robert Lafayette Francisco—son of James and Judith and grandson of Peter Francisco and his late first wife Susannah. General Lafayette was so moved by the gesture that he penned a letter of appreciation to Judith Michaux Francisco that became a treasured family heirloom for generations.[46]

RENOWN

Beyond Lafayette, Peter Francisco served under or fought alongside an astounding number of famous personalities from revolutionary history. Nathanael Greene led him at Brandywine, Germantown, and Guilford Courthouse. With the famed French engineer, Colonel François de Fleury, Francisco faced desperation at Fort Mifflin and scored a stunning victory at Stony Point. Friedrich von Steuben trained him at Valley Forge. General Daniel Morgan led him at Monmouth Courthouse and possibly at Cowpens as well. The giant remained on the field at Camden as Major General Johann von Robais, Baron de Kalb, gave his last. He rode with Lieutenant Colonel William Washington's dragoons through North Carolina to Virginia and fought at Guilford Courthouse (and possibly Scott's Lake and Cowpens). He faced Banastre Tarleton's raiders, survived close-quarters combat (twice on foot at Camden and Amelia), and wreaked havoc as a mounted horseman wielding a gigantic broadsword at Guilford Courthouse. Given his size, strength, courage, and fighting prowess, Francisco was doubtless well known to all of these leaders. Moreover, legend, if not hard physical documentation, indicates to us that his broadsword was fashioned on the orders of the commander in chief himself—General George Washington.

After the war, his station in local society was elevated far beyond his New World origins as a dock urchin at City Point. His fame extended beyond Virginia. We recall that he met Chief Justice John Marshall in the company of Lafayette in 1824. In 1826, he received an audience with the U.S. Secretary of State (and former Speaker of the House) from Kentucky, Henry Clay, at Old Bell Tavern in Richmond.[47] Subsequently, Mr. and Mrs. Francisco hosted Secretary Clay in their home.[48] Born in nearby Ashland, Virginia, Clay observed Francisco's massive frame and inquired if he had ever met his match. Peter related the story of another Kentuckian—Mr. Pamphlet—to which Secretary Clay laughingly stated he was "glad to know that one of the mischievous Pamphlet family has been conquered." Mr. Clay may have been utilizing a double entendre and referring to *pamphlets*, which were published and distributed to impugn the honor of a political opponent in early America.[49]

PENSIONS AND ATTESTATIONS

Beginning in 1784, Peter Francisco began to seek pensions that were available through the federal and state governments. He would receive compensation for two horses killed in combat that he had purchased privately. In 1795, our famed veteran received one hundred bounty acres in Ohio through the Land Office Military Warrant.[50] He assigned the warrant to Mr. John MacDonald for 14 pounds of Virginia currency in 1797.[51] Francisco's petition to Congress in 1818 resulted in the issuance of a monthly pension of $8 the following year. In 1820, the "Virginia Giant" petitioned his adopted state of Virginia for a pension through a letter to the General Assembly. There is a noteworthy by-product to Francisco's initiation of petitions in his postwar life. The applications for compensation resulted in the creation of a more tangible written record of Peter Francisco's wartime exploits.[52] His youthful illiteracy confined us to chasing myth and legend preserved only by word of mouth. His postwar passion for education, however, enabled him to fashion for posterity a solid if not unassailable historical account through his own words in his solicitations for pension and the supporting attestations of his comrades.[53]

DEATH AND REMEMBRANCE

The "Virginia Giant" died on January 16, 1831, at the age of seventy. The cause of death was *indisposition*, which has been hypothesized to indicate acute appendicitis. Many newspapers carried the sad news to a mournful nation. The *Richmond Enquirer* announced on January 17:

> Died-on Sunday, in this city, after a lingering indisposition, PETER FRANCISCO, ESQ., the Sergeant at Arms of the H. of Delegates—and a Revolutionary Soldier, celebrated for his extraordinary strength, his undaunted courage, and his brilliant feats, The House of Delegates have determined to pay him the honors of a Public Funeral, and to bury him with the honors of war. The House have accordingly adjourned until

tomorrow. The Resolutions passed on this occasion, and the Encomiums that were paid to the old Soldier's memory, are detailed in our account of the Proceedings of the House.[54]

The resolutions provided for a House procession in honor of the deceased, burial with military honors, and a committee to plan and execute the funeral. Born Pedro Francisco, the orphan boy who was abandoned on the docks at City Point more than six decades before, he would be eulogized in the House of Delegates Hall where he had served as Sergeant at Arms since 1825. Having previously been inducted into the Freemasons in Charlotte County, Virginia, this warrior's warrior would receive a state funeral with military and masonic decorum in keeping with his wishes.[55] Services were held the following day in the House of Delegates Hall in the State Capitol with the Right Reverend R. C. Moore, Episcopal Bishop of Virginia, presiding. The bishop stated in part: "I have been led to the consideration of the subject which has been discussed, by the death of Peter Francisco, one of the remaining warriors of the Revolutionary War; ... who ... performed many acts of heroism ... in that long and trying conflict. He possessed a degree of strength superior to that of any man of modern times; and that strength with which he was endowed, was exerted in the defense of the country which gave him (a home). . . . It is honorable to the legislative body of the State thus to notice the death of an old revolutionary soldier whose claim in their attention is founded on his love of country." The bishop added that, in his closing hours, Peter stated he was "ready to go."[56] The good bishop assured all assembled that, although Peter Francisco had never before professed publicly his faith, on his death bed he "took refuge in Christ."[57] Moore closed by saying, "We again united in devotional duty, and I bid the old Christian farewell."[58]

At 3:00 p.m., the procession accompanied a cortege bound for the heights of Shockoe Cemetery. The Senate, House of Delegates, Governor, and staff, and various other public officials participated. Military units were assembled in their martial regalia. The report of cannons could be heard throughout the city—perhaps as far as City Point where he first stepped ashore in the New World as a boy. Some weeks later in faraway France, a nobleman formerly in the service of the United States received a message from America. The message carried the sad news of the death of Peter Francisco to his closest of wartime comrades. Upon notification, the French General—Marie-Joseph Paul Yves Roch Gilbert du Motier de La Fayette, our Marquis de Lafayette—wept as though he had lost his own brother. Lafayette penned a heartfelt letter to the widow Francisco conveying his "most respected regards and deepest sympathy" at the loss of her husband and his dear friend.[59]

LEGACY

In his lifetime, Peter Francisco could not have been certain of his Portuguese origin. Upon arrival in America, he knew only that he was not from the New World, and he conjured vague memories of his childhood abroad, abduction, transit, and abandonment on the docks at City Point. Only through subsequent research by historians—most prominently Dr. John E. Manahan in 1960—was evidence of his birth, baptism, and family history determined.[60] In his time, the "Virginia Giant" was known throughout the land for his courage and fierceness in battle. His transition from unknown private to renowned war hero was a testament to his unrivaled strength, fighting prowess, and fearlessness in the face of mortal danger. Once a penniless boy, Francisco broke the barrier of eighteenth-century wartime fame normally reserved for the sons of nobility and gentry. But this was a new nation in the New World—a nation where a man from nothing could achieve things beyond the wildest dreams of his counterparts in the old world. Of this transformation, descendant authors Nannie Francisco Porter and Catherine Fauntleroy Albertson recounted a tribute to his service from an old Richmond periodical:

> It is but the misfortune of the rank and file of an army that while they do all of the hard fighting and encounter the greatest of perils on the battle fields, they receive the smallest portion of the glory and applause which follows victory. They have the lion's share of danger and their officers the lion's share of renown. Sometimes, however, there is among the rank and file of the private soldiers an individual whose peculiar powers and soldierly qualities single him out from the multitude and rivet upon him the attention and admiration of his countrymen. The eyes of the world then pass by the glittering group of officers and fix upon the hero of nature in his plain attire with his countenance blackened by the smoke of battle, yet whose valiant spirit exalts the most humble station. Such a man was Peter Francisco, who in extraordinary strength, lion-like courage, yet gentleness of disposition, was one of the most remarkable of the Revolutionary warriors of Virginia.[61]

Peter Francisco Monument, Peter Francisco Square, New Bedford, Massachusetts.
Wikimedia Commons

Arrival monument at City Point (now Hopewell), Virginia.
Photo by J. T. Palmer

Burial site at Shockoe Cemetery.
Photo by J. T. Palmer

To his friends, he displayed a more complex blend of apex warrior and congenial gentleman. He manifested the very essence of a dutiful yet humble citizen-soldier in our newly independent United States. Mr. McGraw, his postwar schoolmaster, related:

> Francisco could take me in his right hand and pass me over the room, playing my head against the ceiling as though I had been a doll. My weight was one hundred and ninety pounds. He evidently inherited eloquence, his range of information was a revelation of deep thinking, and he possessed the rare but simple formula of originality and directness. His ability was striking, his personality charming. He possessed a high sense of honor, there was never a shadow of self seeking. He crossed any frontier of disappointment with a fixed manliness of purpose and strength that made him all the more beloved by those who knew his earnest efforts for success and knowledge. He possessed vast physical courage with a gentleness whose foundation was fixed. He had a true reverence for God.[62]

Today, Peter Francisco is memorialized by several markers and monuments and a familial Society of the Descendants of Peter Francisco. Specifically, the battlefields at Guilford Courthouse in North Carolina and Amelia in Virginia hold a monument and marker, respectively. Massachusetts gave Francisco his first official recognition in 1953, assigning March 15, the date of the Battle of Guilford Courthouse, as Peter Francisco Day. Shortly thereafter, Rhode Island marked the same date as their annual day in his honor. In deference to his place of birth, the Portuguese Continental Union of USA established in 1957 the Peter Francisco Award for meritorious service. As one might expect, the Commonwealth of Virginia also set aside a day in memory of their most formidable adopted son. Subsequently, various municipalities have erected memorials to Francisco or placed his name upon locales, including Newark, New Jersey (an obelisk and park); New Bedford, Massachusetts (Peter Francisco Park); Hopewell, Virginia—formerly City Point—(a historical marker and monument); and Pawtucket, Rhode Island (memorial).[63] Virginia now has a variety of markers in places such as New Store, Crewe, and Buckingham County.[64] The town of Francisco, North Carolina, is his namesake, and a statue of him as a boy was erected in his home island of Terceira in the Azores.[65] Present-day memorials aside, Peter Francisco goes largely unknown in the United States save for a few history buffs and Revolutionary War reenactors. Author Robert Buckner may have said it best: "One of the most remarkable mysteries of American history is the fact that our greatest soldier (Peter Francisco) is almost entirely unknown ... today not one American in ten thousand can say they ever heard of Peter Francisco."[66]

The stories, history, and legend of our first, greatest warrior can be recaptured, but only if we choose to do so. It takes a patriotic appreciation of our noble past, a recognition of America's unique exceptionalism, and a willingness to accept the mantle and match the high standards of the heroes who have blazed the path for us to follow. Perhaps the best testament to the legend of Francisco may be the reputed words of the first Commander in Chief of the Continental Army, the first President of the United States, and the father of our country—George Washington: "Without him we would have lost two crucial battles, perhaps the War, and with it our freedom. He was truly a One-Man-Army."[67]

Chapter 16

EPILOGUE OF COMRADES

The list of Peter Francisco's friends, famous associations, and collaborators is astonishing. In the aftermath of the American Revolution, the following is an accounting of Francisco's famous colleagues—most of whom he met when he was poor, abandoned, penniless, or holding only the entry-level rank of private within the army of his adopted nation.

GEORGE WASHINGTON

Although technically a compatriot of the commander in chief in all engagements of the Revolutionary War, Private Francisco shared with George Washington the same encampments or battlefields with certainty at Brandywine, Germantown, Valley Forge, Monmouth Courthouse, and Yorktown. The victory at Yorktown made matters increasingly clear for parties on both sides of the Atlantic—America had won its independence. How the country would fare was a persistent topic of debate. British and French evacuations were paced by peace negotiations, and General Washington was eager to return to Mount Vernon to resume his life as a planter.

First, he had to close out his service as commander in chief. In March 1783, he deftly defused the Newburgh Conspiracy—a near mutiny of military officers who were bent on confronting Congress to demand payment of promised war compensation. The general did so by calmly addressing them. He appealed to their sense of honor, recalled their shared purity of motive in the fight for independence, and admonished them that the army's wartime achievements would be diminished by attempts to leverage Congress through the threat of force. With the Treaty of Paris and British departure from New York, General Washington resigned his position and delivered an emotional farewell to his officers in December 1783. Of his reported intent to voluntarily relinquish power, King George III stated that, if Washington were to do that, "he will be the greatest man in the world."[1]

Back at Mount Vernon, Washington outperformed the more educated class of Virginia planters such as Thomas Jefferson and James Madison by diversifying his farm operations. He achieved an uncommon level of agricultural success and sustainability for this age. He raised horses, cattle, sheep, donkeys, and pigs, and he bred some of North America's first mules. Eschewing the labor-intensive, tobacco-centric debt trap of his fellow landowners, he raised a variety of other crops, including hemp, corn, and grains, to support his on-site milling operation. He established a vibrant whiskey distillery, and he harvested herring and shad from the Potomac that would be salted and barreled for sale domestically and internationally. The enterprises at Mount Vernon were fueled by some three hundred enslaved men and women. Only a third were able to contribute to the plantation operations owing to age and infirmity. Where he could have added to his fortune by selling those in bondage who were not participating actively in the plantation undertakings, his desire to preserve family continuity within his enslaved workforce gave him cause to resist the export of slaves from his properties.

The retired general answered a second call to service in 1787 as president of the Constitutional Convention and a third by serving two terms as President of the United States from 1789 to 1797. That he was forced to confront the first generation of factions (or opposing political parties) frustrated him greatly. Still, President Washington charted the course and established many of the customs, courtesies, and precedents that would shape the interaction among the republic's three branches of government to this day. He kept his countrymen from follow-on wars against established, powerful European countries and warned against entangling alliances at the close of his final term. He set the example for a peaceful transfer of power in the new republic as he passed the mantle of the presidency on to John Adams on March 4, 1797.

The father of our country died on December 14, 1799—two days after a five-hour inspection of his fields on horseback during a winter storm. The chill made him ill, and he rapidly declined and died from epiglottitis (inflammation of the epiglottis). His condition was made worse by the medical practices of the day, which included bleeding him four times for a total of five pints of blood. Although often financially illiquid, he died with a net worth of $530,000—making him one of the wealthiest men in America. In addition to livestock and agricultural operations, Washington owned thousands of acres in Virginia, Maryland, New York, Pennsylvania, and the

Federal City (later named District of Columbia). Ironically, it was in British service during the French and Indian War where he was granted massive land tracts in Ohio, which bolstered his fortune significantly.

Of the enslaved Mount Vernon workforce totaling 317 at his death, Washington owned 124 outright. The remainder were part of Martha Washington's estate brought into the marriage. Washington directed in his will that those servants he owned in his own right were to receive their freedom. He forbade sale or transport to counter his orders of manumission. Washington expressed that his instructions in this particular matter were to be "religiously fulfilled" by his executors. He also made provisions for clothing and feeding by his heirs in support of those too old and infirmed to care for themselves. The youngest of those to be freed were to be cared for, taught to read, and instructed in a trade until adulthood, which he clarified to be twenty-five years of age. The people of the United States were shocked to learn of Washington's abrupt death. Any cross-party angst that had been engendered during his presidency melted away immediately. The periods of mourning, platitudes, and eulogies were many. Perhaps he was best and most succinctly remembered by cavalryman "Light Horse" Harry Lee who remarked of Washington: "First in War, First in Peace, and First in the Hearts of his Countrymen."[2]

Washington and Francisco Postscript

In addition to the previous discussion of the Guilford Courthouse broadsword, one final point of issue exists with some historians regarding General George Washington and Private Peter Francisco, fellow Virginians. Legend, literature, and some monuments to history attribute a quote to the commander in chief summarizing the outsized contributions made to the war effort by Francisco. As carved in stone in New Bedford, Massachusetts: "Without him we would have lost two crucial battles, perhaps the War, and with it our freedom. He was truly a One-Man-Army."[3] Some researchers maintain there is no supporting documentation showing where or when Washington spoke or wrote these words. Still, it is doubtful Washington was unaware of Francisco as his exploits were common knowledge, he was also a Virginian, he fought with or was in close proximity to the general on multiple occasions, and the giant served with so many other senior officers in the commander in chief's professional circles (generals Nathanael Greene, the Marquis de Lafayette, Friedrich von Steuben, Horatio Gates, Baron de Kalb, Daniel Morgan, Anthony Wayne, and George Weedon as well as colonels William Washington and "Light Horse" Harry Lee to name a few). Though

Francisco only held the rank of private, the fame of the gargantuan warrior most certainly would have found its way to General Washington. We are left only to ponder the veracity of the compliment that has manifested itself so frequently in Francisco history and lore.

PATRICK HENRY

On March 23, 1775, Judge Anthony Winston's nephew, Patrick Henry, fired the revolutionary passions of the colonies as well as Peter Francisco with his master stroke of oratory ending with "Give me Liberty or Give me Death!" The following month, Virginia's Royal Governor—John Murray, 4th Earl of Dunmore—ordered the seizure of the colony's gunpowder from the Williamsburg arsenal. A provincial colonel, Patrick Henry mustered the Hanover militia, marched to the outskirts of Williamsburg, and was able to force compensation for the powder. Shortly thereafter, he took leave from militia obligations to serve in the Continental Congress but soon returned to duty. He did not see significant action during the war and continued his work in the Virginia conventions. Henry was instrumental in shaping the state constitution in June 1776, and he was elected the first governor of the state of Virginia. From this position, he supported the Continental Army with supplies. After serving the maximum of three terms, he yielded the governorship to Thomas Jefferson.

After the war, he was reelected as Virginia's governor in 1785. He vehemently opposed the constitution fearing an overabundance of executive power, yet he supported the treatise after ratification. He departed the governorship in 1790. He was offered positions in President Washington's cabinet, the Supreme Court, and an ambassadorship, but he declined. After a bout with stomach cancer, Patrick Henry died on June 6, 1799.[4] He is buried in Charlotte County, Virginia. Over time, several military installations, ships, and schools, including Emory and Henry College, were named in his honor.

NATHANAEL GREENE

Peter Francisco served under Nathanael Greene's command at Brandywine, Germantown, and lastly at Guilford Courthouse. Both bivouacked at Valley Forge in winter 1778, and they served in separate units at Monmouth Courthouse. After Guilford Courthouse, Francisco would convalesce with Quakers while General Greene would shadow Charles Cornwallis's withdrawal to Wilmington, North Carolina. The general would try unsuccessfully to lure the British commander back into the wilderness. After Lord Cornwallis redeployed his forces to Virginia, North Carolina was largely free of British influence. Nathanael Greene would move south to sweep the British from South Carolina and Georgia. The general would engage in a series of clashes with British units in the field led by Lord Francis Rawdon. On September 8, 1781, Greene would pit two thousand patriots against twenty-three hundred redcoats at Eutaw Springs. Although essentially a draw, Lord Rawdon's forces were diminished to the point that they withdrew to the safety of the garrison in Charleston. Most of the state was in the hands of patriots. Greene would continue applying pressure in South Carolina and Georgia while Washington laid siege to Yorktown.

As the American commander in the south, Nathanael Greene's reputation was sealed into military history. Of the former Quaker, Cornwallis stated: "Greene is as dangerous as Washington. I never feel secure when encamped in his neighborhood." Washington himself added: "It is with a pleasure which friendship alone is susceptible of that I congratulate you on the glorious end you have put to hostilities in the southern states."[5] At the close of the war, Georgia rewarded General Greene with two thousand acres on the Savannah River that he dubbed Mulberry Grove. He threw his efforts into making his plantation a success. While visiting a neighbor in June 1786, he suffered overexposure to the harsh Georgia sun. General Nathanael Greene died of sunstroke on June 19. Various monuments and statues were erected in memory of Washington's general, and fourteen states named counties in his honor.[6]

GILBERT DU MOTIER, MARQUIS DE LAFAYETTE

The Marquis de Lafayette was perhaps the closest friend of all of Peter Francisco's powerful associates. They served together at Brandywine, Germantown, Monmouth Courthouse, and Yorktown, and they endured the winter encampment at Valley Forge. Lafayette's 1824 tour of America was a welcome respite from years of turmoil in France. After Yorktown, he departed for France from Boston in December 1781. Caught in the torrent of the French Revolution, he was both an aristocratic noble and an officer who had fought in service to a democratic revolution. He sought a middle ground but found no quarter from either faction. Lafayette was pilloried by the king's court and firebrands of the revolution alike.

As a lieutenant general, he led a French army against Austria in 1792. Back in his home country, things became so untenable that he attempted a journey to America. While seeking safe passage off the continent, he was captured and jailed by Austrians until 1797. The marquis was not forgotten by his American allies who provided funds for his maintenance and tried in vain to arrange a release. Ultimately, Napoleon bartered his return to France, but Lafayette refused to swear allegiance to the future emperor. He lived an unsettled existence. An admirer of a constitutional monarchy, the marquis would continue to navigate the choppy political waters of the French court, revolution, empire, and a fledgling representative government throughout his senior years. Lafayette died on May 20, 1834, of complications from pneumonia. He is buried alongside his wife in a soil mixture from Bunker Hill at Picpus Cemetery in Paris. To this day, Lafayette is lionized as a hero in the American Revolution with a host of United States' cities, counties, and schools named in his honor.[7]

FRIEDRICH WILHELM AUGUST HEINRICH FERDINAND VON STEUBEN

Peter Francisco was one of the thousands of American soldiers trained by the venerable Baron von Steuben at Valley Forge. After the winter encampment, Francisco and von Steuben shared the same battlefields at Monmouth Courthouse and Yorktown. While tasked with defending Virginia, the baron also provided key reinforcements and resupply to Major General Greene's southern army. Von Steuben's security and supplies were vital after the conclusion of the Race to the Dan and in preparation for the Battle of Guilford Courthouse. The baron took ill in 1781 but was able to resume duties as a division commander for the siege at Yorktown. Postwar, he assisted George Washington to achieve an orderly demobilization of the army. He also was a key figure in the establishment of the Society of Cincinnati. After receiving a discharge from the army, von Steuben became a U.S. citizen in March 1784. He made his home on sixteen thousand acres he received from the state of New York. Major General von Steuben died on November 28, 1794, at his New York home. He left his estate to two of his military aides de camp from the Revolution. In addition to monuments and memorials, the town of Steuben, New York—near his estate—bears his name. Each September, several towns and cities celebrate Von Steuben Day to memorialize America's Prussian drillmaster.[8]

Comrades and associates of Peter Francisco.
Library of Virginia, Metropolitan Museum of Art, U.S. Senate, National Park Service, Palace of Versailles, Pennsylvania Academy of the Fine Arts, Independence National Historic Park, New York Historical Society, Wikimedia Commons

DANIEL MORGAN

Daniel Morgan was a key veteran of Saratoga where his sharpshooters mortally wounded British Brigadier Simon Fraser and sent General John Burgoyne's redcoats into disarray. Victorious American General Horatio Gates would say the British feared Morgan's corps more than any other, and he praised the colonel's leadership effusively. After Valley Forge, Morgan took charge of the advance forces at Monmouth Courthouse with Peter Francisco assigned as an infantryman. Morgan and Francisco would also join forces in the south at a time when he served as a Virginia militia cavalryman assigned under William Washington—commander of the famed 3rd Continental Light Dragoons. After the Race to the Dan, General Morgan and Private Francisco would part ways in February 1781—Morgan to retire to Virginia owing to chronic and debilitating back injuries and Francisco to continue the fight at Guilford Courthouse and beyond.

Morgan would recover his health after the war, and he built a successful and sizable estate in Virginia. He was recalled briefly into service in 1794 to deal with the Whiskey Rebellion. Promoted to major general and serving under the command of fellow veteran Harry Lee, Morgan led one wing of the U.S. Army into western Pennsylvania. With Morgan's demonstration of force, resistance dissipated quickly. Morgan would go on to represent Virginia in the Congress from 1797 to 1799. He died in his home of Winchester, Virginia, on July 6, 1802, and he is buried in Mount Hebron Cemetery. Many memorials to Daniel Morgan were erected. Nearby the site of his most famous victory at Cowpens, South Carolina, the city of Spartanburg named *Morgan Square* in his honor with an impressive statue of the general placed upon a pillar.[9]

"MAD" ANTHONY WAYNE

General Wayne and Peter Francisco served together at Brandywine, Germantown, and Monmouth Courthouse, and Wayne commanded Francisco at Stony Point. After service in Pennsylvania, General Wayne would march south in 1781 to serve with Lafayette in Virginia. Wayne was present for the siege and surrender at Yorktown along with Lafayette and Francisco.

Immediately after Yorktown, Wayne was detailed to South Carolina and Georgia to usher the British out of the southernmost states. Never one to shrink from combat, Wayne clashed several times with the British near

Savannah, Georgia, and the Crown forces evacuated on July 11, 1782. The state of Georgia would later reward General Wayne with an estate. From Savannah, Wayne moved toward Charleston, South Carolina, and marched into the city on the heels of the British departure. Congress would recognize Wayne's dogged service to the new nation with a promotion to major general in October 1783.

After the war, Wayne would return to Pennsylvania, and he was forced to sell his Georgia property due to financial challenges. He would serve in the Pennsylvania assembly and participate in the Constitutional Convention. In 1793, President George Washington would appoint General Wayne as commander in chief of the U.S. Army for the task of Indian pacification in the northwest territory. "Mad" Anthony would also conduct an overdue reorganization of the U.S. Army that would include the formative processes for standardized basic training of new recruits. Namesake Fort Wayne in Indiana would be built under the general's direction. After several engagements with midwestern tribes, Wayne compelled a treaty in 1795 at Camp Greeneville (named for his old comrade Nathanael Greene) roughly twenty miles northwest of present-day Dayton, Ohio. At the conclusion, he returned to adoring crowds in his hometown of Chester, Pennsylvania, after a three-year absence. A year later, he was conducting a trip on business in the western part of the state when he died at Fort Presque Isle near Erie. He is buried at St. David's Church in Radnor, Pennsylvania. A host of statues and markers detail the life and achievements of General Anthony Wayne. In addition to the Indiana city of Fort Wayne, Wayne County, Michigan—and, by extension, Wayne State University—bear the general's name.[10]

HENRY LEE III
"LIGHT HORSE" HARRY LEE

In August 1779, fellow Virginian and cavalry commander "Light Horse" Harry Lee led Peter Francisco's unit at the Battle of Paulus Hook in New Jersey. Major Lee, Private Francisco, and the accompanying patriots inflicted more than two hundred British casualties against only a handful of American losses. Although serving under William Washington at the time, Peter Francisco and Lee raced to the Dan River, they were both at Guilford Courthouse, and the two men participated in siege activity at Fort Watson, South Carolina—although the exact timing is unclear. Lee was also present at the surrender of Cornwallis at Yorktown. Along with William Washington, Lee would be hailed as an American-born, iconic founder of U.S. cavalry.

Throughout the war, Lee found equal parts success against the enemy and friction within the U.S. Army. If subordinate troops in his charge and superior officers in his chain of command held fondness and respect for Lee, his fellow officers did not. Regardless, "Light Horse" Harry's courage and audacity were undeniable. On February 24, 1781, Lee's horse and Andrew Pickens's militia achieved a stunning victory at Holt's Race Paths near present-day Hillsboro, North Carolina. Mistaking Lee's green-clad cavalrymen for Banastre Tarleton's dragoons, a contingent of four hundred loyalist soldiers led by Colonel John Pyle hailed the patriots as they approached their column. Lee recognized the confusion and, purporting to be Tarleton, requested the loyalist commander yield the road to his troops. Pyle complied. With Pickens's patriot militia concealed in nearby woods, Lee maneuvered his horsemen alongside the loyalist column. At the critical moment, Lee deftly ordered his men (who were joined by Andrew Pickens's militia) to fire upon the unsuspecting loyalists. The great slaughter known to some as "Pyle's Massacre" ensued.[11] A majority of the loyalists were killed or wounded. Lee lost no men.

Owing to his penchant for bold recklessness and a short temper, Lee was the target of many fellow officers who did not hold him in high esteem. "Light Horse" Harry could carry good order and discipline to an extreme as he once sentenced a deserter to death by beheading and displayed his head as a warning to his men. He was court-martialed on more than one occasion but never convicted. As for General George Washington, he did not always agree with Lee's methods, but he appreciated and accommodated his bold cavalry commander.

After the war, Lee was a Virginia delegate to Congress under the Articles of Confederation. He supported a strong federal government and ratification of the U.S. Constitution. During President George Washington's first term, Lee served in the Virginia General Assembly and was elected governor for three consecutive one-year terms from 1791 to 1794. He was recalled to uniformed service by President Washington, promoted to major general, and placed in command of U.S. forces charged with putting down the Whiskey Rebellion in Pennsylvania. A show of force with an army of twelve thousand was enough to quash the insurgents. He later served one term in the U.S. House of Representatives from 1799 to 1801.

Although Henry Lee III married twice and married well, he struggled with his personal finances and was even consigned to debtors' prison for two years beginning in 1809. In 1812, he was a victim of mob violence stemming from rival factions regarding the second war against Great Britain. He was nearly killed, and his health suffered thereafter. After some years battling his physical challenges, Lee traveled throughout the Caribbean in an attempt to recover his well-being. Upon returning to the United States, he was the house guest of Louisa Shaw—the daughter of Nathanael Greene who resided on Cumberland Island, Georgia. Major General Lee died at the Shaw home on March 25, 1818. With his two wives, he fathered nine children—the most famous of whom was his eighth issue who would become known to history as General Robert E. Lee, Confederate States Army, of American Civil War fame. Henry Lee III is interred next to his son Robert at Washington and Lee University in Lexington, Virginia. Lee County in Virginia is named in his honor.[12]

WILLIAM WASHINGTON

Cousin of George, William Washington led Peter Francisco throughout his cavalry service. It is beyond dispute that they served together during the Race to the Dan and shortly thereafter at Guilford Courthouse, North Carolina. Moreover, Washington and Francisco may have also served simultaneously at Fort Watson and Hannah's Cowpens in South Carolina. After Guilford Courthouse, Peter Francisco recuperated in the care of Quakers while Washington moved south with General Greene to press the patriot efforts in South Carolina and Georgia. On September 8, 1781, at Eutaw Springs, Washington was pinned under his horse, bayonetted, and captured. He was imprisoned in Charleston where he recovered from his wounds. He would remain in British custody until the end of the war.

In April 1782, Washington married his wartime sweetheart Miss Jane Riley Elliot. They would reside on Miss Elliot's low country plantation called *Sandy Hill*. As a planter, he would serve in the state legislature. Made a brigadier general in 1792, he served in this capacity until 1800. In 1802, he would visit friend and comrade Daniel Morgan at his deathbed. William Washington died on March 6, 1820, and he is buried at a nearby Charleston plantation.[13] In reflecting upon the American Revolution, Lord Cornwallis paid the following compliment: "there could be no more formidable antagonist in a charge, at the head of his cavalry, than Colonel William Washington."[14]

JOHN MARSHALL

Born in 1755 in Fauquier County, Virginia, John Marshall was the fourth Chief Justice of the U.S. Supreme Court. In conjunction with Lafayette's return tour, he received the French general and Peter Francisco in his home in 1824. The trio had much in common as Marshall had served in the Continental Army's 11th Virginia Regiment at Brandywine, Germantown, and Monmouth Courthouse, and he wintered at Valley Forge. Although largely self-educated, Marshall attended his first legal lectures at William & Mary College while on military leave, and he read law under Chancellor George Wythe, spawning his professional vocation. After the war, the future chief justice served in the Virginia legislature and the U.S. House of Representatives, as an envoy to France, and as the fourth U.S. Secretary of State under President John Adams. In the waning months of his presidential term, Adams nominated Marshall to serve as Chief Justice of the U.S. Supreme Court. Marshall served during the terms of five U.S. presidents over three decades and is considered one of the finest jurists to hold the premier office in the judicial branch. Marshall died in 1835 and is buried in Richmond's Shockoe Cemetery—a few paces from the grave of Peter Francisco.[15]

HENRY CLAY

Secretary of State Henry Clay met war veteran Peter Francisco twice—first at Old Bell Tavern in Richmond, Virginia, in 1826 and afterward at the giant's home. Clay was a native Virginian from Hanover County—the same area where Patrick Henry and many of the Winstons had resided. Educated at William & Mary, Clay moved to Lexington, Kentucky, where he practiced law and went on to serve the fifteenth state as a representative in the State House, a U.S. senator, a U.S. representative and Speaker of the House, and the ninth U.S. Secretary of State. Although seventeen years younger than Francisco, Henry Clay was cobbling together a career as one of the great statesmen of his age. He was known as the *Great Pacificator* and worked to bind the union and stem the passions of civil war through the Missouri Compromise, the Compromise Tariff of 1833, and the Compromise of 1850. He ran for the presidency three times unsuccessfully and stated he would "rather be right than president."[16] He died of tuberculosis in 1852 and is buried at Lexington Cemetery in Kentucky. Counties in sixteen states bear his name.[17]

ILLUSTRATIONS

Cover. *George Washington's One-Man Army: The Life, Legend, and Battles of Peter Francisco*. Compilation.

- Engraving depicting Francisco's Fight in Amelia (now Nottoway) County, Virginia, by Augustus Kollner. Courtesy of Peter Francisco Society member Ed Bowman.
- Peter Francisco Portrait by unknown. Wikicommons (Magicpiano). Virginia Historical Society (Public domain).
- Comrades and associates of Peter Francisco. Library of Virginia, Metropolitan Museum of Art, U.S. Senate, National Park Service, Palace of Versailles, Pennsylvania Academy of the Fine Arts, Independence National Historic Park, New York Historical Society, Wikimedia Commons.

Title Page. Peter Francisco Portrait by unknown. From Wikimedia Commons (Magicpiano). Virginia Historical Society (Public Domain). https://commons.wikimedia.org/w/index.php?curid=11312409.

Page xiii, top. Between the Old and New Worlds, Azores and Terceira.

Page 11, bottom right. Henrico Parish Church hosted the Second Virginia Convention, site of Patrick Henry's famous oratory. Photo by J. T. Palmer.

Page 12, top left. Patrick Henry. By George Bagby Matthews (1857–1943), after Thomas Sully (1783–1872). From Wikimedia Commons (Complex01). Artist employed by the federal government (Public Domain). https://commons.wikimedia.org/wiki/File:Patrick_henry.JPG.

Page 26, bottom left. General George Washington. By Charles Willson Peale. From Wikimedia Commons (Signaleer). U.S. Senate Collection (Public Domain). https://commons.wikimedia.org/wiki/File:WashingtonPeale.jpg.

Page 28, bottom. The Battle of Brandywine, September 11, 1777, during the American Revolutionary War. From History Department, United States Military Academy, April 16, 2021 (Public Domain). https://commons.wikimedia.org/wiki/File:Map_of_Battle_of_Brandywine.jpg.

Page 32, bottom. The Battle of Brandywine. Positioning of Greene's division for rear guard action: Francisco in 2nd Virginia Brigade.

- Positioning of Greene's division for rear guard Action.

Page 33, top right. Peter Francisco. Artist unknown. From Porter and Albertson, *The Romantic Record of Peter Francisco* (1929). https://ia802900.us.archive.org/9/items/romanticrecordof00port/romanticrecordof00port.pdf.

Page 41, top. The Battle of Germantown—October 4, 1777. From History Department, U.S. Military Academy (Public Domain). https://www.westpoint.edu/sites/default/files/inline-images/academics/academic_departments/history/Am%20Rev/26GermantownBattle.pdf.

Page 43, bottom. The Battle of Germantown—the American attack on Chew House. Compilation.

- The American attack on Chew House at the Battle of Germantown on October 4, 1777, in the American Revolutionary War. By Edward Lamson Henry. Art Institute of Chicago (BritishBattles.com). https://www.britishbattles.com/war-of-the-revolution-1775-to-1783/battle-of-germantown/.
- Upper right insert: Chew House today. Photo by J. T. Palmer.

Page 51, top right. Map of Philadelphia and surrounding Delaware River. Compilation.

- Map of Philadelphia and surrounding Delaware River area drafted by the British troops (1777). Library of Congress (Public Domain). https://commons.wikimedia.org/w/index.php?curid=98802636.
- Textboxes and arrows added by J. T. Palmer.

Page 52, bottom. Mud Island: Fort Mifflin with the Delaware River and New Jersey in the background. From Wikimedia Commons (Surfsupusa). https://commons.wikimedia.org/wiki/File:Fort_mifflin_from_airplane_arriving_at_PHL.jpg.

- Creative Commons License Link: https://creativecommons.org/licenses/by-sa/4.0/deed.en.

Page 69, bottom. American and British troop movement to Monmouth Courthouse.

- American and British troop movement to Monmouth Courthouse.

Page 71, top. British withdrawal and American attacks during the Battle of Monmouth, June 28, 1778. Mark Lender and Garry Stone, *Fatal Sunday: George Washington, the Monmouth Campaign, and the Politics of Battle* (Norman: University of Oklahoma Press, 2016). From Wikimedia Commons (Factotem).

- Creative Commons License Link: https://creativecommons.org/licenses/by-sa/4.0/deed.en.

Page 73, top left. Colonel Daniel Morgan. By Alonzo Chappel. U.S. House of Representatives (Public Domain). https://historica.fandom.com/wiki/Daniel_Morgan.

Page 73, top right. Private, 6th Virginia Regiment. From the Monmouth Battlefield State Park Collection, Division of Parks, Forestry, and Historic Sites, New Jersey Department of Environmental Protection.

Page 80, top. King's Ferry. Compilation.

- King's Ferry between Stony Point and Verplanck's Point. By John Wright. From Stony Point Battlefield State Historic Site.
- Inserts and arrows added by J. T. Palmer.

Page 80, bottom left. Brigadier "Mad" Anthony Wayne. By Edward Savage. From Wikimedia Commons (WMrapids). New York Historical Society (Public Domain). https://commons.wikimedia.org/wiki/File:Anthony_Wayne_(1745–1796).jpg.

Page 80, bottom middle. Lieutenant Colonel Richard Butler. By John Trumbull. From Yale University Art Gallery (Public Domain). https://artgallery.yale.edu/collections/objects/122.

Page 80, bottom right. George Washington at Verplanck's Point. By John Trumbull. From Wikimedia Commons (Zeete). Winterthur Museum (Public Domain). https://en.wikipedia.org/wiki/File:Washington_at_Verplanck%27s_Point_by_John_Trumbull.jpg.

Page 85, bottom. American Strategy. Compilation.

- American strategy: demonstration west to east along the causeway with pincers from the north. By John Wright. From Stony Point Battlefield State Historic Site. Textbox and arrow added by J. T. Palmer.

Page 93, bottom left. Horatio Gates. By Gilbert Stuart. From the Metropolitan Museum of Art. https://www.metmuseum.org/art/collection/search/12667.

Page 93, bottom right. Lieutenant General Charles Earl Cornwallis. By Thomas Gainsborough. From Wikimedia Commons (Materialscientist). From National Portrait Gallery, London (Public Domain). https://commons.wikimedia.org/wiki/File:Lord_Cornwallis.jpg.

Page 97, top. The Battle of Camden. From History Department, United States Military Academy (Public Domain). https://s3.amazonaws.com/usma-media/inline-images/academics/academic_departments/history/Am%20Rev/37CamdenBattle-01.jpg.

Page 97, bottom left. Peter Francisco impales the British dragoon. Artist unknown. From Porter and Albertson, *The Romantic Record of Peter Francisco* (1929).

Page 97, bottom right. Francisco transfers his mount to Captain Mayo. Artist unknown. From Porter and Albertson, *The Romantic Record of Peter Francisco* (1929).

Page 102, bottom. Peter Francisco carries a cannon from Camden Battlefield. From U.S. Postal Service (1975). https://peterfrancisco.org/military-service/.

Page 108, top. South Carolina, Scott's Lake, and Hannah's Cowpens.

Page 111, top. Fort Watson today, Francisco's "Sugar Loaf." Photo by J. T. Palmer.

Page 114, top. The Battle of Cowpens.

Page 116, top left. Brigadier Daniel Morgan. By Charles Willson Peale. From Wikimedia Commons (Sebastian Wallroth). Independence National Historic Park (Public Domain). https://en.m.wikipedia.org/wiki/File:DanielMorgan.jpeg.

Page 126, bottom. The Battle of Guilford Courthouse. By H. Charles McBarron. From Wikimedia Commons (Kordas). Center of Military History (Public Domain). https://commons.wikimedia.org/w/index.php?curid=6274659.

Page 129, bottom. Peter Francisco Monument, Guilford Courthouse National Military Park. Photo by J. T. Palmer. https://www.nps.gov/guco/index.htm.

Page 136, bottom left. Francisco slashes the dragoon paymaster at Ward's Tavern. Artist unknown. From Virginia State Library.

- Fair use link: https://www.virginia.gov/privacy-policy/.
- U.S. Copyright Office Fair Use Index: https://www.copyright.gov/fair-use/.

Page 137, top right. Engraving depicting Francisco's Fight in Amelia (now Nottoway) County, Virginia. By Augustus Kollner. Lithograph drawn by Kollner in 1845 after the 1814 copper engraving by Webster and Worral. Lithographed by Thos. Sinclair, Philadelphia. Provided by Peter Francisco Society member Ed Bowman (Public Domain).

Page 141, bottom. The Siege of Yorktown. From Wikimedia Commons (BotMultichillT). History Department, United States Military Academy (Public Domain). https://commons.wikimedia.org/w/index.php?curid =8259519.

Page 143, bottom. The storming of redoubt 10 at Yorktown. By H. Charles McBarron. From Wikimedia Commons (BotMultichillT). U.S. Army Center of Military History (Public Domain). https://commons.wikimedia .org/w/index.php?curid=8259517.

Page 150, bottom. Locust Grove. Artist unknown. Courtesy of Brian Carlton of the *Farmville Herald* (VA).

Page 153, top. Peter Francisco throws Mr. Pamphlet over the fence. Artist unknown. Library of Virginia.

- Library of Virginia user permissions: https://www.lva.virginia.gov/ about/policies/photo-reproductions.php.

Page 161, top. Peter Francisco Monument, Peter Francisco Square, Kempton Street, New Bedford, Massachusetts. From Wikimedia Commons (Ohioforestman2000). https://commons.wikimedia.org/w/index.php ?curid=106371370.

- Creative Commons License Link: https://creativecommons.org/ licenses/by-sa/4.0/deed.en.

Page 161, bottom left. Arrival monument at City Point (now Hopewell), Virginia. Photo by J. T. Palmer.

Page 161, bottom right. Burial site at Shockoe Cemetery in Richmond, Virginia. Photo by J. T. Palmer.

Page 171. Comrades and associates of Peter Francisco. Compilation. Identification begins with center portrait and then proceeds from the top (clockwise).

- Center: Peter Francisco. Artist unknown. Library of Virginia. https:// www.lva.virginia.gov/about/policies/photo-reproductions.php.

Illustrations 183

- George Washington. By Gilbert Stuart. From Wikimedia Commons (DCoetzee). Metropolitan Museum of Art (Public Domain). https://commons.wikimedia.org/w/index.php?curid=2030921.
- Patrick Henry. By George Bagby Matthews after Thomas Sully. From Wikimedia Commons (Complex01). U.S. Senate (Public Domain). https://commons.wikimedia.org/wiki/File:Patrick_henry.JPG.
- Nathanael Greene. By Charles Willson Peale. From Wikimedia Commons (Fryed-peach). National Park Service (Public Domain). https://en.m.wikipedia.org/wiki/File:Greene_portrait.jpg.
- Marquis de Lafayette. By Joseph-Désiré Court. From Wikimedia Commons (Guise). Palace of Versailles (Public Domain). https://commons.wikimedia.org/w/index.php?curid=12059524.
- Baron Friedrich Wilhelm von Steuben. By Charles Willson Peale. From Wikimedia Commons (Hohum). Pennsylvania Academy of the Fine Arts (Public Domain). https://commons.wikimedia.org/w/index.php?curid=17206505.
- Daniel Morgan. By Charles Willson Peale. From Wikimedia Commons (Sebastian Wallroth). Independence National Historic Park (Public Domain). https://commons.wikimedia.org/w/index.php?curid=126478.
- Anthony Wayne. By Edward Savage. From Wikimedia Commons (WMrapids). New York Historical Society (Public Domain). https://commons.wikimedia.org/w/index.php?curid=119843943.
- Henry Lee III. By William Edward West after Gilbert Stuart. From Wikimedia Commons (Holly Cheng). Private Collection (Public Domain). https://commons.wikimedia.org/w/index.php?curid=1654124.
- William Washington. By Rembrandt Peale. From Wikimedia Commons (Adam sk). Independence National Historic Park (Public Domain). https://commons.wikimedia.org/w/index.php?curid=4199065.
- John Marshall. By Henry Inman. From Wikimedia Commons (Screwing). Library of Virginia (Public Domain). https://commons.wikimedia.org/w/index.php?curid=9538002.
- Henry Clay. By Henry F. Darby. From Wikimedia Commons (wow). U.S. Senate (Public Domain). https://commons.wikimedia.org/w/index.php?curid=73530886.

Page 213. Author image. Photo by Brooks Mahaffey Palmer.

NOTES

EPIGRAPH

1. Cadet First Lieutenant Arthur Preston Price '43, "Alma Mater," The Citadel—The Military College of South Carolina, 1943, https://www.citadel.edu/cadet-life-resources/the-citadel-alma-mater/.

INTRODUCTION

1. Pedro De Merelim, "Pedro Francisco, Heroi (americano) e Tercierense," *Uniao*, July 4, 1978.
2. J. K. Hall, MD, "Peter Francisco—Hyperpituitary Patriot," *Annals of Medical History*, n.s., 8, no. 5 (1936): 449.
3. Mark Mayo Boatner III, *Encyclopedia of the American Revolution* (New York: Van Rees, 1996), 392–93.
4. Benjamin M. Francisco, *Biography of Peter Francisco of Revolutionary Notoriety*, pamphlet located at the University of Virginia Library, 1879, 1.
5. Nannie Francisco Porter and Catherine Fauntleroy Albertson, *The Romantic Record of Peter Francisco* (Staunton, VA: McClure, 1929), 29.
6. Mervyn Williamson, "Peter Francisco—Washington's One-Man Regiment," *Iron Worker*, August 1972, 5; Page Smith, *A New Age Begins* (New York: McGraw-Hill, 1976), 1:1.
7. William Shakespeare, *Henry V*, act 4, scene 3.

CHAPTER 1

1. Nannie Francisco Porter and Catherine Fauntleroy Albertson, *The Romantic Record of Peter Francisco* (Staunton, VA: McClure, 1929), 8, 17.
2. Mervyn Williamson, "Peter Francisco—Washington's One-Man Regiment," *Iron Worker*, August 1972, 4.
3. Porter and Albertson, *The Romantic Record of Peter Francisco*, 11.
4. Michael D. Hull, "Peter Francisco: American Revolutionary War Hero," HistoryNet, July 25, 2006, https://www.historynet.com/peter-francisco-american-revolutionary-war-hero/.
5. Benjamin M. Francisco, *Biography of Peter Francisco of Revolutionary Notoriety*, pamphlet located at the University of Virginia Library, 1879, 1.
6. Hull, "Peter Francisco."
7. Porter and Albertson, *The Romantic Record of Peter Francisco*, 12, 18.
8. William Arthur Moon, *Peter Francisco: The Portuguese Patriot* (Pfafftown, NC: Colonial; Winston-Salem, NC: Bradford Printing Service, 1980), 1.

CHAPTER 2

1. Nannie Francisco Porter and Catherine Fauntleroy Albertson, *The Romantic Record of Peter Francisco* (Staunton, VA: McClure, 1929), 13–19.
2. Adelaide Fries, Stuart Thomas Wright, and J. Edwin Hendricks, *Forsyth: The History of a County on the March* (Chapel Hill: University of North Carolina Press, 1960), 50.
3. R. W. Brock, *Vestry Book of Henrico Parish Virginia 1730–1773* (n.p.: University of Virginia Library, 1874), 107.
4. William Arthur Moon, *Peter Francisco: The Portuguese Patriot* (Pfafftown, NC: Colonial; Winston-Salem, NC: Bradford Printing Service, 1980), 1–2.
5. Porter and Albertson, *The Romantic Record of Peter Francisco*, 19.
6. Mervyn Williamson, "Peter Francisco—Washington's One-Man Regiment," *Iron Worker*, August 1972, 2.
7. Office of Public Affairs, *A History of Roads in Virginia: The Most Convenient Ways* (Richmond: Virginia Department of Transportation, 2006), 4–6.
8. Porter and Albertson, *The Romantic Record of Peter Francisco*, 15.
9. Moon, *Peter Francisco*, 1.
10. Moon, *Peter Francisco*, 2–3.
11. Christopher Tomlins, "Reconsidering Indentured Servitude: European Migration and the Early American Labor Force, 1600–1775," *Labor History* 42, no. 1 (2001): 5–43.
12. Lerone Bennett Jr., "White Servitude in America," *Ebony Magazine*, November 1969, 31–40.

13. David McCullough, *John Adams* (New York: Simon & Schuster, 2001), 447, 529; Jane Harrington Scott, *A Gentleman as Well as a Whig: Caesar Rodney and the American Revolution* (Newark: University of Delaware Press, 2000), 16–18.

14. Anonymous, *The Blacksmith in Eighteenth-Century Williamsburg: An Account of His Life and Times and of His Craft* (Williamsburg, VA: Colonial Williamsburg, 1978), https://www.gutenberg.org/files/58318/58318-h/58318-h.htm.

15. Donald N. Moran, "Peter Francisco, Giant of the American Revolution," Sons of Liberty California Society SAR, December 14, 2007–November 12, 2022, https://web.archive.org/web/20190507011049/http://www.revolutionarywararchives.org/francisco.html.

16. Michael D. Hull, "Peter Francisco: American Revolutionary War Hero," HistoryNet, July 25, 2006, https://www.historynet.com/peter-francisco-american-revolutionary-war-hero/.

17. Moran, "Peter Francisco, Giant of the American Revolution."

18. Jon Kukla, "Patrick Henry (1736–1799)," *Encyclopedia Virginia*, December 7, 2020, https://encyclopediavirginia.org/entries/henry-patrick-1736-1799.

19. Edwin Slipek, "St. John's Episcopal Church and Churchyard," Architecture Richmond, 2020, https://architecturerichmond.com/inventory/st-johns-episcopal-church-and-churchyard-5/; Helena Lane, "History of St. John's Church: Richmond, Virginia," Genealogy Trails, April 22, 2024, http://genealogytrails.com/vir/henrico/st_johns_church_history.html.

20. "The Second Virginia Convention," Historic St. John's Church, March 20–27, 1775, https://www.historicstjohnschurch.org/2nd-virginia-convention.

21. Porter and Albertson, *The Romantic Record of Peter Francisco*, 26.

22. Patrick Henry, "On the Resolution to Put the Commonwealth into a State of Defence," address delivered before the Second Virginia Convention, March 23, 1775, https://avalon.law.yale.edu/18th_century/patrick.asp.

23. Harry Kollatz Jr., "American Hercules, Peter Francisco, 'One Man Regiment' of the Revolution," *Richmond Magazine*, July 2012, 191–92.

24. Brock, *Vestry Book*, 171.

CHAPTER 3

1. Brigadier General John A. Klein (Acting Adjutant General), "Letter to Howard E. Baker" (responding to a request for Peter Francisco's military record), National Archives, September 13, 1951.

2. National Archives, "Muster Rolls of the Revolution," 10th Virginia Regiment, May–August 1777 (Washington, DC: General Services Administration, n.d.).

3. Ron Chernow, *Washington: A Life* (New York: Penguin, 2010), 300.

4. National Archives, "Muster Rolls of the Revolution."

5. George Washington's Mount Vernon, "Revolutionary War Reenacting Part 1," YouTube, July 4, 2017, https://www.youtube.com/watch?v=1gAZZWsswHY&t=61s.

6. Jamestown Yorktown Foundation, "JYF Cribs/Layout of Continental Army Encampments," YouTube, October 16, 2021, https://www.youtube.com/watch?v=Dv9_aSLZePE&t=146s.

7. Jamestown Yorktown Foundation, "Revolutionary War Army Kitchens in Continental Army Camps," YouTube, September 6, 2023, https://www.youtube.com/watch?v=2hi01WuYdds.

8. George Washington's Mount Vernon, "Revolutionary War Reenacting Part 1."

9. "The Fighting Man of the Continental Army: Daily Life as a Soldier," American Battlefield Trust, 2023, https://www.battlefields.org/learn/articles/fighting-man-continental-army.

10. Michael B. Gunn, "Revolutionary War Uniforms," Cincinnati Chapter of the Sons of the American Revolution, April 4, 2014, https://cincinnatisar.files.wordpress.com/2015/11/revolutionarywaruniforms.pdf.

11. Jamestown Yorktown Foundation, "Continental Army Basic Training," YouTube, January 10, 2024, https://www.youtube.com/watch?v=X8kADOfBqp0.

12. Guilford Courthouse Battlefield, "On the March" Display, Guilford Courthouse National Military Park, National Park Service, 2024, https://www.nps.gov/guco/index.htm.

13. William J. Bahr, "Revolutionary War: The Things They Carried," YouTube, October 19, 2019, https://www.youtube.com/watch?v=OFhoUlFx5dc.

14. "The Fighting Man of the Continental Army."

15. William J. Bahr, "Revolutionary War Cartridge Making," YouTube, September 10, 2013, https://www.youtube.com/watch?v=AYUPaX-F_nA.

16. "Brown Bess Bayonet: The Gun That Freed America," Revolutionary War, March 4, 2020, https://www.revolutionary-war.net/brown-bess-bayonet/.

17. John S. Pancake, *This Destructive War: The British Campaign in the Carolinas, 1780–1782* (Tuscaloosa: University of Alabama Press, 1985), 38–39.

18. "The Fighting Man of the Continental Army."

CHAPTER 4

1. Independence Hall Association, "Timeline of the Revolutionary War," USHistory, 2023, https://www.ushistory.org/declaration/revwartimeline.html.

2. Brandon Fisichella, "Who Were the British Grenadiers?," YouTube, June 10, 2021, https://www.youtube.com/watch?v=wzf5cDMSCpE.

3. Colonel Christopher Bopp (Professor of Naval Science at The Citadel and Revolutionary War reenactor), historical commentary with the author, May 4, 2025, regarding *George Washington's One-Man Army: The Life, Legend, and Battles of Peter Francisco*, by John T. Palmer (Essex, CT: Stackpole Books, 2026).

4. Brandon Fisichella, "Who Were the British Light Infantry of the American War of Independence?," YouTube, December 30, 2021, https://www.youtube.com/watch?v=A-tSAtRF9_E.

5. John S. Pancake, *This Destructive War: The British Campaign in the Carolinas, 1780–1782* (Tuscaloosa: University of Alabama Press, 1985), 38–39.

6. Brandywine Battlefield, "The Battle of Brandywine," Pennsylvania Historical & Museum Commission, 2023, https://www.brandywinebattlefield.org/battle/.

7. Robert Middlekauff, *The Glorious Cause: The American Revolution, 1763–1789* (New York: Oxford University Press, 1982), 386.

8. National Archives, "Muster Rolls of the Revolution," 10th Virginia Regiment, September 1777 (Washington, DC: General Services Administration, n.d.).

9. Chester County Planning Commission, *The Army Marched at Dawn—Southern Battlefield Strategic Landscapes Plan: A Specific Plan of the Brandywine Battlefield Preservation Plan* (Chester County, PA: Chester County Planning Commission and Commonwealth Heritage Group, 2020), 3–5, https://www.landscapes3.com/Historic/Campaign1777/South.pdf.

10. Middlekauff, *The Glorious Cause*, 387.

11. Chester County Planning Commission, "Battle of Brandywine—Part 3—Washington's Perspective," YouTube, February 19, 2014, https://www.youtube.com/watch?v=qdqi4j1CHRM.

12. Laura Auricchio, *The Marquis: Lafayette Reconsidered* (New York: Knopf, 2014), 51.

13. Michael Harris, "Battle of Brandywine," YouTube, August 11, 2022, https://www.youtube.com/watch?v=8Fyode2Grro&t=2282s.

14. Brandywine Battlefield, "The Battle of Brandywine."

15. Samuel S. Smith, *The Battle of Brandywine* (Monmouth Beach, NJ: Phillip Freneau, 1976), 21.

16. Robert Buckner, "Peter Francisco," *Elks Magazine* 15, no. 6 (November 1936): 7, https://www.elks.org/magazinescans/1936-11E.pdf.

17. William Arthur Moon, *Peter Francisco: The Portuguese Patriot* (Pfafftown, NC: Colonial; Winston-Salem, NC: Bradford Printing Service, 1980), 7.

18. Edward G. Lengel, "The Battle of Brandywine," George Washington's Mount Vernon, Mount Vernon Ladies Association, 2024, https://www.mountvernon.org/george-washington/the-revolutionary-war/washingtons-revolutionary-war-battles/the-battle-of-brandywine/.

19. Michael C. Harris, *Brandywine: A Military History of the Battle That Lost Philadelphia but Saved America, September 11, 1777* (El Dorado Hills, CA: Savas Beatie, 2016), 344.

20. Smith, *The Battle of Brandywine*, 21, 24.

21. Harris, *Brandywine*, 362.

22. Gerald M. Carbone, *Nathanael Greene: A Biography of the American Revolution* (New York: Palgrave Macmillan, 2008), 73–74.

23. Harris, *Brandywine*, 368.

24. Ronald S. Gibbs, MD, "Medicine in the American Revolution," lecture to the Society of Cincinnati hosted by the American Revolution Institute, Washington, DC, June 21, 2022, https://www.youtube.com/watch?v=4EdPlpjLaW4&t=2890s.

25. David Raymond, Eric Gimbi, and Mike Graham, "Revolutionary War Medicine, Battlefield Surgery, Amputation, and Smallpox Inoculation," YouTube, May 27, 2021, https://www.youtube.com/watch?v=xggzGL3Jbc0.

26. Gibbs, "Medicine in the American Revolution."

27. Nannie Francisco Porter and Catherine Fauntleroy Albertson, *The Romantic Record of Peter Francisco* (Staunton, VA: McClure, 1929), 44.

28. Moon, *Peter Francisco*, 5, 7.

29. Middlekauff, *The Glorious Cause*, 389–91.

CHAPTER 5

1. Gerald M. Carbone, *Nathanael Greene: A Biography of the American Revolution* (New York: Palgrave Macmillan, 2008), 75–79.

2. Joseph J. Ellis, *His Excellency George Washington* (New York: Vintage Books, 2004), 103.

3. History.com Editors, "Battle of Germantown," History.com, February 6, 2020, https://www.history.com/topics/american-revolution/battle-of-germantown.

4. Robert Middlekauff, *The Glorious Cause: The American Revolution, 1763–1789* (New York: Oxford University Press, 1982), 393.

5. Eric Niderost, "George Washington and Lord Cornwallis at Germantown," Warfare History Network, February 2005, https://warfarehistorynetwork.com/article/george-washington-and-lord-cornwallis-at-germantown/.

6. John Mackenzie, "Battle of Germantown," BritishBattles.com, 2002–2011, https://www.britishbattles.com/war-of-the-revolution-1775-to-1783/battle-of-germantown/.

7. Thomas J. McGuire, *The Surprise of Germantown—October 4th, 1777* (Gettysburg, PA: Thompson, 1994), 81.

8. Terry Golway, *Washington's General—Nathanael Greene and the Triumph of the American Revolution* (New York: Holt, 2005), 147.

9. William Arthur Moon, *Peter Francisco: The Portuguese Patriot* (Pfafftown, NC: Colonial; Winston-Salem, NC: Bradford Printing Service, 1980), 8.

10. Mackenzie, "Battle of Germantown."

11. Niderost, "George Washington and Lord Cornwallis at Germantown."

12. George Washington, "From General Washington to General William Howe, 6 October 1777," Founders Online, National Archives, February 2024, https://founders.archives.gov/documents/Washington/03-11-02-0432#GEWN-03-11-02-0432-fn-0001.

13. Michael C. Harris, *Brandywine: A Military History of the Battle That Lost Philadelphia but Saved America, September 11, 1777* (El Dorado Hills, CA: Savas Beatie, 2016), 404.

14. Ron Chernow, *Washington: A Life* (New York: Penguin, 2010), 311.

15. Harris, *Brandywine*, 395–96.

16. Michael C. Harris, "George Washington and the Battle of Germantown," virtual lecture hosted by Frauncis Tavern Museum, New York, October 19, 2021, https://www.youtube.com/watch?v=1Nj1sXjnF7E.

17. Harris, *Brandywine*, 402.

18. Ellis, *His Excellency George Washington*, 106.

19. Mackenzie, "Battle of Germantown."

CHAPTER 6

1. Brady Crytzer, "American Revolution: The Siege of Fort Mifflin," YouTube, February 23, 2022, https://www.youtube.com/watch?v=HvA4gOrPZvk&t=1797s.

2. William Arthur Moon, *Peter Francisco: The Portuguese Patriot* (Pfafftown, NC: Colonial; Winston-Salem, NC: Bradford Printing Service, 1980), 8.

3. Patrick K. O'Donnell, *Washington's Immortals: The Untold Story of an Elite Regiment Who Changed the Course of a Revolution* (New York: Atlantic Monthly, 2016), 167.

4. John F. Reed, *Campaign to Valley Forge—July 1, 1777–December 19, 1777* (Philadelphia: University of Pennsylvania Press, 1965), 296–303.

5. Bob Drury and Tom Clavin, *Valley Forge* (New York: Simon & Schuster, 2018), 96.

6. O'Donnell, *Washington's Immortals*, 166.

7. Reed, *Campaign to Valley Forge*, 340.

8. Drury and Clavin, *Valley Forge*, 96.

9. Crytzer, "American Revolution."

10. Thomas J. McGuire, *The Philadelphia Campaign* (Mechanicsburg, PA: Stackpole Books, 2007), 2: 204–5.

11. Donald N. Moran, "Peter Francisco, Giant of the American Revolution," Sons of Liberty California Society SAR, December 14, 2007–November 12, 2022, https://web.archive.org/web/20190507011049/http://www.revolutionarywararchives.org/francisco.html.

12. Crytzer, "American Revolution."

13. Ambrose Serle (Secretary to General Sir William Howe), "Eyewitness," Fort Mifflin National Historic Landmark, n.d.

14. Reed, *Campaign to Valley Forge*, 334.

15. Rachel Christian, "A Furious Cannonade, and a Great Explosion," *Naval History* 36, no. 1 (February 2022), https://www.usni.org/magazines/naval-history-magazine/2022/february/furious-cannonade-and-great-explosion.

CHAPTER 7

1. Robert Middlekauff, *The Glorious Cause: The American Revolution, 1763–1789* (New York: Oxford University Press, 1982), 411–12.
2. National Historic Park Pennsylvania, "What Happened at Valley Forge," National Park Service, June 13, 2023, https://www.nps.gov/vafo/learn/historyculture/valley-forge-history-and-significance.htm.
3. National Archives, "Muster Rolls of the Revolution," 10th Virginia Regiment, January–February 1778 (Washington, DC: General Services Administration, n.d.).
4. William Arthur Moon, *Peter Francisco: The Portuguese Patriot* (Pfafftown, NC: Colonial; Winston-Salem, NC: Bradford Printing Service, 1980), 8.
5. Thomas Fleming, *Washington's Secret War: The Hidden History of Valley Forge* (New York: HarperCollins, 2005), 12, 15.
6. Middlekauff, *The Glorious Cause*, 413.
7. Bob Drury and Tom Clavin, *Valley Forge* (New York: Simon & Schuster, 2018), 163.
8. Joseph J. Ellis, *His Excellency George Washington* (New York: Vintage Books, 2004), 111–12.
9. Moon, *Peter Francisco*, 8.
10. Brandon Fisichella, "'The 1764 Manual Exercise': The British Army's Revolutionary War Era Drill Manual," YouTube, April 4, 2021, https://www.youtube.com/watch?v=RF-mA3kbUzY.
11. Middlekauff, *The Glorious Cause*, 417–18.
12. Paul Lockart, *The Drillmaster of Valley Forge: The Baron de Steuben and the Making of the American Army* (New York: HarperCollins, 2008), 28–29, 87–88, 98.
13. Lockart, *The Drillmaster of Valley Forge*, 76–77.
14. Lockart, *The Drillmaster of Valley Forge*, 82–83.
15. Drury and Clavin, *Valley Forge*, 272–73.
16. Lockart, *The Drillmaster of Valley Forge*, 81.
17. Drury and Clavin, *Valley Forge*, 267.
18. Lockart, *The Drillmaster of Valley Forge*, 97–102, 111.
19. Lockart, *The Drillmaster of Valley Forge*, 88.
20. Ellis, *His Excellency George Washington*, 117.
21. Brandon Fisichella, "How 18th-Century Armies Shot at Each Other," YouTube, January 29, 2022, https://www.youtube.com/watch?v=EURWwDbKvWY.
22. Fisichella, "How 18th-Century Armies Shot at Each Other."
23. Brandon Fisichella, "The Continental Army's Manual Exercise, as Ordered by Baron de Steuben," YouTube, March 31, 2021, https://www.youtube.com/watch?v=JWXn-_B41Dc.

CHAPTER 8

1. National Archives, "Muster Rolls of the Revolution," 10th Virginia Regiment, April–August 1778 (Washington, DC: General Services Administration, n.d.).

2. Captain John Mountjoy, "Pension Application of John Mountjoy," Southern Campaigns American Revolution Pension Statements and Rosters, June 16, 1818, https://www.revwarapps.org/s36175.pdf.

3. "John Green," Find a Grave Memorial ID: 12593, Find a Grave, September 16, 2000, https://www.findagrave.com/memorial/12593/john-green; Arlington National Cemetery, "John Green," Facebook, July 4, 2020, https://www.facebook.com/ArlingtonNatl/photos/a.200950083975/10159895119373976/?type=3.

4. Monmouth Courthouse Battlefield State Park, "June 1778, The Continentals' Route through New Jersey," static display, February 29, 2024.

5. N. B. Winston, *Peter Francisco, Soldier of the Revolution* (Richmond, VA: West, Johnson, 1893), 20.

6. Albert Louis Zambone, *Daniel Morgan: A Revolutionary Life* (Yardley, PA: Westholme, 2018), 9, 22–24.

7. James Kirby Martin and Mark Edward Lender, *A Respectable Army: The Military Origins of the Republic, 1763–1789* (Arlington Heights, IL: Harlan Davidson, 1982), 76.

8. "Daniel Morgan," American Battlefield Trust, 2023, https://www.battlefields.org/learn/biographies/daniel-morgan.

9. Winston, *Peter Francisco, Soldier of the Revolution*, 19.

10. Mark Edward Lender and Gary Wheeler Stone, *Fatal Sunday—George Washington, the Monmouth Campaign, and the Politics of Battle* (Norman: University of Oklahoma Press, 2016), 168; Peter Francisco, "Petition for Reimbursement to Virginia General Assembly," Virginia State Library, November 11, 1828, https://revwarapps.org/w11021.pdf.

11. Zambone, *Daniel Morgan*, 174.

12. Lender and Stone, *Fatal Sunday*, 181.

13. Zambone, *Daniel Morgan*, 177–79.

14. Monmouth Courthouse Battlefield State Park, "Private, Rifle Company 6th Virginia Regiment," static display, February 29, 2024.

15. Joseph G. Bilby and Katherine Bilby Jenkins, *Monmouth Court House: The Battle That Made the American Army* (Yardley, PA: Westholme, 2010), 195.

16. Lender and Stone, *Fatal Sunday*, 194.

17. Bilby and Jenkins, *Monmouth Court House*, 211.

18. Bilby and Jenkins, *Monmouth Court House*, 238–47.

19. Monmouth Courthouse Battlefield State Park, "The Battle of Monmouth," static display, February 29, 2024.

20. Zambone, *Daniel Morgan*, 181.

21. Francisco, "Petition for Reimbursement to Virginia General Assembly."

CHAPTER 9

1. William Arthur Moon, *Peter Francisco: The Portuguese Patriot* (Pfafftown, NC: Colonial; Winston-Salem, NC: Bradford Printing Service, 1980), 9.
2. Don Loprieno, *Enterprise in Contemplation: The Midnight Assault of Stony Point* (Westminster, MD: Heritage Books, 2004), 4–5.
3. Loprieno, *Enterprise in Contemplation*, 3.
4. Henry P. Johnston, *The Storming of Stony Point on the Hudson Midnight July 15, 1779—Its Importance in the Light of Unpublished Documents* (New York: Da Capo, 1971), 59.
5. Johnston, *The Storming of Stony Point*, 64.
6. Loprieno, *Enterprise in Contemplation*, 5.
7. Loprieno, *Enterprise in Contemplation*, 6.
8. Johnston, *The Storming of Stony Point*, 65.
9. Johnston, *The Storming of Stony Point*, 62.
10. Loprieno, *Enterprise in Contemplation*, 1.
11. Loprieno, *Enterprise in Contemplation*, 9.
12. Loprieno, *Enterprise in Contemplation*, 12.
13. Moon, *Peter Francisco*, 9.
14. Johnston, *The Storming of Stony Point*, 69.
15. Loprieno, *Enterprise in Contemplation*, 20–21.
16. Moon, *Peter Francisco*, 9.
17. Loprieno, *Enterprise in Contemplation*, 24.
18. Loprieno, *Enterprise in Contemplation*, 23.
19. Johnston, *The Storming of Stony Point*, 74–76.
20. Mark Miller, "18 C. & Early 19th C. Axes," Fur Trade Axes and Tomahawks, 2009–2015, 24, https://www.furtradetomahawks.com/18th-c--early-19th-c-axes---24.html; Mark Miller, "About Iron and Steel," Fur Trade Axes and Tomahawks, 2009–2015, 25, https://www.furtradetomahawks.com/about-iron-and-steel---25.html.
21. Moon, *Peter Francisco*, 9–10.
22. Loprieno, *Enterprise in Contemplation*, 23.
23. Johnston, *The Storming of Stony Point*, 82.
24. Loprieno, *Enterprise in Contemplation*, 28.
25. Loprieno, *Enterprise in Contemplation*, 22.
26. Stony Point Battlefield State Historic Site, "The American Strategy," February 27, 2024, Battlefield Station 4.
27. Loprieno, *Enterprise in Contemplation*, 27.
28. Stony Point Battlefield State Historic Site, "Leading the Assault," February 27, 2024, Battlefield Station 15.
29. Stony Point Battlefield State Historic Site, "Flanking the Lower Works," February 27, 2024, Battlefield Station 6.
30. Johnston, *The Storming of Stony Point*, 80.

31. Stony Point Battlefield State Historic Site, "The Cannons Rendered Useless," February 27, 2024, Battlefield Station 9.

32. Johnston, *The Storming of Stony Point*, 82.

33. Moon, *Peter Francisco*, 9.

34. Nannie Francisco Porter and Catherine Fauntleroy Albertson, *The Romantic Record of Peter Francisco* (Staunton, VA: McClure, 1929), 29.

35. Patrick K. O'Donnell, *Washington's Immortals: The Untold Story of an Elite Regiment Who Changed the Course of a Revolution* (New York: Atlantic Monthly, 2016), 220.

36. Loprieno, *Enterprise in Contemplation*, 33.

37. Stony Point Battlefield State Historic Site, "Leading the Assault."

38. Loprieno, *Enterprise in Contemplation*, 32, 35.

39. Loprieno, *Enterprise in Contemplation*, 35.

40. Loprieno, *Enterprise in Contemplation*, 57.

41. Ronald S. Gibbs, MD, "Medicine in the American Revolution," lecture to the Society of Cincinnati hosted by the American Revolution Institute, Washington, DC, June 21, 2022, https://www.youtube.com/watch?v=4EdPlpjLaW4&t=2890s.

42. Moon, *Peter Francisco*, 10.

43. Porter and Albertson, *The Romantic Record of Peter Francisco*, 29.

44. Moon, *Peter Francisco*, 10.

45. Mervyn Williamson, "Peter Francisco—Washington's One-Man Regiment," *Iron Worker*, August 1972, 5.

46. Loprieno, *Enterprise in Contemplation*, 76.

47. "Stony Point," American Battlefield Trust, August 24, 2023, https://www.battlefields.org/learn/revolutionary-war/battles/stony-point#:~:text=One%20of%20the%20first%20Americans,at%20least%20three%20British%20soldiers.

48. "Peter Francisco: The American Soldier," *William and Mary Quarterly Historical Magazine* 13, no. 4 (April 1905): 217.

49. O'Donnell, *Washington's Immortals*, 379.

50. Moon, *Peter Francisco*, 93.

51. Michael Schellhammer, "Peter Francisco—Distinguishing Fact from Fiction," *Journal of the American Revolution*, July 23, 2013, https://allthingsliberty.com/2013/07/peter-francisco-fact-or-fiction/.

CHAPTER 10

1. Jim Piecuch, *The Battle of Camden: A Documentary History* (Charleston, SC: The History Press, 2006), 10.

2. Piecuch, *The Battle of Camden*, 17.

3. James B. Legg, Steven D. Smith, and Tamara S. Wilson, *Understanding Camden: The Revolutionary War Battle of Camden as Revealed through Historical, Archaeological, and Private Collections Analysis* (Columbia: South Carolina Institute of Archaeology and Anthropology, 2005), 16.

4. Piecuch, *The Battle of Camden*, 14–15.

5. Legg, Smith, and Wilson, *Understanding Camden*, 17–18, 20.

6. Robert Middlekauff, *The Glorious Cause: The American Revolution, 1763–1789* (New York: Oxford University Press, 1982), 454–57.

7. Piecuch, *The Battle of Camden*, 17.

8. John S. Pancake, *This Destructive War: The British Campaign in the Carolinas, 1780–1782* (Tuscaloosa: University of Alabama Press, 1985), 104.

9. John W. Gordon, *South Carolina and the American Revolution: A Battlefield History* (Columbia: University of South Carolina Press, 2003), 92–94.

10. Donald N. Moran, "Peter Francisco, Giant of the American Revolution," Sons of Liberty California Society SAR, December 14, 2007–November 12, 2022, http://www.revolutionarywararchives.org/francisco.html.

11. Michael D. Hull, "Peter Francisco: American Revolutionary War Hero," HistoryNet, July 25, 2006, https://www.historynet.com/peter-francisco-american-revolutionary-war-hero/; Moran, "Peter Francisco, Giant of the American Revolution."

12. Benjamin M. Francisco, *Biography of Peter Francisco of Revolutionary Notoriety*, pamphlet located at the University of Virginia Library, 1879, 3.

13. Moran, "Peter Francisco, Giant of the American Revolution."

14. William Arthur Moon, *Peter Francisco: The Portuguese Patriot* (Pfafftown, NC: Colonial; Winston-Salem, NC: Bradford Printing Service, 1980), 11–12.

15. Legg, Smith, and Wilson, *Understanding Camden*, 43.

16. Anna Inbody, "Maj. Gen. Baron Johann de Kalb's Original Gravesite," Historical Marker Database, November 9, 2011, https://www.hmdb.org/m.asp?m=49354.

17. Rob Orrison, "'In the Deepest Distress and Anxiety of Mind . . .' Gen. Gates Letter to Congress on the Battle of Camden," Emerging Revolutionary War Era, August 16, 2018, https://emergingrevolutionarywar.org/2018/08/16/in-the-deepest-distress-and-anxiety-of-mind-gen-gates-letter-to-congress-on-the-battle-of-camden/.

18. Legg, Smith, and Wilson, *Understanding Camden*, 44.

19. Rear Admiral John Palmer (U.S. Navy [Retired]), *From Bluegrass to Blue Water—Lessons in Farm Philosophy and Navy Leadership* (Nashville, TN: Fidelis, 2022), 74–75.

20. John Knight, *War at Saber Point—Banastre Tarleton and the British Legion* (Yardley, PA: Westholme, 2023), 94–104.

21. Francisco, *Biography of Peter Francisco of Revolutionary Notoriety*, 3.

22. Moon, *Peter Francisco*, 12.

23. Nannie Francisco Porter and Catherine Fauntleroy Albertson, *The Romantic Record of Peter Francisco* (Staunton, VA: McClure, 1929), 29–30.

24. Moon, *Peter Francisco*, 12, 25, 28.

25. Karl G. Elsea, "Peter Carried a Cannon, the Real Story," Emerging Revolutionary War Era, August 15, 2021, https://emergingrevolutionarywar.org/2021/08/15/peter-carried-a-cannon-the-real-story/.

26. Nick Best, Eddie Hall, Robert Oberst, and Brian Shaw, *The Strongest Man in History*, season 1, episode 7, "Revolutionary Strongmen," aired August 14, 2019, on History Channel, https://www.youtube.com/watch?v=gwHWrRaVfQg.

27. Adam Hadhazy, "How It's Possible for an Ordinary Person to Lift a Car," BBC, May 1, 2016, https://www.bbc.com/future/article/20160501-how-its-possible-for-an-ordinary-person-to-lift-a-car.

28. J. K. Hall, MD, "Peter Francisco—Hyperpituitary Patriot," *Annals of Medical History*, n.s., 8, no. 5 (1936): 452.

CHAPTER 11

1. Terry Golway, *Washington's General—Nathanael Greene and the Triumph of the American Revolution* (New York: Holt, 2005), 12–15.

2. Golway, *Washington's General*, 38–39.

3. John S. Pancake, *This Destructive War: The British Campaign in the Carolinas, 1780–1782* (Tuscaloosa: University of Alabama Press, 1985), 130.

4. John W. Gordon, *South Carolina and the American Revolution: A Battlefield History* (Columbia: University of South Carolina Press, 2003), 127.

5. James B. Legg, Steven D. Smith, and Tamara S. Wilson, *Understanding Camden: The Revolutionary War Battle of Camden as Revealed through Historical, Archaeological, and Private Collections Analysis* (Columbia: South Carolina Institute of Archaeology and Anthropology, 2005), 18.

6. Lionheart Filmworks, "The U.S. Cavalry during the American Revolution: A History," YouTube, January 5, 2020, https://www.youtube.com/watch?v=o9sf_J9gATw.

7. Travis Shaw, "Cavalry in the American Revolution," American Battlefield Trust, April 4, 2024, https://www.battlefields.org/learn/articles/cavalry-american-revolution?ms=googlepaid&gad_source=1&gclid=Cj0KCQjwn7mwBhCiARIsAGoxjaJbJi0SWSLilB2BDgCovPyHvOc6Ve_k89GYYu7DCizE9BIjmSJbDzMaAn-VEALw_wcB.

8. Lionheart Filmworks, "The U.S. Cavalry during the American Revolution."

9. Captain Charles Yerba, "Attestation on Behalf of Peter Francisco," Southern Campaigns American Revolution Pension Statements and Rosters, March 6, 1780, http://revwarapps.org/w11021.pdf.

10. Don Troiani, "Cavalry Arms of the American Revolution," *American Rifleman*, April 12, 2022, https://www.americanrifleman.org/content/cavalry-arms-of-the-american-revolution/.

11. Daniel Murphy, historical commentary with the author, September 10, 2024, regarding *George Washington's One-Man Army: The Life, Legend, and Battles of Peter Francisco*, by John T. Palmer (Essex, CT: Stackpole Books, 2026).

12. Nannie Francisco Porter and Catherine Fauntleroy Albertson, *The Romantic Record of Peter Francisco* (Staunton, VA: McClure, 1929), 32.

13. Daniel Murphy, "A Short History of the 3rd Continental Dragoons," SChistory.net, 2012, http://www.schistory.net/3CLD/Articles/3dragoon.html.

14. Don Pruitt, "Scotch Lake," Peter Francisco Society, 2023, https://peterfrancisco.org/scotch-lake/.

15. "Peter Francisco: The American Soldier," *William and Mary Quarterly Historical Magazine* 13, no. 4 (April 1905): 217, https://books.google.com/books?id=WtURAAAAYAAJ&printsec=frontcover#v=onepage&q&f=false.

16. Leland G. Ferguson, "Archeology at Scott's Lake: Exploratory Research 1972, 1973," Institute of Archeology and Anthropology, University of South Carolina, February 1975, 1, 6, 11–13, https://scholarcommons.sc.edu/cgi/viewcontent.cgi?article=1140&context=archanth_books.

17. William Arthur Moon, *Peter Francisco: The Portuguese Patriot* (Pfafftown, NC: Colonial; Winston-Salem, NC: Bradford Printing Service, 1980), 12.

18. Gordon, *South Carolina and the American Revolution*, 125–26.

19. Cowpens National Battlefield, "Order to Daniel Morgan from General Nathanael Greene, December 16, 1780," battlefield placard, National Park Service, 2024, https://www.nps.gov/cowp/index.htm.

20. Patrick K. O'Donnell, *Washington's Immortals: The Untold Story of an Elite Regiment Who Changed the Course of a Revolution* (New York: Atlantic Monthly, 2016), 277–287.

21. Gordon, *South Carolina and the American Revolution*, 129–36.

22. Cowpens National Battlefield, "Morgan's Army the Night before the Battle," museum display, Patriot Army, National Park Service, 2024, https://www.nps.gov/cowp/index.htm.

23. John Mackenzie, "Battle of Cowpens," BritishBattles.com, 2002–2011, https://www.britishbattles.com/war-of-the-revolution-1775-to-1783/battle-of-cowpens/.

24. Cowpens National Battlefield, After-action statements by Lord Cornwallis, Lieutenant Colonel Tarleton, Major General Greene, and Brigadier General Morgan, museum display, National Park Service, 2024, https://www.nps.gov/cowp/index.htm.

25. Moon, *Peter Francisco*, 12.

26. "Peter Francisco, Buckingham's Hero of the Revolution," *Appomattox-Buckingham Times*, July 24, 1901, 2, https://virginiachronicle.com/?a=d&d=ABT19010724.1.2&e=-------en-20--1--txt-txIN--------.

27. "Siege of Fort Watson," American Battlefield Trust, 2024, https://www.battlefields.org/learn/revolutionary-war/battles/siege-fort-watson.

28. Santee National Wildlife Refuge, "Fort Watson," Clarendon County, SC, March 8, 2024, https://www.fws.gov/refuge/santee/about-us.

CHAPTER 12

1. John S. Pancake, *This Destructive War: The British Campaign in the Carolinas, 1780–1782* (Tuscaloosa: University of Alabama Press, 1985), 156–58.
2. J. D. Lewis, "The Race to the Dan—January 18th to February 15th, 1781," American Revolution in North Carolina, 2011, https://www.carolana.com/NC/Revolution/revolution_race_to_the_dan_river_1781.html.
3. Pancake, *This Destructive War*, 168.
4. Pancake, *This Destructive War*, 161–71.
5. Terry Golway, *Washington's General—Nathanael Greene and the Triumph of the American Revolution* (New York: Holt, 2005), 253.
6. Pancake, *This Destructive War*, 174–75.
7. Nannie Francisco Porter and Catherine Fauntleroy Albertson, *The Romantic Record of Peter Francisco* (Staunton, VA: McClure, 1929), 31.
8. William Arthur Moon, *Peter Francisco: The Portuguese Patriot* (Pfafftown, NC: Colonial; Winston-Salem, NC: Bradford Printing Service, 1980), 15; Mervyn Williamson, "Peter Francisco—Washington's One-Man Regiment," *Iron Worker*, August 1972, 5.
9. Golway, *Washington's General*, 255.
10. Golway, *Washington's General*, 256.
11. Golway, *Washington's General*, 257.
12. Golway, *Washington's General*, 258.
13. Patrick K. O'Donnell, *Washington's Immortals: The Untold Story of an Elite Regiment Who Changed the Course of a Revolution* (New York: Atlantic Monthly, 2016), 322.
14. Stephen F. Haller, *William Washington—Cavalryman of the Revolution* (Bowie, MD: Heritage Books, 2001), 110–11.
15. William Henry Foote, *Sketches of North Carolina, Historical and Biographical, Illustrative of the Principles of a Portion of Her Early Settlers* (New York: Carter, 1846), 278.
16. Haller, *William Washington*, 111–12.
17. O'Donnell, *Washington's Immortals*, 322.
18. Golway, *Washington's General*, 259.
19. Golway, *Washington's General*, 260–61.
20. Moon, *Peter Francisco*, 16.
21. Michael D. Hull, "Peter Francisco: American Revolutionary War Hero," HistoryNet, July 25, 2006, https://www.historynet.com/peter-francisco-american-revolutionary-war-hero/.
22. Porter and Albertson, *The Romantic Record of Peter Francisco*, 40–41.
23. Guilford Courthouse Battlefield, "The Battle of Guilford Courthouse: A Victory within a Defeat," museum placard, Guilford Courthouse National Military Park, National Park Service, September 28, 2023, https://www.nps.gov/guco/index.htm.

24. Guilford Courthouse Battlefield, "The Battle of Guilford Courthouse," Guilford Courthouse National Military Park, National Park Service, December 2, 2002, https://www.nps.gov/parkhistory/online_books/hh/30/hh30a.htm.
25. Moon, *Peter Francisco*, 15–16.
26. Golway, *Washington's General*, 261.
27. Michael Schellhammer, "Peter Francisco—Distinguishing Fact from Fiction," *Journal of the American Revolution*, July 23, 2013, https://allthingsliberty.com/2013/07/peter-francisco-fact-or-fiction/.
28. Robert Buckner, "Peter Francisco," *Elks Magazine* 15, no. 6 (November 1936): 38, https://www.elks.org/magazinescans/1936-11E.pdf.
29. Moon, *Peter Francisco*, 46.
30. Ian McDowell, "Peter Francisco: Hercules of the Revolution and Washington's One-Man Army," *Yes! Weekly*, March 3, 2021, https://www.yesweekly.com/news/peter-francisco-hercules-of-the-revolution-and-washington-s-one-man-army/article_b78786b0-7c3e-11eb-8b33-a3f220222ee6.html.
31. Moon, *Peter Francisco*, 46.
32. McDowell, "Peter Francisco."
33. Schellhammer, "Peter Francisco—Distinguishing Fact from Fiction."

CHAPTER 13

1. Greg Eanes, *Tarleton's Southside Raid and Peter Francisco's Famous Fight* (Crewe, VA: Eanes Group, 2014), 18.
2. "Green Spring," American Battlefield Trust, 2024, https://www.battlefields.org/learn/revolutionary-war/battles/green-spring.
3. Eanes, *Tarleton's Southside Raid*, 10–13, 17.
4. William Arthur Moon, *Peter Francisco: The Portuguese Patriot* (Pfafftown, NC: Colonial; Winston-Salem, NC: Bradford Printing Service, 1980), 16.
5. Eanes, *Tarleton's Southside Raid*, 30.
6. Moon, *Peter Francisco*, 17.
7. Eanes, *Tarleton's Southside Raid*, 30–36.
8. Moon, *Peter Francisco*, 18; Nannie Francisco Porter and Catherine Fauntleroy Albertson, *The Romantic Record of Peter Francisco* (Staunton, VA: McClure, 1929), 39.
9. Eanes, *Tarleton's Southside Raid and Peter Francisco's Famous Fight*, 32, 36.

CHAPTER 14

1. Harry Kollatz Jr., "American Hercules, Peter Francisco, 'One Man Regiment' of the Revolution," *Richmond Magazine*, July 2012, 191.

2. Nannie Francisco Porter and Catherine Fauntleroy Albertson, *The Romantic Record of Peter Francisco* (Staunton, VA: McClure, 1929), 44.

3. Joseph J. Ellis, *His Excellency George Washington* (New York: Vintage Books, 2004), 131.

4. Patrick K. O'Donnell, *Washington's Immortals: The Untold Story of an Elite Regiment Who Changed the Course of a Revolution* (New York: Atlantic Monthly, 2016), 357–60.

5. Robert Middlekauff, *The Glorious Cause: The American Revolution, 1763–1789* (New York: Oxford University Press, 1982), 563.

6. Ellis, *His Excellency George Washington*, 132–36.

7. Lord Charles Cornwallis, "Cornwallis to Clinton," Teaching American History, 2006–2023, https://teachingamericanhistory.org/document/cornwallis-to-clinton/.

8. John Mackenzie, "Battle of Yorktown," BritishBattles.com, 2002–2011, https://www.britishbattles.com/war-of-the-revolution-1775-to-1783/battle-of-yorktown/.

CHAPTER 15

1. William Arthur Moon, *Peter Francisco: The Portuguese Patriot* (Pfafftown, NC: Colonial; Winston-Salem, NC: Bradford Printing Service, 1980), 21.

2. Nannie Francisco Porter and Catherine Fauntleroy Albertson, *The Romantic Record of Peter Francisco* (Staunton, VA: McClure, 1929), 45–46.

3. Porter and Albertson, *The Romantic Record of Peter Francisco*, 47–50.

4. Mervyn Williamson, "Peter Francisco—Washington's One-Man Regiment," *Iron Worker*, August 1972, 8–9.

5. Porter and Albertson, *The Romantic Record of Peter Francisco*, 53.

6. Porter and Albertson, *The Romantic Record of Peter Francisco*, 61–62.

7. Moon, *Peter Francisco*, 19–20.

8. Moon, *Peter Francisco*, 19.

9. Moon, *Peter Francisco*, 22–23.

10. Porter and Albertson, *The Romantic Record of Peter Francisco*, 55–56.

11. Moon, *Peter Francisco*, 23–25.

12. Moon, *Peter Francisco*, 32.

13. Moon, *Peter Francisco*, 35.

14. Williamson, "Peter Francisco," 9.

15. Moon, *Peter Francisco*, 35, 37.

16. Moon, *Peter Francisco*, 27, 31, 35.

17. Williamson, "Peter Francisco," 7.

18. Williamson, "Peter Francisco," 6.

19. Moon, *Peter Francisco*, 21, 31, 41.

20. Porter and Albertson, *The Romantic Record of Peter Francisco*, 20.

21. Williamson, "Peter Francisco," 7.
22. Moon, *Peter Francisco*, 31.
23. Benjamin M. Francisco, *Biography of Peter Francisco of Revolutionary Notoriety*, pamphlet located at the University of Virginia Library, 1879, 5.
24. Williamson, "Peter Francisco," 8.
25. Francisco, *Biography of Peter Francisco of Revolutionary Notoriety*, 6.
26. Moon, *Peter Francisco*, 24.
27. Moon, *Peter Francisco*, 31.
28. Porter and Albertson, *The Romantic Record of Peter Francisco*, 67–68.
29. Williamson, "Peter Francisco," 6–7.
30. Williamson, "Peter Francisco," 6.
31. Francisco, *Biography of Peter Francisco of Revolutionary Notoriety*, 7.
32. Moon, *Peter Francisco*, 27.
33. Moon, *Peter Francisco*, 29, 30.
34. Moon, *Peter Francisco*, 28.
35. Porter and Albertson, *The Romantic Record of Peter Francisco*, 65.
36. Williamson, "Peter Francisco," 9–10.
37. Williamson, "Peter Francisco," 6.
38. Porter and Albertson, *The Romantic Record of Peter Francisco*, 64.
39. Williamson, "Peter Francisco," 6.
40. Moon, *Peter Francisco*, 29.
41. Moon, *Peter Francisco*, 31.
42. Francisco, *Biography of Peter Francisco of Revolutionary Notoriety*, 5.
43. Moon, *Peter Francisco*, 37.
44. Moon, *Peter Francisco*, 38.
45. Williamson, "Peter Francisco," 9.
46. Moon, *Peter Francisco*, 38.
47. Moon, *Peter Francisco*, 25.
48. Porter and Albertson, *The Romantic Record of Peter Francisco*, 60.
49. Francisco, *Biography of Peter Francisco of Revolutionary Notoriety*, 7.
50. Williamson, "Peter Francisco," 9.
51. Moon, *Peter Francisco*, 24.
52. C. Leon Harris, compilation of attestations on behalf of Peter Francisco, transcribed and annotated, Southern Campaigns American Revolution Pension Statements and Rosters, April 2, 2015, http://revwarapps.org/w11021.pdf.
53. Moon, *Peter Francisco*, 95.
54. Moon, *Peter Francisco*, 41–42.
55. Gail Tonkens, "Masonic Lodge Membership," *Virginia Giant* 2, no. 10 (September 2014).
56. Moon, *Peter Francisco*, 42–44.
57. Williamson, "Peter Francisco," 10.
58. Moon, *Peter Francisco*, 44.
59. Moon, *Peter Francisco*, 38.

60. Moon, *Peter Francisco*, 52.
61. Porter and Albertson, *The Romantic Record of Peter Francisco*, 82–83.
62. Porter and Albertson, *The Romantic Record of Peter Francisco*, 84.
63. "Monuments," Peter Francisco Society, 2024, https://peterfrancisco.org/monuments/.
64. Moon, *Peter Francisco*, 46–50, 59–61.
65. Society of the Descendants of Peter Francisco, "Walking in Peter's Footsteps," *Virginia Giant* 2, no. 12 (September 2015), https://web.archive.org/web/20160312005922/; http://www.peterfrancisco.org/wp-content/uploads/2015/09/TheVirginiaGiant_Sept2015.pdf.
66. Robert Buckner, "Peter Francisco," *Elks Magazine* 15, no. 6 (November 1936): 4, https://www.elks.org/magazinescans/1936-11E.pdf. https://www.elks.org/magazinescans/1936-11E.pdf.
67. Page Smith, *A New Age Begins* (New York: McGraw-Hill, 1976), 1.

CHAPTER 16

1. Julie Miller, "George Washington: 'The Greatest Man in the World'?," Library of Congress Blogs, December 15, 2022, https://blogs.loc.gov/manuscripts/2022/12/george-washington-the-greatest-man-in-the-world/#_ftn3.
2. Joseph J. Ellis, *His Excellency George Washington* (New York: Vintage Books, 2004), 52, 244, 262–63, 268–70.
3. Wikipedia, s.v. "Monument to Francisco in New Bedford, Massachusetts," June 10, 2016, https://en.m.wikipedia.org/wiki/File:Monument_to_Francisco_in_New_Bedford,_Massachusetts_.jpg.
4. "Patrick Henry," American Battlefield Trust, 2024, https://www.battlefields.org/learn/biographies/patrick-henry.
5. Guilford Courthouse Battlefield, "Nathanael Greene Monument," Guilford Courthouse National Military Park, National Park Service, September 28, 2023, https://www.nps.gov/guco/index.htm.
6. Independence Hall Association, "Nathanael Greene," USHistory, 2024, https://www.ushistory.org/valleyforge/served/greene.html.
7. Independence Hall Association, "The Marquis de Lafayette," USHistory, 2024, https://www.ushistory.org/valleyforge/served/lafayette.html.
8. Independence Hall Association, "Baron Von Steuben," USHistory, 2024, https://www.ushistory.org/valleyforge/served/steuben.html.
9. Ariel Wilks, "Daniel Morgan," George Washington's Mount Vernon, Mount Vernon Ladies Association, 2024, https://www.mountvernon.org/library/digitalhistory/digital-encyclopedia/article/daniel-morgan/.
10. Independence Hall Association, "General Anthony Wayne," USHistory, 2024, https://www.ushistory.org/valleyforge/served/wayne.html.

11. Jim Piecuch, "'Light Horse Harry' Lee and Pyle's Massacre," *Journal of the American Revolution*, June 19, 2013, https://allthingsliberty.com/2013/06/light-horse-harry-lee-and-pyles-massacre/.

12. Colin Woodward, "Henry Lee (1756–1818)," *Encyclopedia Virginia*, May 2, 2022, https://encyclopediavirginia.org/entries/lee-henry-1756-1818/.

13. Cowpens National Battlefield, "William Washington," National Park Service, 2024, https://www.nps.gov/articles/000/william-washington.htm.

14. Samuel K. Fore, "William Washington," George Washington's Mount Vernon, Mount Vernon Ladies Association, 2024, https://www.mountvernon.org/library/digitalhistory/digital-encyclopedia/article/william-washington/.

15. "John Marshall, the Great Chief Justice," William & Mary Law School, 2024, https://law.wm.edu/about/ourhistory/John%20Marshall,%20the%20Great%20Chief%20Justice.php.

16. *Political Dictionary*, s.v. "I'd Rather Be Right," 2024, https://politicaldictionary.com/words/id-rather-be-right/.

17. Office of the Historian, "Biographies of the Secretaries of State: Henry Clay (1777–1852)," Foreign Service Institute, United States Department of State, 2024, https://history.state.gov/departmenthistory/people/clay-henry.

BIBLIOGRAPHY

American Battlefield Trust (Website). 2024. https://www.battlefields.org.
Anonymous. *The Blacksmith in Eighteenth-Century Williamsburg: An Account of His Life and Times and of His Craft*. Williamsburg, VA: Colonial Williamsburg, 1978. https://www.gutenberg.org/files/58318/58318-h/58318-h.htm.
Arlington National Cemetery. "John Green." Facebook, July 4, 2020. https://www.facebook.com/ArlingtonNatl/photos/a.200950083975/10159895119373976/?type=3.
Auricchio, Laura. *The Marquis: Lafayette Reconsidered*. New York: Knopf, 2014.
Bahr, William J. YouTube channel. 2024. https://www.youtube.com/@BillBahr11.
Bennett, Lerone, Jr. "White Servitude in America." *Ebony Magazine,* November 1969.
Best, Nick, Eddie Hall, Robert Oberst, and Brian Shaw. *The Strongest Man in History*. Season 1, episode 7, "Revolutionary Strongmen." Aired August 14, 2019, on History Channel. https://www.youtube.com/watch?v=gwHWrRaVfQg.
Bilby, Joseph G., and Katherine Bilby Jenkins. *Monmouth Court House: The Battle That Made the American Army*. Yardley, PA: Westholme, 2010.
Boatner, Mark Mayo, III. *Encyclopedia of the American Revolution*. New York: Van Rees, 1996.
Bopp, Colonel Christopher (Professor of Naval Science at The Citadel and Revolutionary War reenactor). Historical commentary with the author, May 4, 2025, regarding *George Washington's One-Man Army: The Life, Legend, and Battles of Peter Francisco*, by John T. Palmer. Essex, CT: Stackpole Books, 2026.
Brandywine Battlefield. "The Battle of Brandywine." Pennsylvania Historical & Museum Commission, 2023. https://www.brandywinebattlefield.org/battle/.
Brock, R. W. *Vestry Book of Henrico Parish Virginia 1730–1773*. N.p.: University of Virginia Library, 1874.
Buckner, Robert. "Peter Francisco." *Elks Magazine* 15, no. 6 (November 1936): 4–7. https://www.elks.org/magazinescans/1936-11E.pdf.

Carbone, Gerald M. *Nathanael Greene: A Biography of the American Revolution.* New York: Palgrave Macmillan, 2008.

Chernow, Ron. *Washington: A Life.* New York: Penguin, 2010.

Chester County Planning Commission. "Battle of Brandywine—Part 3—Washington's Perspective." YouTube, February 19, 2014. https://www.youtube.com/watch?v=qdqi4j1CHRM.

———. *The Army Marched at Dawn—Southern Battlefield Strategic Landscapes Plan: A Specific Plan of the Brandywine Battlefield Preservation Plan.* Chester County, PA: Chester County Planning Commission and Commonwealth Heritage Group, 2020. https://www.landscapes3.com/Historic/Campaign1777/South.pdf.

Christian, Rachel. "A Furious Cannonade, and a Great Explosion." *Naval History* 36, no. 1 (February 2022). https://www.usni.org/magazines/naval-history-magazine/2022/february/furious-cannonade-and-great-explosion.

Cornwallis, Lord Charles. "Cornwallis to Clinton." Teaching American History, 2006–2023. https://teachingamericanhistory.org/document/cornwallis-to-clinton/.

Cowpens National Battlefield. National Park Service (Website). 2024. https://www.nps.gov/cowp/index.htm.

Crytzer, Brady. "American Revolution: The Siege of Fort Mifflin." YouTube, February 23, 2022. https://www.youtube.com/watch?v=HvA4gOrPZvk&t=1797s.

De Merelim, Pedro. "Pedro Francisco, Heroi (americano) e Tercierense." *Uniao*, July 4, 1978.

Drury, Bob, and Tom Clavin. *Valley Forge.* New York: Simon & Schuster, 2018.

Eanes, Greg. *Tarleton's Southside Raid and Peter Francisco's Famous Fight.* Crewe, VA: Eanes Group, 2014.

Ellis, Joseph J. *His Excellency George Washington.* New York: Vintage Books, 2004.

Elsea, Karl G. "Peter Carried a Cannon, the Real Story." Emerging Revolutionary War Era, August 15, 2021. https://emergingrevolutionarywar.org/2021/08/15/peter-carried-a-cannon-the-real-story/.

Ferguson, Leland G. "Archeology at Scott's Lake: Exploratory Research 1972, 1973." Institute of Archeology and Anthropology, University of South Carolina, February 1975. https://scholarcommons.sc.edu/cgi/viewcontent.cgi?article=1140&context=archanth_books.

Find a Grave. "John Green." Find a Grave Memorial ID 12593. September 16, 2000. https://www.findagrave.com/memorial/12593/john-green.

Fisichella, Brandon. YouTube channel. 2024. https://www.youtube.com/@BrandonF.

Fleming, Thomas. *Washington's Secret War: The Hidden History of Valley Forge.* New York: HarperCollins, 2005.

Foote, William Henry. *Sketches of North Carolina, Historical and Biographical, Illustrative of the Principles of a Portion of Her Early Settlers.* New York: Carter, 1846.

Fore, Samuel, K. "William Washington." George Washington's Mount Vernon, Mount Vernon Ladies Association, 2024. https://www.mountvernon.org/library/digitalhistory/digital-encyclopedia/article/william-washington/.

Francisco, Benjamin M. *Biography of Peter Francisco of Revolutionary Notoriety.* Pamphlet located at the University of Virginia Library, 1879.
Francisco, Peter. "Petition for Reimbursement to Virginia General Assembly." Virginia State Library, November 11, 1828. https://revwarapps.org/w11021.pdf.
Fries, Adelaide, Stuart Thomas Wright, and J. Edwin Hendricks. *Forsyth: The History of a County on the March.* Chapel Hill: University of North Carolina Press, 1960.
George Washington's Mount Vernon. "Revolutionary War Reenacting Part 1." YouTube, July 4, 2017. https://www.youtube.com/watch?v=1gAZZWsswHY&t=61s.
———. "Revolutionary War Reenacting Part 2." YouTube, July 11, 2017. https://www.youtube.com/watch?v=aGEgdIllSNo.
Gibbs, Ronald S., MD. "Medicine in the American Revolution." Lecture to the Society of Cincinnati hosted by the American Revolution Institute, Washington, DC, June 21, 2022. https://www.youtube.com/watch?v=4EdPlpjLaW4&t=2890s.
Golway, Terry. *Washington's General—Nathanael Greene and the Triumph of the American Revolution.* New York: Holt, 2005.
Gordon, John W. *South Carolina and the American Revolution: A Battlefield History.* Columbia: University of South Carolina Press, 2003.
Guilford Courthouse Battlefield. Guilford Courthouse National Military Park. National Park Service (Website). 2024. https://www.nps.gov/guco/index.htm.
Gunn, Michael B. "Revolutionary War Uniforms." Cincinnati Chapter of the Sons of the American Revolution, April 4, 2014. https://cincinnatisar.files.wordpress.com/2015/11/revolutionarywaruniforms.pdf.
Hadhazy, Adam. "How It's Possible for an Ordinary Person to Lift a Car." BBC, May 1, 2016. https://www.bbc.com/future/article/20160501-how-its-possible-for-an-ordinary-person-to-lift-a-car.
Hall, J. K., MD. "Peter Francisco—Hyperpituitary Patriot." *Annals of Medical History,* n.s., 8, no. 5 (1936): 448–52.
Haller, Stephen F. *William Washington—Cavalryman of the Revolution.* Bowie, MD: Heritage Books, 2001.
Harris, C. Leon. Compilation of attestations on behalf of Peter Francisco, transcribed and annotated. Southern Campaigns American Revolution Pension Statements and Rosters, April 2, 2015. http://revwarapps.org/w11021.pdf.
Harris, Michael C. "Battle of Brandywine." YouTube, August 11, 2022. https://www.youtube.com/watch?v=8Fyode2Grro&t=2282s.
———. *Brandywine: A Military History of the Battle That Lost Philadelphia but Saved America, September 11, 1777.* El Dorado Hills, CA: Savas Beatie, 2016.
———. "George Washington and the Battle of Germantown." Virtual lecture hosted by Frauncis Tavern Museum, New York, October 19, 2021. https://www.youtube.com/watch?v=1Nj1sXjnF7E.

Henry, Patrick. "On the Resolution to Put the Commonwealth into a State of Defence." Address delivered before the Second Virginia Convention, March 23, 1775. https://avalon.law.yale.edu/18th_century/patrick.asp.

Historic St. John's Church. "The Second Virginia Convention." March 20–27, 1775. https://www.historicstjohnschurch.org/2nd-virginia-convention.

History.com Editors. "Battle of Germantown." History.com, February 6, 2020. https://www.history.com/topics/american-revolution/battle-of-germantown.

Hull, Michael D. "Peter Francisco: American Revolutionary War Hero." HistoryNet, July 25, 2006. https://www.historynet.com/peter-francisco-american-revolutionary-war-hero/.

Inbody, Anna. "Maj. Gen. Baron Johann de Kalb's Original Gravesite." Historical Marker Database, November 9, 2011. https://www.hmdb.org/m.asp?m=49354.

Independence Hall Association. USHistory (Website). 2024. https://www.ushistory.org/.

Jamestown Yorktown Foundation. JYF Museums (Website). https://www.jyfmuseums.org/about.

Johnston, Henry P. *The Storming of Stony Point on the Hudson Midnight July 15, 1779—Its Importance in the Light of Unpublished Documents.* New York: Da Capo, 1971.

Klein, Brigadier General John A. (Acting Adjutant General). "Letter to Howard E. Baker" (responding to a request for Peter Francisco's military record). National Archives, September 13, 1951.

Knight, John. *War at Saber Point—Banastre Tarleton and the British Legion.* Yardley, PA: Westholme, 2023.

Kollatz, Harry, Jr. "American Hercules, Peter Francisco, 'One Man Regiment' of the Revolution." *Richmond Magazine*, July 2012, 191–92.

Kukla, Jon. "Patrick Henry (1736–1799)." *Encyclopedia Virginia*, December 7, 2020. https://encyclopediavirginia.org/entries/henry-patrick-1736-1799.

Lane, Helena. "History of St. John's Church: Richmond, Virginia." Genealogy Trails, April 22, 2024. http://genealogytrails.com/vir/henrico/st_johns_church_history.html.

Legg, James B., Steven D. Smith, and Tamara S. Wilson. *Understanding Camden: The Revolutionary War Battle of Camden as Revealed through Historical, Archaeological, and Private Collections Analysis.* Columbia: South Carolina Institute of Archaeology and Anthropology, 2005.

Lender, Mark Edward, and Gary Wheeler Stone. *Fatal Sunday—George Washington, the Monmouth Campaign, and the Politics of Battle.* Norman: University of Oklahoma Press, 2016.

Lengel, Edward G. "The Battle of Brandywine." George Washington's Mount Vernon, Mount Vernon Ladies Association, 2024. https://www.mountvernon.org/george-washington/the-revolutionary-war/washingtons-revolutionary-war-battles/the-battle-of-brandywine/.

Lewis, J. D. "The Race to the Dan—January 18th to February 15th, 1781." American Revolution in North Carolina, 2011. https://www.carolana.com/NC/Revolution/revolution_race_to_the_dan_river_1781.html.

Lionheart Filmworks. "The U.S. Cavalry during the American Revolution: A History." YouTube, January 5, 2020. https://www.youtube.com/watch?v=o9sf_J9gATw.

Lockart, Paul. *The Drillmaster of Valley Forge: The Baron de Steuben and the Making of the American Army.* New York: HarperCollins, 2008.

Loprieno, Don. *Enterprise in Contemplation: The Midnight Assault of Stony Point.* Westminster, MD: Heritage Books, 2004.

Mackenzie, John. BritishBattles (Website). 2002–2011. https://www.britishbattles.com.

Martin, James Kirby, and Mark Edward Lender. *A Respectable Army: The Military Origins of the Republic, 1763–1789.* Arlington Heights, IL: Harlan Davidson, 1982.

McCullough, David. *John Adams.* New York: Simon & Schuster, 2001.

McDowell, Ian. "Peter Francisco: Hercules of the Revolution and Washington's One-Man Army." *Yes! Weekly,* March 3, 2021. https://www.yesweekly.com/news/peter-francisco-hercules-of-the-revolution-and-washington-s-one-man-army/article_b78786b0-7c3e-11eb-8b33-a3f220222ee6.html.

McGuire, Thomas J. *The Philadelphia Campaign.* Vol. 2. Mechanicsburg, PA: Stackpole Books, 2007.

———. *The Surprise of Germantown—October 4th, 1777.* Gettysburg, PA: Thompson, 1994.

Middlekauff, Robert. *The Glorious Cause: The American Revolution, 1763–1789.* New York: Oxford University Press, 1982.

Miller, Julie. "George Washington: 'The Greatest Man in the World'?" Library of Congress Blogs, December 15, 2022. https://blogs.loc.gov/manuscripts/2022/12/george-washington-the-greatest-man-in-the-world/#_ftn3.

Miller, Mark. "About Iron and Steel." Fur Trade Axes and Tomahawks, 2009–2015. https://www.furtradetomahawks.com/about-iron-and-steel---25.html.

———. "18 C. & Early 19th C. Axes." Fur Trade Axes and Tomahawks, 2009–2015. https://www.furtradetomahawks.com/18th-c--early-19th-c-axes---24.html.

Monmouth Courthouse Battlefield State Park. Static displays. February 29, 2024.

Moon, William Arthur. *Peter Francisco: The Portuguese Patriot.* Pfafftown, NC: Colonial; Winston-Salem, NC: Bradford Printing Service, 1980.

Moran, Donald N. "Peter Francisco, Giant of the American Revolution." Sons of Liberty California Society SAR, December 14, 2007–November 12, 2022. https://web.archive.org/web/20190507011049/http://www.revolutionarywararchives.org/francisco.html.

Mountjoy, John. "Pension Application of John Mountjoy." Southern Campaigns American Revolution Pension Statements and Rosters, June 16, 1818. https://www.revwarapps.org/s36175.pdf.

Murphy, Daniel. "A Short History of the 3rd Continental Dragoons." SChistory.net, 2012. http://www.schistory.net/3CLD/Articles/3dragoon.html.

———. Historical commentary with the author, September 10, 2024, regarding *George Washington's One-Man Army: The Life, Legend, and Battles of Peter Francisco*, by John T. Palmer. Essex, CT: Stackpole Books, 2026.

National Archives. "Muster Rolls of the Revolution." 10th Virginia Regiment, May–September 1777, January–February 1778, and April–August 1778. Washington, DC: General Services Administration, n.d.

National Historic Park Pennsylvania. "What Happened at Valley Forge." National Park Service, June 13, 2023. https://www.nps.gov/vafo/learn/historyculture/valley-forge-history-and-significance.htm.

Niderost, Eric. "George Washington and Lord Cornwallis at Germantown." Warfare History Network, February 2005. https://warfarehistorynetwork.com/article/george-washington-and-lord-cornwallis-at-germantown/.

O'Donnell, Patrick K. *Washington's Immortals: The Untold Story of an Elite Regiment Who Changed the Course of a Revolution*. New York: Atlantic Monthly, 2016.

Office of Public Affairs. *A History of Roads in Virginia: The Most Convenient Ways*. Richmond: Virginia Department of Transportation, 2006.

Office of the Historian. "Biographies of the Secretaries of State: Henry Clay (1777–1852)." Foreign Service Institute, United States Department of State, 2024. https://history.state.gov/departmenthistory/people/clay-henry.

Orrison, Rob. "'In the Deepest Distress and Anxiety of Mind . . .': Gen. Gates Letter to Congress on the Battle of Camden." Emerging Revolutionary War Era, August 16, 2018. https://emergingrevolutionarywar.org/2018/08/16/in-the-deepest-distress-and-anxiety-of-mind-gen-gates-letter-to-congress-on-the-battle-of-camden/.

Palmer, Rear Admiral John (U.S. Navy [Retired]). *From Bluegrass to Blue Water—Lessons in Farm Philosophy and Navy Leadership*. Nashville, TN: Fidelis, 2022.

Pancake, John S. *This Destructive War: The British Campaign in the Carolinas, 1780–1782*. Tuscaloosa: University of Alabama Press, 1985.

"Peter Francisco, Buckingham's Hero of the Revolution." *Appomattox-Buckingham Times*, July 24, 1901. https://virginiachronicle.com/?a=d&d=ABT19010724.1.2&e=-------en-20--1--txt-txIN--------.

Peter Francisco Society. "Monuments." 2024. https://peterfrancisco.org/monuments/.

"Peter Francisco: The American Soldier." *William and Mary Quarterly Historical Magazine* 13, no. 4 (April 1905): 213–16.

Piecuch, Jim. *The Battle of Camden: A Documentary History*. Charleston, SC: History Press, 2006.

———. "'Light Horse Harry' Lee and Pyle's Massacre." *Journal of the American Revolution*, June 19, 2013. https://allthingsliberty.com/2013/06/light-horse-harry-lee-and-pyles-massacre/.

Political Dictionary, s.v. "I'd Rather Be Right." 2024. https://politicaldictionary.com/words/id-rather-be-right/.

Porter, Nannie Francisco, and Catherine Fauntleroy Albertson. *The Romantic Record of Peter Francisco*. Staunton, VA: McClure, 1929.

Price, Cadet First Lieutenant Arthur Preston '43. "Alma Mater." The Citadel—The Military College of South Carolina, 1943. https://www.citadel.edu/cadet-life-resources/the-citadel-alma-mater/.

Pruitt, Don. "Scotch Lake." Peter Francisco Society, 2023. https://peterfrancisco.org/scotch-lake/.

Raymond, David, Eric Gimbi, and Mike Graham. "Revolutionary War Medicine, Battlefield Surgery, Amputation, and Smallpox Inoculation." YouTube, May 27, 2021. https://www.youtube.com/watch?v=xggzGL3Jbc0.

Reed, John F. *Campaign to Valley Forge—July 1, 1777–December 19, 1777*. Philadelphia: University of Pennsylvania Press, 1965.

Revolutionary War. "Brown Bess Bayonet: The Gun That Freed America." March 4, 2020. https://www.revolutionary-war.net/brown-bess-bayonet/.

Santee National Wildlife Refuge. "Fort Watson." Clarendon County, SC, March 8, 2024. https://www.fws.gov/refuge/santee/about-us.

Schellhammer, Michael. "Peter Francisco—Distinguishing Fact from Fiction." *Journal of the American Revolution*, July 23, 2013. https://allthingsliberty.com/2013/07/peter-francisco-fact-or-fiction/.

Scott, Jane Harrington. *A Gentleman as Well as a Whig: Caesar Rodney and the American Revolution*. Newark: University of Delaware Press, 2000.

Serle, Ambrose (Secretary to General Sir William Howe). "Eyewitness." Fort Mifflin National Historic Landmark, n.d.

Shakespeare, William. *Henry V*. 1599. London: Blackie, 1903. https://archive.org/details/henryfifth00shakuoft.

Shaw, Travis. "Cavalry in the American Revolution." American Battlefield Trust, April 4, 2024. https://www.battlefields.org/learn/articles/cavalry-american-revolution?ms=googlepaid&gad_source=1&gclid=Cj0KCQjwn7mwBhCiARIsAGoxjaJbJi0SWSLilB2BDgCovPyHvOc6Ve_k89GYYu7DCizE9BIjmSJbDzMaAn-VEALw_wcB.

Slipek, Edwin. "St. John's Episcopal Church and Churchyard." Architecture Richmond, 2020. https://architecturerichmond.com/inventory/st-johns-episcopal-church-and-churchyard-5/.

Smith, Page. *A New Age Begins*. Vol. 1. New York: McGraw-Hill, 1976.

Smith, Samuel S. *The Battle of Brandywine*. Monmouth Beach, NJ: Phillip Freneau, 1976.

Society of the Descendants of Peter Francisco. "Walking in Peter's Footsteps." *Virginia Giant* 2, no. 12 (September 2015). https://web.archive.org/web/20160312005922/; http://www.peterfrancisco.org/wp-content/uploads/2015/09/TheVirginiaGiant_Sept2015.pdf.

Southern Battlefield Strategic Landscapes Plan. *The Army Marched at Dawn: A Specific Plan of the Brandywine Battlefield Preservation Plan*. Chester County, PA: Chester County Planning Commission & Commonwealth Heritage Group, 2020. https://www.chesco.org/DocumentCenter/View/60800/Southern-BB-Plan-entire-document.

Stony Point Battlefield State Historic Site. February 27, 2024.

Tomlins, Christopher. "Reconsidering Indentured Servitude: European Migration and the Early American Labor Force, 1600–1775." *Labor History* 42, no. 1 (2001): 5–43.

Tonkens, Gail. "Masonic Lodge Membership." *Virginia Giant* 2, no. 10 (September 2014).

Troiani, Don. "Cavalry Arms of the American Revolution." *American Rifleman*, April 12, 2022. https://www.americanrifleman.org/content/cavalry-arms-of-the-american-revolution/.

Washington, George. "From General Washington to General William Howe, 6 October 1777." Founders Online, National Archives, February 2024. https://founders.archives.gov/documents/Washington/03-11-02-0432#GEWN-03-11-02-0432-fn-0001.

Wikipedia, s.v. "Monument to Francisco in New Bedford, Massachusetts." June 10, 2016. https://en.m.wikipedia.org/wiki/File:Monument_to_Francisco_in_New_Bedford,_Massachusetts_.jpg.

Wilks, Ariel. "Daniel Morgan." George Washington's Mount Vernon, Mount Vernon Ladies Association, 2024. https://www.mountvernon.org/library/digitalhistory/digital-encyclopedia/article/daniel-morgan/.

William & Mary Law School. "John Marshall, the Great Chief Justice." 2024. https://law.wm.edu/about/ourhistory/John%20Marshall,%20the%20Great%20Chief%20Justice.php.

Williamson, Mervyn. "Peter Francisco—Washington's One-Man Regiment." *Iron Worker*, August 1972.

Winston, N. B. *Peter Francisco, Soldier of the Revolution*. Richmond, VA: West, Johnson, 1893.

Woodward, Colin. "Henry Lee (1756–1818)." *Encyclopedia Virginia*, May 2, 2022. https://encyclopediavirginia.org/entries/lee-henry-1756-1818/.

Yerba, Captain Charles. "Attestation on Behalf of Peter Francisco." Southern Campaigns American Revolution Pension Statements and Rosters, March 6, 1780. http://revwarapps.org/w11021.pdf.

Zambone, Albert Louis. *Daniel Morgan: A Revolutionary Life*. Yardley, PA: Westholme, 2018.

ABOUT THE AUTHOR

Rear Admiral (retired) John T. Palmer is a native of Lexington, Kentucky. He is married to the former Elizabeth Brooks Mahaffey (Brooks) of Spartanburg, South Carolina. They are the proud parents of two children, Elizabeth Palmer Sanders and John Taylor Palmer Jr., and they are blessed with five grandchildren. The Palmers live among family in Spartanburg, where Brooks works as a registered nurse.

Palmer is a graduate of The Citadel—The Military College of South Carolina (BS in business administration), the Naval Postgraduate School (MS in systems management), and the Columbia University Graduate School of Business (Senior Executive Program). He is owner of JT Palmer Enterprises LLC, a South Carolina corporation, where he serves as an independent consultant, advisory board member, college guest lecturer, and author.

Palmer's first book is titled *From Bluegrass to Blue Water: Lessons in Farm Philosophy and Navy Leadership* (2022). He is a frequent guest lecturer at various colleges and universities, including his most recent appearance at Columbia University's Columbia Business School in the Executive MBA Program. He performs as a public speaker to an array of civic groups

John T. Palmer
Photo by Brooks Mahaffey Palmer

throughout the southeast and as a commentator for various media, including Fox News, as a subject matter expert. He also participates in managing two family farms in Kentucky.

The Palmers served for more than thirty-two years as a U.S. Navy family, with John retiring at the rank of rear admiral. Palmer was assigned to four ships for nearly nine years. He was entrusted with command on three occasions culminating with his final tour as Commander of the Defense Logistics Agency (DLA) Land & Maritime—a $6 billion per year procurement activity supporting U.S. Army/Marine Corps wheeled and tracked vehicles and Navy surface vessels and submarines. During his naval career, Palmer earned several warfare and professional qualifications and is entitled to wear various personal, unit, and service awards, including the Defense Superior Service Medal and the Combat Action Ribbon.

"*George Washington's One-Man Army* is a must read about a giant of a man, Peter Francisco, who never rose in rank above private but was crucial to the Colonies winning the American Revolution. This book goes into great detail about each of Peter's most famous engagements, from military strategy, to the everyday life of soldiers, and, most interestingly, to his larger-than-life accomplishments on and off the battlefield during the war with Great Britain. Retired Rear Admiral John Palmer brings the American Revolution to life through the strength, bravery, and heroics of Peter Francisco."—**Ed Bowman**, president of the Peter Francisco Society and descendant of Peter Francisco

"One-Man Army" was George Washington's nom de guerre for Peter Francisco. Abducted from the Azores and deposited in the colony of Virginia at the age of four, little Pedro Francisco was an orphan from a strange land in the New World. Renamed Peter Francisco, the youngster found a home under indenture to Patrick Henry's uncle as a blacksmith. Peter was present for Henry's famous speech, hearing firsthand the words "Give me liberty or give me death." By the age of fourteen, he stood at 6-foot-6 and 260 pounds. He would fashion himself an apex warrior, serving both in the patriot infantry and cavalry.

In his capacity as a soldier, Francisco participated in some of the fiercest fighting, witnessed the greatest events, and met an astounding number of luminaries from early America headlined by generals George Washington, Nathanael Greene, and the Marquis de Lafayette. Francisco fought in at least ten battles and received six gruesome wounds as he dispatched over twenty enemy soldiers, mostly by the bayonet and a six-foot broadsword commissioned for him by Washington. His feats of courage and strength were legendary as he is reputed to have carried a half-ton cannon from the battlefield at Camden.

Postwar, Francisco became a planter and businessman. Endeavoring to educate himself, he overcame illiteracy and developed into a voracious reader. As a veteran, the "Virginia Giant" was sought out for meetings by the Secretary of State and was received in the home of the Chief Justice of the Supreme Court. He was thrice married into Virginia society, a father of six, and a fixture in the Commonwealth serving as Sergeant at Arms for the legislature late in life. Known to all throughout the newly independent thirteen states, Peter Francisco's exploits were all but lost to history . . . until now.

Rear Admiral John T. Palmer, U.S. Navy (Ret.), is a native of Lexington, Kentucky, and a graduate of The Citadel, the Naval Postgraduate School, and Columbia University's Senior Executive Program. As owner of JT Palmer Enterprises, he serves as a consultant, advisory board member, and college lecturer, and he helps manage two family farms in Kentucky. Palmer's first book was *From Bluegrass to Blue Water: Lessons in Farm Philosophy and Navy Leadership* (2022).

www.ingramcontent.com/pod-product-compliance
Lightning Source LLC
LaVergne TN
LVHW090054080526
838200LV00082B/5